D0426363

LAS VEGAS-CLARK COUNTY
LIBRARY DISTRICT
833 LAS VEGAS BLVD, N
LAS VEGAS, NEVADA 89101

THE GREAT GENERALS SERIES

"Palgrave's Great Generals Series is an important and inspiring contribution to our understanding of modern-day warfare. Every book in the series will provide invaluable insight into the legacies of eminent military leaders and take the reader on a gripping tour of the most spectacular maneuvers, missions, and battles in world history."

—Gen. Wesley K. Clark

This distinguished new series will feature the lives of eminent military leaders who changed history in the United States and abroad. Top military historians will write concise but comprehensive biographies including the personal lives, battles, strategies, and legacies of these great generals, with the aim to provide background and insight into today's armies and wars.

Patton by Alan Axelrod

Grant by John Mosier

Eisenhower by John Wukovits

Lemay by Barrett Tillman

MacArthur by Richard B. Frank

Stonewall Jackson by Donald A. Davis

Patton

A BIOGRAPHY

Alan Axelrod

palgrave
macmillan

PATTON: A BIOGRAPHY
Copyright © Alan Axelrod, 2006.
Copyright forword © Palgrave Macmillen, 2006.
All rights reserved. No part of this book may be used or reproduced in any manner whatsoever without written permission except in the case of brief quotations embodied in critical articles or reviews.

First published 2006 by
PALGRAVE MACMILLAN™
175 Fifth Avenue, New York, N.Y. 10010 and
Houndmills, Basingstoke, Hampshire, England RG21 6XS.
Companies and representatives throughout the world.

PALGRAVE MACMILLAN is the global academic imprint of the Palgrave Macmillan division of St. Martin's Press, LLC and of Palgrave Macmillan Ltd. Macmillan® is a registered trademark in the United States, United Kingdom and other countries. Palgrave is a registered trademark in the European Union and other countries.

ISBN 1–4039–7139–0 hardback

Library of Congress Cataloging-in-Publication Data
Axelrod, Alan, 1952-
Patton/Alan Axelrod.
    p.   cm.
Includes bibliographical references and index.
ISBN 1–4039–7139–0
    1. Patton, George S. (George Smith), 1885–1945   2. Generals—United States—Biography.   3. United States. Army—Biography.
4. United States—History, Military—20th century.   I. Title

A catalogue record for this book is available from the British Library.

Design by Letra Libre, Inc.

First edition: February 2006
10 9 8 7 6 5 4 3 2 1

Printed in the United States of America

Contents

Photosection appears between pages 99 and 100

For Anita, as always

Foreword

THE WORLD HAS CHANGED SIGNIFICANTLY SINCE George Patton's day, as has warfare. The struggle for imperial dominance that led to World War I continued as Germany fought for recovery and revenge in World War II. But the advent of the atomic bomb marked the beginning of mutual deterrence between potential adversaries in the west and the Soviet Union. The risks of nuclear escalation were so daunting that the struggle for world dominance was carried on largely by subterfuge and proxy wars fought on the margins of Western civilization.

But while there were no more World Wars, the United States was engaged in action after action, some difficult and bloody, others marked by nuance and maneuver. Still, these were operations Patton would surely have recognized as his own—forces with armored vehicles and air support, often engaged in intense ground combat. Indeed, there were battles in Korea—the breakout from the Pusan perimeter—and in Vietnam—the incursion into Cambodia—that could have been lifted straight from Patton's playbook.

American military interests in Korea, Vietnam and during the forty-year Cold War were in many ways the legacy not just of Patton's generation, but rather of Patton himself. Patton's tactical vision for maneuver warfare suffused the post–World War II US Army. His former subordinates and family kept alive not only his reputation but also his principles and spirit.

When the army built its first postwar tank, it was named for Patton. And at many an army post there was a Patton Hall, a Patton barracks, or a Patton museum. The spirit of maneuver warfare, and the use of combined arms, including airpower, as taught by Patton, became hallmarks of army war-fighting doctrine. Patton's tough training regimen became the stuff of legend, with a whole generation of officers claiming to carry his torch. One of the army's greatest chiefs of staff, he was best known for his leadership of the tank battalion that spearheaded Third Army's relief of Bastogne during the Battle of the Bulge. In the case studies of battles and leadership at the U.S. Army Armor School at Fort Knox, Patton was simply lionized.

At the US Military Academy, some fifty classes of West Pointers have walked daily past the inspirational statue of Patton in front of the library. With his feats near enough to make us glance over self-consciously, we dreamed and prayed that we might have the opportunity and courage to live up to his legacy.

After the difficult decade of the Vietnam War, as the army struggled to recover its bearings, army leaders returned to the foundations laid by Patton: the Desert Training Center. Just a few miles north of where Patton located his training camp in 1942, the army created a National Training Center, dedicated to teaching the art of combined arms, maneuver warfare. I was privileged to serve there twice, the last time as its commander. At the Center we made sure that, in true Patton style, the army sought to teach better fighting techniques and develop the requirements for better equipment. The result was an army that was trained, transformed, and ready for a fight.

With the fall of the Berlin Wall in 1989, some of the restraints on the use of U.S. forces were released. Patton would have been proud of the army's sweeping maneuver to push Saddam Hussein's legions out of Kuwait. He would have positively rejoiced as American armor, including a brigade from his own 2nd Armored Division, knocked out enemy vehicles from ranges of up to two miles with precision tank gunnery or defeated a large defending force at night in one of the largest tank battles in military history.

And certainly Patton's spirit was there with army generals Dave McKiernan, the Land Force Commander, and Scott Wallace, commanding V

Corps, as they sped deep into Iraq to penetrate Saddam's forces and seize Baghdad in the spring of 2003. Maneuver warfare, risk taking . . . it was all there, and Patton would have been proud to acknowledge his legacy.

Technology is far advanced now, of course. Unmanned aircraft fly over the enemy and send pictures to the ground, tanks communicate by internet-like messages, and with infrared technology we own the night. But Patton would see all this as the natural evolution of warfare along his own design.

It would be a mistake to limit Patton's influence to a form of warfare. In fact, it is also his character that has exerted a magnetic pull on the officer corps. His "tone-deafness" to politics, his aggressive swagger, his "fight where we're told, win where we fight" attitude marked a line of professional ethics that many officers have followed. He was the consummate professional warrior, committed to learning his profession, the "master of the sword."

Despite his swagger, Patton had a large dose of self-doubt. But only fools are always certain in leadership and war, two of mankind's most unpredictable activities. Patton's willingness to admit his doubts to himself may have been a key factor in his continuing professional growth, for as you will read in the following pages, Patton was able to look over the "edge of the cliff," and work to avoid the failures foreseen.

Many of my mentors at West Point and later would work hard to produce a "Patton-plus" mentality—hard-charging in combat, yes, but also able to deal with the intricacies of strategy and statecraft. In view of the challenges we face in peacekeeping operations today, we've never needed the "Patton-plus" mindset more.

Patton was a master of the media (at least most of the time), as you will read in Alan Axelrod's book. For all his appreciation of and use of the media however, he also discovered that it was truly a double-edged sword—the publicity that could make a career could also finish it.

No doubt Patton would have his frustrations with the global war on terror, nation-building, and peacekeeping. In the pages that follow Axelrod describes Patton's difficulties in postwar Germany, difficulties that are reflected in our current peacekeeping missions. But Patton was a student, perpetually studying how best to accomplish each mission. And it is this mindset, more than any other, that Patton has to offer today's leaders. He was a winner, a morale- and team-builder who adapted quickly and sought to master every challenge. We need leaders like that today.

—General Wesley K. Clark

Command and Controversy

FIELD MARSHAL GERD VON RUNDSTEDT WAS the brilliant German commander of World War II whose daring and desperate Ardennes offensive—"the Bulge"—was pounded into disaster by George S. Patton's Third Army. Asked, after the war, to name the American commander who most impressed him, Rundstedt did not hesitate: "Patton was your best." [1]

In a stunningly candid appraisal, Marshal Joseph Stalin declared: "The Red Army could not have conceived and certainly could not have executed the advance made by the Third Army across France."[2]

Americans also offered praise. Patton's subordinate, Lucian Truscott, a hard-bitten old cavalry commander who clashed bitterly with his chief during operations in Sicily, called him "perhaps the most colorful, as he was certainly the most outstanding battle leader of World War II." As for ordinary GIs, many certainly did not love the general. Patton's partially self-invented nickname, "Old Blood and Guts," was ubiquitous during much of the war, and many a GI griped, with sarcasm typical of the American army, "Yeah. *His* guts. *Our* blood." Yet probably to a man, the soldiers of the Third United States Army took very hard and very personally Patton's death on December 21, 1945. As one private wrote to his parents, all the boys in his outfit were "in mourning for . . . one of the greatest men that ever lived. . . . The rest of the world thinks of him as just another guy with stars on his shoulders. The men that served under him know him as a soldier's leader. I am proud to say that I have served under him in the Third Army." [3]

Some other Americans had very different feelings. The critic and cultural historian Dwight Macdonald, who served in World War II, called Patton "a swaggering bigmouth, a Fascist-minded aristocrat . . . brutal and hysterical, coarse and affected, violent and empty, . . . compared to the dreary run of us, General Patton was quite mad." Andy Rooney, a young war correspondent who today is best known as the curmudgeonly commentator on CBS Television's *60 Minutes,* minced no words. He "detested Patton and everything about the way he was. It was because we had so few soldiers like him that we won the war. . . . Patton was the kind of officer that our wartime enlisted man was smarter than." [4]

It is easy to find scores of paeans to George S. Patton Jr. and just as easy to find at least as many indictments lodged against him. What *cannot* be found is anything in between. No one seems to have had a moderate, let alone objective, opinion of the general.

Why did Patton so powerfully polarize opinion and, indeed, why does he continue to do so?

Historians, armchair generals, and professional soldiers routinely dissect and debate the campaigns of Napoleon, Grant, and Lee, apportioning praise or blame, merit or criticism, based on tactics and troop movements. This is not the case with Patton. No one disputes the results he achieved.

Patton was a highly effective pioneer, advocate, and exponent of modern mechanized warfare as well as a doctrine of highly mobile offensive, which enabled American ground forces to prevail against the army that invented blitzkrieg. On the eve of American entry into World War II, in the largest, most ambitious war games the U.S. Army had ever staged, Patton was universally acknowledged to have outgeneraled all of his colleagues. Subsequently assigned to create a desert warfare training center outside of Indio, California, Patton turned out America's first generation of desert warriors. When the U.S. II Corps, in the army's first major contest against the Germans, suffered humiliating defeat at Kasserine Pass, Tunisia, Dwight D. Eisenhower, commanding the U.S. Army in North Africa, called for Patton. Within days he transformed the thoroughly demoralized American force into the kernel of a victorious army that defeated the vaunted Afrika Korps. When Anglo-American forces jumped off from North Africa to invade Sicily, Patton unilaterally revised the subordinate role his Seventh Army had been assigned and, with lightning speed, took Palermo and then beat British general Bernard Law Montgomery to the conquest of Messina.

Following the D-Day landings at Normandy, Patton was assigned command of the Third Army and, with it, amplified Operation Cobra— General Omar Bradley's modest plan for breaking out of the Norman hedgerow country—into the most spectacular and productive advance of World War II. *The Third Army's After Action Report,* the official account, begins: "In nine months and eight days of campaigning, Third U.S. Army compiled a record of offensive operations that could only be measured in superlatives, for not only did the Army's achievements astonish the world but its deeds in terms of figures challenged the imagination." During this brief period, Patton's men liberated or gained 81,522 square miles in France, 1,010 in Luxembourg, 156 in Belgium, 29,940 in Germany, 3,485 in Czechoslovakia, and 2,103 in Austria. The Third Army liberated or captured some 12,000 cities, towns, and villages, 27 of which contained more than 50,000 people. It captured 1,280,688 prisoners of war between August 1, 1944, and May 13, 1945. It killed 47,500 enemy soldiers and wounded 115,700 more. During this same period, Third Army logistics troops brought in by rail, truck, and air 1,234,529 tons of supplies, including 533,825 tons of ammunition. Its engineers built 2,498 bridges—about 8.5 miles—and repaired or reconstructed 2,240 miles of road and 2,092 miles of railroad. Its Signal Corps troops laid 3,747 miles of open wire and

36,338 miles of underground cable. Its telephone operators handled an average of 13,986 calls daily. Its ambulances evacuated 269,187 patients. Its officers and men administered civil affairs in Belgium, Czechoslovakia, France, and Luxembourg, as well as providing military governments for parts of Germany and Austria, ultimately regulating the lives and welfare of some 30 million men, women, and children.[5]

In the midst of the great Allied drive eastward, Field Marshal von Rundstedt launched the Ardennes offensive, hitting the American line at its weakest point and threatening to split the Allied forces in two with an all-out advance targeting the crucial Allied-held port of Antwerp. Patton performed a miracle of tactics, logistics, and human endurance when he turned the bulk of his army—troops exhausted by three months of continual battle and advance—90 degrees north to launch a bold counterattack into the southern flank of the German advance. The Battle of the Bulge, which began as a stunning catastrophe for the Allies, was converted into a U.S. victory that broke the back of the German army.

Despite such prodigies, Patton was almost continually on the verge of being removed from command. That fact is but the sum of the many contradictions that orbit this man. He was a cavalry officer steeped in romantic military tradition, holder of the grandly archaic U.S. Army title of "Master of the Sword," which had been invented expressly for him. Yet it was he who was instrumental in pulling a hidebound and reluctant American military into the most advanced realms of mobile armored warfare. An autocratic snob, scion of old California and even older Virginia gentry, wedded to a New England heiress, Patton still managed to create unparalleled rapport with the lowliest private in his command. An outspoken racist, he nevertheless relied heavily on African American combat troops, whereas most of his contemporaries relegated them to menial service and support units. Exuberant in his profanity, he was a deeply religious man, who believed God had destined him to military greatness. He professed to have a personal relationship with God, and he was a believer in the efficacy of prayer. Patton was afflicted with dyslexia that exacerbated his childhood insecurities and, as an adult, he was tortured by self-born intimations of cowardice. Throughout his life, but especially in middle age, he suffered profound depression and episodes others described as hysteria (he called it "biliousness"); and yet he inspired the men of his Seventh and then his Third Army to a level of absolute self-confidence and consistent victory.

As theater commander in North Africa, and later as supreme Allied commander in Europe, Dwight David Eisenhower—whom Patton had befriended in 1919 when both were stationed at Camp Meade, Maryland—was Patton's boss, although he was junior to Patton both in age and years in service. No one was more painfully aware of Patton's failings than Eisenhower. To close colleagues, he expressed fears about what he called Patton's "instability." For the public, in the pages of his postwar memoir, *Crusade in Europe,* he wrote of Patton's "emotional tenseness and impulsiveness," traits that led Patton to make outrageous statements and to spout streams of profanity that delighted many enlisted men, but embarrassed some. Most notoriously, his "impulsiveness" caused him to assault two soldiers suffering from battle fatigue (see chapter 9), and those incidents, in turn, led politicians, the press, and the public to demand Patton's immediate removal. Eisenhower was tempted to yield to the pressure of those demands and even appealed to *his* boss, George C. Marshall, army chief of staff, for instructions. Marshall turned the decision back to Eisenhower. After a period of soul-searching, Eisenhower wrote to Marshall: "I would want Patton as one of my Army commanders" for the upcoming invasion of Europe. "For certain types of action," he wrote, George S. Patton "was the most outstanding soldier our country has produced." Yet Eisenhower regarded Patton as something like a hero of Greek tragedy—the very elements of his greatness always threatened to destroy him. "His emotional tenseness and his impulsiveness were the very qualities that made him, in open situations, such a remarkable leader of an army. In pursuit and exploitation there is need for a commander who sees nothing but the necessity of getting ahead; the more he drives his men the more he will save their lives."[6]

On December 14, 1943, Eisenhower replied to a letter from June Jenkins Booth. Mrs. Booth, upon reading that Patton had slapped soldiers suffering from battle fatigue, wrote that she had one son in the service and another slated to go the following year, and that she hoped Patton would not remain in command, where he might "repeat his fits of temper on another unfortunate victim." She appealed to the supreme commander, telling him that she would "die of worry" if her sons had to serve under "such a cruel, profane, impatient officer."

Eisenhower replied:

> . . . You are quite right in deploring acts such as [Patton's] and in being incensed that they could occur in an American army. But in Sicily General Patton saved thousands of American lives. By his boldness, his speed, his drive, he won his part of the campaign by marching, more than he did by fighting. He drove himself and his men almost beyond human endurance, but because of this he minimized tragedy in American homes.
>
> . . . I decided [that Patton] should not be lost to us in the job of winning this war . . . even though the easy thing for me would have been to send General Patton home. I hope that, as the mother of two American soldiers, you will understand.[7]

In essence, Eisenhower was asking this soldier's mother to do as he did: to close her eyes to everything except the life-saving results this "cruel, profane, impatient officer" produced. It was a great deal to ask of a mother— or of a supreme Allied commander. It was, in fact, a great deal to ask of a democratic nation that was sending its sons to fight the most brutal and destructive tyranny the world had ever seen.

Much as Eisenhower forced himself to accept Patton with all of his formidable failings, today's military leaders continue to value the legacy of this controversial commander. Both of Patton's major wars, the two world wars, were predicated on a military strategy and political policy of maximum effort for total victory, whereas the wars that followed World War II were "limited" conflicts dominated by the principle of "containment," a need to achieve victory without igniting a potentially civilization-destroying third world war. Nevertheless, within the context of limited warfare, maximum effort combined with great speed, intensive violence of attack, flexibility of response, and the highest possible degree of mobility were often required. Patton laid the groundwork for these, as was evident in General Douglas MacArthur's masterpiece assault on Inchon during the Korean War, the use of "airmobile cavalry" in the Vietnam War, the sweeping armored assault that constituted the major action of the first Persian Gulf War (Operation Desert Storm) in 1991, and the race across Iraq and into Baghdad during the opening phase of Operation Iraqi Freedom in 2003. Such operations constitute the tactical legacy of George S. Patton Jr., but no modern commander would look at this list and say that it adequately summarizes Patton's place in the living history of America's military. Patton also imbued the American army with a commitment to victory through individual initiative and personal leadership. To be sure, this aspect of his legacy is less tangible than the tactical lessons, but, for the commanders of today and tomorrow, it is even more urgently indispensable.

No one questions the results Patton unfailingly produced, but in a democracy, which has never been congenial to a standing army and never wanted to raise a military caste, a born-and-bred warrior must always find himself the object of questions, doubts, disdain, fear, and even loathing. We admire Patton the captain, we relish Patton the legend, but we are, at the very least, uneasy with Patton the man. This brief biography seeks a balanced appreciation of a great and greatly flawed figure, whose contributions to modern military doctrine and modern world history are profound and whose greatness and failings alike reveal as much about America—who we were, who we are, and who we have imagined ourselves to be—as they do about George Smith Patton Jr.

CHAPTER 1

To the Army Born

GEORGE SMITH PATTON JR. WAS BORN TO THE ARMY, born on November 11, 1885, at Lake Vineyard, his family's home outside of Los Angeles. He was named after both his father, George William Patton (who changed his middle name to Smith to honor both his father and his stepfather, George Hugh Smith), and after his grandfather, George Smith Patton. Grandfather graduated from Virginia Military Institute (VMI) in 1852 (having been a student of Thomas "Stonewall" Jackson) and rose to command the 22nd Virginia Infantry in the Civil War. Wounded, then captured during the Shenandoah campaign, he was exchanged, only to be killed on September 19, 1864, at the Third Battle of Winchester. Similarly, Grandfather's brother, Waller Tazewell Patton, was wounded at Second Bull Run, and then fell in Pickett's Charge at the Battle of Gettysburg.

George William—the Patton children called him Papa—was a Virginian who attended VMI, just as his father had. In his senior year, during the 1876 national centennial, George William led the cadets in a parade at Philadelphia as top-ranked first captain. It was the very first southern military formation to march in the North after the Civil War. Papa did not pursue a military career, but left Virginia and became a lawyer in California, where he became district attorney of Los Angeles County before giving it all up to manage the estate and vineyard of his wife's family.

George Smith Patton Jr. learned well the names of his ancestors, together with those of many cousins who had held command rank in the army of the Confederacy, and, before them, Great-Great Grandfather Robert Patton, who settled in Fredericksburg, Virginia, in 1771. Robert Patton married Anne Gordon Mercer, daughter of Hugh Mercer who had fought at Culloden in his native Scotland. Mercer immigrated to America and fought in the French and Indian War and finally, as a close comrade of General George Washington, in the American Revolution, he fell at the Battle of Princeton.

Young George was selective in his ancestor worship. Enthralled by the martial glory of his father's ancestors, he paid little attention to the family of his mother, Ruth Wilson Patton. Great-Grandfather David Wilson had been a major in the American Revolution, a Tennessee pioneer, and, later, speaker of the Tennessee territorial assembly; grandfather Benjamin Davis Wilson worked in Mississippi and New Mexico as a trapper, Indian trader, and storekeeper before moving to southern California, where he bought a ranch and made money in the hide and tallow trade. He married a Mexican woman of Spanish descent and became the *alcalde* (justice of the peace) for San Bernardino, called universally and with affectionate respect Don Benito. Later moving to Los Angeles, he lived on a small vineyard and, operating from what would one day be the site of Union Station, became a prosperous merchant, saloon keeper, hotelier, and minor real estate tycoon. Widowed in 1849, Don Benito married his housekeeper, Margaret Hereford (after her husband died); it was she who gave birth to George's mother. Wilson ultimately achieved great local prominence, becoming the first mayor of Los Angeles and acquiring a ranch of 14,000 acres, encompassing what is now Pasadena, South Pasadena, San Marino, Alhambra, and San Gabriel. He transformed his home, Lake Vineyard, into the biggest producer of wine and brandy in California.

A pioneer, politician, and magnate, Don Benito nevertheless failed to cast over his grandson the same spell as the military paternal forebears. Worse, when Don Benito died, his son-in-law and business partner, James de Barth Shorb, who lived in sumptuous style, mismanaged the winery through a period of drought and frosts, running the business into serious debt. Determined to come to the rescue of the enterprise, George's Papa gave up his law practice and moved the family to Lake Vineyard. George idolized his father, and he resented how the winery and myriad other business affairs attendant on Shorb's financial train wreck monopolized his time.

One of the activities Mr. Patton had less time for was reading to his son. Those who knew Patton as an adult could not help but observe that he was an avid reader. Yet, as a child, his difficulties in learning to read were such that his father continued reading aloud to him well beyond the age when most parents have stopped. (That he learned not only to read but to love reading is a testament to the strength of his will and determination.) Favorites of father and son were the novels of Sir Walter Scott, which nurtured the youngster's growing sense of romance and chivalry, as well as an appreciation for his Scots heritage; the *Iliad* and *Odyssey*, classic evocations of heroic ideals; the tragedies of Shakespeare; the stories and verse of Rudyard Kipling; and the Old Testament. Unbidden, George memorized long passages from the books his papa read to him.

Anyone who spent much time with "the Boy," as his father fondly called him, realized he was highly intelligent. However, his family—and no one more than George himself—was baffled and frustrated by his struggle with reading and writing. Today his learning disability would be readily diagnosed as dyslexia, a common disorder characterized by a difficulty in recognizing and comprehending written words. In young Patton's day, the problem would have branded the boy as "slow." Determined to avoid that stigma, his parents hired tutors to school him at home until he was eleven years old. By that time, they decided he was ready for a good private school and enrolled him in Stephen Cutter Clark's School for Boys in Pasadena. From the beginning, his favorite subject was history. He immersed himself in the stories of the leaders of ancient times, particularly the great captains, including Scipio Africanus, Hannibal, and Caesar. Moving into the more modern era, his favorites included Joan of Arc and Napoleon Bonaparte. To the schoolboy, figures such as these joined seamlessly with the heroes nearer to his own time, including Robert E. Lee and Stonewall Jackson. John Singleton Mosby, the famed "Gray Ghost" of the Confederacy, had become a lawyer for the Southern Pacific Railroad and from time to time, during Patton's boyhood, visited the family, regaling a rapt George with stories of his daring cavalry raids.

Beginning in childhood, the past, in the form of vivid ghosts of heroism and ageless models of command, was always present for Patton. The historical figures of whom he read were superimposed upon his own experience. Lifelong, he devoured libraries of history, especially the history of ancient conquest, general military history, and the memoirs of celebrated generals. Prior to flying into Normandy to assume command of the Third Army a month after D-Day, he "read *The Norman Conquest* by Freeman, paying particular attention to the roads William the Conqueror used in his operations in Normandy and Brittany." When he proposed crossing the Seine at Melun, it was entirely natural for him to toss off the observation that the "Melun crossing is the same as that used by Labienus with his Tenth Legion about 55 B.C." His absorption in military history was more than intellectual or even professional, for he made no secret of his belief in reincarnation. In 1943, before the Allies stepped off from North Africa to invade Sicily, British general Sir Harold Alexander admiringly observed, "You know, George, you would have made a great marshal for Napoleon if you had lived in the 19th century." Patton replied dryly: "But I did." He was never embarrassed to confess his belief in reincarnation, his conviction that he had marched with Napoleon or with Bohemia's John the Blind against the Turks in the fourteenth century, or even that, as a Roman legionnaire, "Perhaps I stabbed our Savior / In His sacred helpless side."[1]

The past, for Patton, was not all in books or even in lives earlier lived. It was his very birthright. After he had proposed to Beatrice during Christmas of 1908, he wrote a letter to her father, Frederick Ayer, justifying his choice of career. Patton admitted that there was no rational reason for embarking on a life so financially unrewarding as that of an officer in the U.S. Army, but, he explained, "I only feel it inside. It is as natural for me to be a soldier as it is to breathe and would be as hard to give up all thought of it as it would to stop breathing." [2]

The very first childhood game he remembered playing was "soldiers," with his sister Anne, called Nita, assuming the rank of major "while I claimed to be a private which I thought was superior," Patton recalled. Their father joined in, snapping a salute to brother and sister each morning and asking "how the private and major were." Not much later, George came to understand that "private" was superior to nothing, and he began referring to himself as "Georgie S. Patton, Jr., Lieutenant General."[3]

Out of doors in the golden California sunshine, George learned to ride early. While Papa happily fashioned wooden swords for his son and taught him how to build forts, he could not keep up with the boy's energy, drive, and endless craving for exercise and endless activity.

Family heritage, the reading of heroic tales and military history, love of horses, boundless energy, and exuberant play—these were the elements of George Patton's boyhood, and the adult Patton would never leave them far behind. There is no evidence that he ever seriously thought about becoming anything other than a soldier. More to the point, all the evidence reveals an early and ever-growing desire to be a leader, a commander, a winner of great glory and universal recognition. During the six years he spent at Clark's School for Boys, he strove to excel despite his dyslexia, which earned him the ridicule of fellow students whenever he stumbled over words he read aloud or wrote on the blackboard. It must have been painful for him, but he was never discouraged. Raised on the romance of his Scots and Confederate ancestors, people beaten but unbowed, he saw defeat as a challenge to win *next time* or to triumph *in the end.* Later, as a mature commander, he would inscribe, using all uppercase letters, in one of his field notebooks: "YOU ARE NOT BEATEN UNTIL YOU ADMIT IT. HENCE DON'T."[4] In any event, no matter what happened to him, his adoring father and mother never allowed him to feel defeated.

But for the limitations of dyslexia, George Smith Patton Jr. was, as he himself later recalled, "the happiest boy in the world,"[5] and the idyll was made complete by summers spent on Catalina Island, which the sons of B. D. Wilson's business partner Phineas Banning had purchased in 1892 to turn into an upscale vacation resort. There is where the Pattons had a summer place, and it was there, in 1902, that 17-year-old George met Beatrice Banning Ayer, privileged daughter of a Boston industrialist named Frederick Ayer and his second wife, Ellen Barrows Banning, niece of Phineas Banning. Beatrice had arrived in California with her parents to visit the Bannings. George was smitten. In some ways, it was an instance of the attraction of opposites. George was tall, muscular, and rough, whereas 16-year-old Beatrice was small, slender, and graceful. Yet, in other ways, they were perfectly matched: the only thing she loved more than sailing was horseback riding, which she did fiercely and fearlessly, despite a nearsightedness so severe that she could barely see where she was going.

After that Catalina summer, when Beatrice had returned to Boston, the two began writing one another, and, come Christmas, Beatrice sent George a tiepin. "Please believe me when I say that it was the very thing I most wanted," Patton wrote in a letter of January 10, 1903, "and that when I first wore it and looked into a glass to see if it was in straight, I involuntarily raised my hat."[6] Before meeting Beatrice, George had shown little interest in girls. Clearly, new he was growing up. Not only did he have a girlfriend, who, eight years later, he would marry, but, by the fall of 1902, he was ready to tell his parents that he had definitely decided on his life's work. He would become an officer in the United States Army.

From the moment his son made the decision, Papa embarked on a tireless campaign to obtain for him an appointment to West Point. On September 29, he wrote to Senator Thomas R. Bard, who had the power to recommend the boy for a cadet slot. He then set about appealing to his many prominent and influential friends to prevail upon Senator Bard on his boy's behalf. Despite all of the campaigning, the best that could be elicited from Bard was a promise that he would allow George to compete with other young men in an examination, which would determine his choice of nominee.

Mr. Patton loved his son, but he was a realist. On spelling alone, George would likely fail the exam. To cover all bases, he looked into the University of Arizona, where the corps of cadets was commanded by his cousin, and at ROTC programs at Princeton and Cornell. He also looked into securing for his son another year of pre-college education at the Morristown Preparatory School in New Jersey. And then there was VMI—his alma mater and that of his father and two uncles. The faculty was populated by Patton friends and relatives, and it occurred to him that the Virginia Military Institute would perhaps be the ideal place for George to gain a year of training, education, and maturity before he applied for entrance to West Point "by certificate," which would allow him to bypass the entrance examination.

Bombarded by Mr. Patton's letters, Senator Bard never said no, but he did not say yes, either. In June, Princeton accepted George (despite his having failed the plane geometry portion of the entrance examination), but Mr. Patton decided to enroll his son at VMI. If Bard suddenly called him in for the examination, he could always return to California in the spring.

The trip to Virginia that September, to his ancestral and spiritual home, as well as the far-off focus of his boyish imaginings, was George's very first journey outside of California. Two dozen years later, Patton recalled: "Just before I went away to the V.M.I. I was walking with Uncle Glassell Patton and told him that I feared that I might be cowardly. He told me that no Patton could be a coward." Characteristically, George confided this exchange to his father, who obligingly interpreted his uncle's words for him. "While ages of gentility might make a man of [your] breeding reluctant to engage in a fist fight," he told his son, "the same breeding made him perfectly willing to face death from weapons with a smile." That hardly ended Patton's inner debate over issues of courage. He would question himself, and even doubt himself, on the subject for his entire life. Yet, almost hopefully, some 24 years later, he wrote of Papa's explanation: "I think that this is true."[7]

CHAPTER 2

Cadet, Soldier, Athlete, Swordsman

As a soldier, George S. Patton Jr. would live and fight in many climes and countries, but his most dramatic journey came in 1903 and took him from the sharp brown hills of southern California to the lush, green, low, and rolling folds of the Blue Ridge that formed the backdrop to the Virginia Military Institute's campus of crenellated gothic buildings outside of Lexington, Virginia. Later in life, Patton would recall how "Papa and Mama took me east to enter the V.M.I. . . . Papa went with me to report. The First Captain, Ragland, was in the room on the left of the salley port which had been Papa's when he was Sergeant Major." So there it was, in this strange, new place: the presence of the past. Papa (VMI, 1877) and his father (VMI, 1852) before him had been cadets here, as had great-uncles John Mercer Patton Jr. (VMI 1846) and Waller Tazewell Patton (VMI 1855). George signed the enrollment papers, and Ragland looked toward Papa: "'Of course you realize Mr. Patton that now your son is a cadet he cannot leave the grounds.' Papa said 'Of course.' I never felt lower in my life."[1]

As far as the faculty and cadets of VMI were concerned, that was precisely the feeling appropriate to a first-year cadet. They were called *rats*. But George had an additional disadvantage. His dyslexia caused him to stumble over a handwritten "no hazing pledge" all incoming cadets were required to read aloud in an assembly. As usual, he kept no secret from his Papa, who wrote on September 27, 1903: "I do not see how you are going to over-come this difficulty, except by practicing reading all kinds of writing." And the words that follow could have been written by General Patton himself. "Do not give up," Papa wrote, "but when you start to read any thing keep at it till you work it out." He continued, helpfully and practically, by pointing out that "hazing" had been mis-spelled as "hazeing" in his son's letter. "The verb is 'to haze' and you should remember the general rule—to drop the final 'e' before 'ing.'"[2] There was never anything pompous or empty in what Papa told his son, but always a mixture of warm encouragement and practical advice. This was at the root of Patton's own command style. A stern and intimidating presence, Patton nevertheless celebrated the high performance of subor-dinates and, when he corrected them, he did so with concrete criticism and practical advice.

As comforting as communication with his father was, Cadet Patton was even more delighted when he presented himself to the school tailor, who not only recognized him as a Patton, but remarked that his uniform measurements were exactly those of his father and his grandfather. He soon felt as if he belonged there, almost as if he had come home. Papa advised him (as Patton recalled years later) "that the first thing was to be a good soldier, next a good scholar." Cadet Patton became a model sol-dier, flawless in appearance and in his execution of every movement of every drill. He memorized VMI regulations and followed them to the letter. An outside of observer might have thought his devotion obsessive, even fanatical, but there were no outsiders at VMI. A third-generation cadet, he had marched into his birthright, as had many of his classmates. They did not think him a grind or a fanatic; they respected and admired him. He had a natural talent for behaving like "one of the fellows," but he never broke the rules or, as he gleefully admitted to Papa, never allowed himself to get caught. He was the first in his class to be initiated into "K.A.," a secret fraternity, which immediately resulted in upperclassmen treating him "almost as an equal." Possessed of a thoroughly sympathetic understanding of the caste system at VMI, George wrote Papa: "Theoretically, I do not approve" of being coddled by upperclassmen, "but practically I do." In this, in his ability to go unwaveringly by the book yet also manage to be popular, was foreshadowed the future commander. General Patton was a stickler for protocol, regulations, impeccable uniforms, and the flawless practice of military courtesy, yet he nurtured within himself an unconventional boldness and an insatiable appetite for glory.[3]

Even as he flourished at VMI, neither George nor Papa took their eyes off the real prize: an appointment to West Point. Papa's ceaseless barrage of letters to Senator Bard and those who could exert influence on the senator finally yielded fruit when, in February 1904, Bard invited George to his office in Los Angeles for an informal examination. He used the long train ride west to study, concentrating on geography and spelling. At home, he greeted his family warmly, then dived back into his books, not emerging until the examination was over and done. He then returned to VMI, playing and replaying the examination in his mind until word came on February 18 that George S. Patton Jr. was among three candidates recommended to Senator Bard.

He had made the first cut. Now Papa swung into action again, calling on a host of his prominent and influential friends to pepper Bard with their letters. The senator at last waved a white flag in the form of a telegram to Mr. Patton on March 3, 1904, announcing his son's nomination. An ecstatic Papa in turn fired off the good news in a telegram to his son then followed up with a letter: "You cannot know," he wrote, "how proud we feel—and how gratified that you have won your first promotion in the battle of life. . . . You have in you good soldier blood."[4]

George S. Patton Jr. left VMI for West Point with a sterling record, grades averaging well above 90 percent, and characterized by VMI commandant Major L. H. Strother as "a young man of exemplary habits and excellent mental ability and attainments. . . . He has an aptitude for military life." Moreover, Major Strother informed him that, had he stayed, he would have been made first corporal, the highest appointment for second-year cadets.[5]

First-year cadets were called *plebes* at the Point, and many a plebe was profoundly shocked by his first year—the rules, the discipline, the hard riding by upperclassmen, and most of all, the nonstop tempo. However, the only thing that bothered Cadet Patton, as he wrote in his first letter home, was the necessity of rising at 5 A.M. and the fact that they "make us shave every day and the only time we get to do this is before rev[eille]," which was also "the only time we are allowed or have time to write except on Sunday." A nightly bath was also required, and cadets were permitted "but eight minutes to take it in." The food was "fine" with "lots of variety," and the "table-cloth is changed every day." *That* was clearly important to Cadet Patton, fine southern gentleman that he saw himself to be, but what disappointed him was the academy's apparent dearth of "gentlemen" of his own caliber. His two roommates were "very nice and work hard and try to keep the room and them selves clean but they are not gentlemen in the sence of being refined and using good grammar. They are just very respectable middle class fellows."[6]

Patton was never a tolerant man. Throughout his life, diaries and letters are laced with racism, anti-Semitism, and miscellaneous xenophobia. To a modern conscience and consciousness, these attitudes are repugnant, yet they reveal as much about the social milieu in which Patton was raised—a prosperous Anglo California household staffed by servants of Mexican descent, a family tree rooted in chivalrous, slave-holding Virginia—and the America of his day than they do about Patton the man. As a lowly plebe, he was indeed a social snob; that is what his entire childhood and his year at VMI had produced. But as George saw it, his social identity ran deeper than mere training or upbringing. It was a matter of *breeding,* in the literal sense; it was a matter of blood. On July 3, 1904, he wrote to Papa about a Fourth of July oration he had just attended in Cullum Hall. The subject was "the modern soldier and what he stood for." The entire audience applauded, and "I believe they all agreed with the speaker. I didn't."

> Infact from what I have seen here and at the [Virginia Military] Institute I belong to a different class a class perhaps almost extinct or one which may have never existed yet as far removed from these lazy, patriotic, or peace soldiers as heaven is from hell. I know that my ambition is selfish and cold yet it is not a selfishnes for instead of sparing me, it makes me exert my self to the utter most to attain an end which will do neither me nor any one else any good. Of course I may be a dreamer but I have a firm conviction I am not and in any case I will do my best to attain what I consider—wrongly perhaps—my destiny.[7]

Young Patton's self-understanding was mature beyond his years and, in fact, was at a level few adults ever attain. His snobbery was a mere symptom of his perception of a special "destiny" (it was a word he would use often in speaking of himself), a destiny compounded of something ancient and archaic ("perhaps almost extinct") or something entirely mythic ("may have never existed"), a destiny that set him apart from anything like the "modern" soldier (as far apart as "heaven is from hell"), a destiny that made him coldly ambitious, apparently selfish, yet utterly unsparing of himself.

Realizing one's destiny, it seems, required a patience that Cadet Patton did not possess in abundance. His goal was to graduate as cadet adjutant, the top senior upperclassman, and by the end of his first year, he wanted to be cadet corporal. At first Patton thought that this might not be so hard to do, for he judged his fellow cadets harshly. They seemed to him lazy, beset by "a languid lacitude—or careless indifference or hazy uncertainty," whereas he, Cadet Patton, was at all times sharp as a razor. But he soon discovered that the academic work was much harder at West Point than at VMI. By November, he was struggling and wrote to his father: "I actually think that if I don't get a corp [promotion to cadet corporal] I will die . . . I fancy that there is no one in my class who so hates to be last or who tries so hard to be first and who so utterly fails. . . . Infact the sum total of me is that I am a character-less, lazy, stupid yet ambitious dreamer; who will degenerate into a third rate second lieutenant and never command any thing more than a platoon." (In adult life, Patton's theatrical arrogance and blustering self-confidence would—sometimes transparently—mask his persistent self-doubts.) His class report for December 1 put him at number 42 in mathematics, 71 in English, and 30 in drill regulations out of a class of 152. In January, he wrote Papa that it was "beastly discouraging to get worse marks than men who you know have less grey matter and not half the ambition." In June, he failed his final French examination, which meant (according to the arcane rules of the academy) that he also had to take an examination in mathematics. On June 12, he dispatched a telegram to Papa: "Did not pass math turned back to next class probably furlough this summer will wire definitely." Mr. Patton sent a return telegram the very next day: "It is all right my boy and all for best God bless you."[8]

Patton returned to California to lick his wounds, and, while vacationing with his family on Catalina, he studied on his own and also worked with a tutor. As if determined to discipline his very thoughts, he bought a notebook so that no passing idea could escape him. Entry number one was: "Do your damdest always."[9]

When he returned to West Point to repeat his first year, he tried out for varsity football, throwing himself so fiercely into practice that he injured his arm and was removed from the squad. That is when he took up the sword and tried out for the track team. He would excel in both. He redeemed himself academically—adequately, if not spectacularly—and he was named second corporal for the second-year class. It was both a disappointment and a vast relief.

During the summer, he was assigned to break in the plebes at summer camp. Second Corporal Patton took to command as a thirsty man to water. Although he commanded merely a company, when the first corporal was absent on other duties, Patton took over the entire battalion. His cadets drilled flawlessly, yet, to a man, they cordially despised Patton. He demanded of them no less than he demanded of himself, and that was simply too much. He withheld all praise, but noted and reported the slightest infraction. However it affected the first-year cadets, for him the result was a valuable lesson in the difference between a demanding commander and a martinet. At the conclusion of summer camp, the tactical officers demoted Patton from second to sixth corporal. As he explained in a letter to Beatrice, he had been "too d—military."[10] Later, as a mature commander, he would learn to blend praise with criticism, though he would remain a stickler for all military courtesies and usages.

During his second year (actually his third year at the Point, if we count his repeated first year), Patton clawed his way to the middle of his class, tried out for football again, was again sidelined with injuries suffered in practice, but became a star when he wielded a sword or mounted a saddle. Although he might not excel in the classroom or have the opportunity to do so on the gridiron, he must have been gratified to have found a home in more martial exploits with saber and steed. Patton pushed himself into the kind of reckless test of courage that he would repeat throughout his career. As a general, Patton believed it important to make himself conspicuous in the front lines, "to show the soldiers that generals could get shot at." As a cadet, while crouching in the target trench on the rifle range—his job was to raise the targets for shooting, then lower them for scoring—Patton decided to discover for himself what it was like to get shot at. Would he have the courage that his father had spoken to him of, the courage to "face death from weapons with a smile"? He suddenly sprang up from the safety of the trench and stood at attention facing the firing line as the bullets zinged about him. He was not afraid. What others thought of this experiment is not recorded.[11]

By the spring of his sophomore year, Patton regained his post as second corporal and, for his junior year, was promoted to cadet sergeant major. This would position him for a plum promotion as a senior. Then, in February 1908, came a wonderful harbinger of destiny itself. He was named cadet adjutant for the following—senior—year. It was not just evidence of achievement, but an opportunity for further glory. The cadet adjutant was the leader of the class and the central figure on the parade ground, the cadet who, every day, marched to the center of the field and read out the orders of the day. All eyes were fixed on him and on him alone.

Almost simultaneously with his appointment as cadet adjutant dawned the realization that he was in love with Beatrice Ayer. The two events seemed intertwined. Responding to Beatrice's congratulations on his promotion, he wrote on February 22: "Do you remember long ago when . . . I said I would like to be adjutant but feared I never would be and you said I would[?]"[12] And while there had been other girls during his West Point years—including one Kate, a beautiful heiress from Vassar, to whom he was briefly attracted by her looks as well as her money—he wrote his father that Beatrice was *the* one. Yet the young man who as a commander would be so swiftly decisive on the field of battle could not bring himself to propose. On a visit to the Ayers during Christmas vacation, he spoke to Beatrice of his love and told her that he wanted to marry her, but he asked her not to answer—not yet. He held the matter of marriage in abeyance, and Beatrice complied, as he completed his final year and threw himself into the knotty problem of what branch of the service to opt for. In the army of the day, there were infantry, cavalry, artillery, and the engineers. The last two were easily discounted. Patton had neither the aptitude nor the academic grades for a posting with the engineers, and, as for the artillery, the big guns were generally well back from the front lines, the region of greatest danger and greatest glory. That left infantry and cavalry. Infantry was the "queen of battle," the branch in which promotion could be expected to come fastest, yet cavalry seemed naturally more suited to Patton, a lover of horses and an outstanding horseman. The branch was more elite than the infantry, its officers typically a better, more uniform class of "gentlemen," like himself. And then there was the historical fact that knights always rode horses while the rabble marched on foot. Nevertheless, Patton wore out anyone who would listen with the pros and cons until he finally decided. He would be a cavalryman.

＋≒＝≒╪

On June 11, 1909, George Smith Patton Jr. graduated from the United States Military Academy 46 out of 103, a ranking not based (as in civilian colleges) on academic standing alone, but "according to general merit." Cadet Patton's mediocre standing was not, of course, predictive of his military career. J. C. H. Lee, whose imperious and uncooperative ways as Eisenhower's chief of Services and Supply in World War II earned him the nickname "Jesus Christ Himself," graduated number 12 in 1909. Number 39, Jacob L. Devers, whom the other cadets thought incurably lazy, went on to command 6th Army Group in Europe. Robert Eichelberger, ranked 68th, became Douglas MacArthur's most brilliant general, commander of the Eighth Army in the Pacific. And William H. Simpson, 101 of 103, went on to command the Ninth Army in Europe. More telling than the numbers or Patton's own self-evaluation was how his classmates regarded him. It was at best with paradoxically respectful condescension. It was hard not to admire his zeal and effort, but it was also hard to take seriously his interminable talk of glory. That it was spoken of in all candor and earnestness made it even harder to accept without a grin or a grimace. Among his classmates, he had no close friends, but there was genuine affection in one of his West Point nicknames, Georgie (which was also used later by the circle of fellow senior commanders in World War II); his other nickname, Quill, betrayed a resentment just as genuine. In cadet jargon, "to quill" was to gratuitously "skin" a fellow cadet—that is, to report him for an offense. The point was not that Cadet Patton was a snitch or vindictive or sadistic but that he was impossibly hard on underclassmen, demanding a level of performance few, if any, could deliver. That he was hardest on himself probably escaped few of his classmates, and that fact saved him from universal condemnation.

In all candor, Patton doubtless admitted all aspects of his classmates' estimate of himself, just as he seems to have accepted the necessity of defending his choice of profession. Beatrice's father, Frederick Ayer, was quite properly concerned about his daughter's dim future as an army wife, moving from one rude military outpost to another, often living among social inferiors, and tied to a man who would never have much money of his own. In a February 16, 1909, letter to Beatrice, Patton explained that sometimes "I get violent with my self in defence of my profession which to me seems very good. It is the oldest and at one time was the only business that was proper. . . . I dare say that for every man remembered for acts of peace there are fifteen made immortal by war and since in my mind all life is a struggle to perpetuate your name war is naturally my choice."[13]

Patton had not so much chosen a career in the army as he had chosen a career that would allow him to go to war. His purpose was to achieve the only kind of glory likely to perpetuate his name. Even to West Point classmates, this was a distasteful attitude. If it disturbed Beatrice, however, she never let on.

But in 1909 there was no war. Posted after graduation to sleepy Fort Sheridan, north of Chicago, Second Lieutenant Patton was consigned to miserable bachelor quarters on the third floor what amounted to a military tenement. His furniture consisted of one mahogany desk and an iron bed. It was all too typical of an army that struggled for its portion of a shoe-string $150 million annual military budget (most of which went to the navy with its big ships) to maintain a force 80,672 men commanded by 4,299 officers. The smallest of European nations had armies many times this size, but few people in pre–World War I America saw much need for a large standing army.

Patton was well aware that there was only one way out of the dreary purgatory of military routine in places like Fort Sheridan: promotion to high rank. But he also knew that promotion in the peacetime army customarily proceeded at a glacial pace. The only hope was, from the very beginning, to draw to himself the positive attention of superiors. He did all he could to curry favor with his commanding officer, Captain Francis C. Marshall, who (as Patton saw things) was at least a gentleman, in contrast to the other officers at Fort Sheridan, many of whom were former militiamen who had gained entry into the regular army by virtue of service in the Spanish-American War of 1898. To impress Marshall, Patton made liberal use of his family connections and military heritage, but he also performed his duties impeccably and enthusiastically, so much so that Marshall rated him an officer "of especial promise" and "the most enthusiastic soldier of my acquaintance," who "misses no chance to improve." [14]

As was the case at West Point, Patton soon earned a reputation for driving his men as hard as he drove himself—which, as the majority of enlisted men saw it, was much harder than necessary. While on stable duty one afternoon, he noticed that a horse had been left untied in its stall. Patton stalked off to find the man responsible for this breach. Locating him at the far end of the stable building, he chewed him out, then, as punishment, ordered him to run to the horse's stall, tie the animal down properly, then run back to him. The soldier obediently turned, then walked—albeit rapidly—toward the stall.

"Run, damn you, run!" Patton bawled after him.

The soldier broke into a run, but the incident preyed on the young second lieutenant's conscience. "Damn it" would have been fine, but "damn you," he decided, was just plain wrong. When the soldier ran back after tying the horse, Patton summoned all bystanders together and apologized to the soldier, not for having cursed, but for having cursed *him*.[15]

Had Patton done nothing more than chew out the soldier, his men would have pegged him as just another second lieutenant throwing around what little weight he had. However, by chewing him out and then apologizing, in public, for having crossed the line, Patton initiated his steady rise into the realm of army legend and lore.

It was, of course, a minor incident. But Patton quickly discovered that he had a natural talent for converting minor incidents into the stuff of minor myth. As he was drilling his troops one day, Patton was suddenly bucked off his horse. He instantly remounted, only to have his horse rear back. But this time Patton held on as the horse fell. Patton extricated his leg from under the animal and sprang to his feet just as the horse also rose and, throwing back its head, caught Patton just above the eyebrow, opening an ugly gash. With blood running down his face and onto his sleeve, Patton spent another twenty minutes completing the drill. He did not even pause to wipe his face. On schedule, he dismissed the men, retired to wash himself, then, as scheduled, taught a class at the school for noncoms, after which, as scheduled, he attended a class for junior officers. Only after having completed these duties did he visit the fort surgeon, who, with considerable admiration for the young man, stitched up the wound.

It is embarrassing for an officer to be thrown by his horse, and Patton had lost control of the animal not once but twice. Yet by refusing even to acknowledge his wound, he transformed potential humiliation into a tale told for quite some time in the Sheridan barracks.

Other than the accident itself, there was nothing accidental about Patton's actions. He was deliberately modeling himself as an exceptional officer. On another occasion, he expressed his annoyance that "for so fierce a warrior, I have a damned mild expression,"[16] and he began practicing before a mirror to cultivate what he would later call his "war face": the hard, glowering image that looks out from so many wartime photographs of the general. Patton was known to practice this war face his whole life, putting it on prior to appearances before the troops, much as actors put on their makeup before setting foot on stage.

Patton spent Christmas leave in 1909 visiting the Ayer family and discussing marriage with Beatrice's father. But he did not yet propose. On February 28, 1910, back at Fort Sheridan, Patton finally sent Beatrice a letter in which he managed to do no better than stammer, "If you marry [me] in June—please do." Beatrice understood, replying by Western Union telegram: "Pa and Ma willing for June if you are rejoice." [17]

The couple was wed at St. John's Episcopal Church at Beverly Farms, Massachusetts, on May 26, 1910, and a lavish reception followed at the Ayer home in Pride's Crossing. The Pattons spent their wedding night in Boston, then traveled to New York, where they boarded the liner *Deutschland*, which took them to a month long honeymoon in Europe. Patton recorded little of the sojourn in his diary, though he did note the singularly unromantic purchase of a copy of Karl von Clausewitz's *On War* in London. Patton also got his first extended look at the French countryside, including some of the region that would become the trench-scarred Western Front of World War I.

After the honeymoon, the couple settled into their half of the two-family house Patton had rented just outside Fort Sheridan. Although accustomed to much grander surroundings, Beatrice easily adapted to life as an army wife. She saw her mission as smoothing her husband's rough social edges and doing everything else in her power to advance his career. By autumn 1910, she was pregnant, and, fluent in French, she passed the time collaborating with her husband on an English translation of a French military article. It was the first of many articles Patton turned out for professional military journals. He wrote not so much out of a burning desire to express his ideas on doctrine and tactics, as to attract attention. Nevertheless, his message was compelling, and, throughout a long career, it varied in detail but never wavered in principle: almost everything he wrote was some variation on *attack, advance, and attack again.* In this way, from very early in his career, before there was even a war to fight, Patton's name became associated throughout the small universe of the professional American army with the doctrine of offensive warfare.

On March 11, 1911, a daughter was born to the Pattons. They named her Beatrice. Now Patton thought harder and harder about how to raise his career to the next level. He prevailed on his father to help clear the way for his advancement by exploiting his connections, which extended as far as the office of the adjutant general, Major General Fred C. Ainsworth, a family friend. Patton also exploited the Ayers' links to President William Howard Taft and his circle. By the end of 1911, Patton had obtained a transfer at to Fort Myer, outside of Washington, D.C.

In the army of this era, Fort Myer was both a showplace and a center of power. It was the home of the Army Chief of Staff, and it attracted the kind of officers Patton had found in such short supply at Fort Sheridan: gentlemen. These men devoted much time to perfecting their horsemanship, which they regularly exhibited in fiercely played polo matches. Fort Myer was the very heart of America's professional army and the place from which some of the most promising careers were launched. The Pattons left their modest midwestern half a house and moved into splendid on-post accommodations at Myer. They were quickly ushered into Washington society, Patton lunched with the movers and shakers at the best Washington clubs. One day, as he was riding along one of the fort's numerous bridle paths, he encountered the secretary of war, Henry L. Stimson. An avid rider himself, Stimson took to the Fort Myer equestrian trails whenever the weather permitted. The two men—one a junior lieutenant, the other chief of the War Department—struck up a friendship destined to last their entire lives. Soon Patton found himself serving as the secretary's uniformed aide at important social functions and was assigned the position of quartermaster for his squadron. This duty freed Patton from mundane troop details and gave him ample time to hone his horsemanship to a degree that earned him a place on the Fort Myer polo team and enabled him to compete in steeplechase competitions, which he did with reckless abandon.

Patton's horsemanship and his skill in fencing led to his nomination as the U.S. Army's entry in a brand-new Olympic sport, the modern pentathlon, scheduled for the Fifth Olympiad to be held in 1912 at Stockholm, Sweden. The modern pentathlon consisted of five events—riding a 5,000-meter steeplechase, shooting a pistol on a 25-meter range, fencing, swimming 300 meters, and running a 4,000-meter foot race—together intended to represent a distinctly military scenario in which an officer carries a message on horseback, encounters an enemy force and has to shoot, fence, and then escape by swimming a river and running cross country. Although Patton was in excellent physical shape, he went on a crash course of training, cutting out tobacco and alcohol and eating a diet of raw steak and salad, as well as running hard. Patton, Beatrice (with little Beatrice), and his father, mother, and sister Nita sailed for Belgium aboard the *Finland* on June 14, then traveled from Belgium to Sweden, arriving on the 29th. Papa accompanied George to every practice before the games. In the end, Patton excelled in the fencing competition, defeating 20 of 29 competitors (an astounding result for anyone, especially an American), and finished third in the steeplechase. His worst showing was, surprisingly enough, on the pistol range, in which he placed twenty-first of 42 competitors. By the time of the final event, the 4,000-meter run, only 15 of the original 42 competitors remained. Although he never claimed to be a runner, Patton came in third. Then he passed out cold.

"Will the boy live?" Papa asked Patton's trainer.

It was a serious question, to which the trainer replied, "I think he will but cant tell."[18]

He did recover, of course, was placed fifth in the overall pentathlon standings, and received generous praise from the Swedish press, which called his energy incredible and remarked of his fencing that his "calm was unusual and calculated. He was skillful in exploiting his opponent's every weakness." [19]

Before leaving Europe, Patton and his wife traveled to Saumur, home of the French army's cavalry school, where Patton took two weeks of private lessons from an officer known to history only as Adjutant Cléry, the school's instructor of fencing and the man generally conceded to be the greatest fencer in Europe. Not only did Patton work on his own technique with sword and saber, he learned the outlines of Cléry's method of instruction, which he wanted to bring back to the U.S. Army.

On his return to Fort Myer, Patton was invited by Army Chief of Staff General Leonard Wood to dinner in company with Secretary Stimson. Patton also joined the Metropolitan Club, watering hole for Washington's power elite, and built an increasingly formidable reputation as a racer, both in flat competition and in the steeplechase. Patton rode like the devil, pushing himself to the edge of danger and beyond and, most of all, ensuring that the right people saw him push himself. "Advertising," he called it.

Making maximum use of Beatrice's fluency in French, Patton wrote a detailed report of his experience with Adjutant Cléry and thereby began to revolutionize mounted saber technique as it had been traditionally taught in the American cavalry. American cavalrymen were trained to slash, whereas, Patton reported, the French use the point of the sword, thrusting with the tip. Patton believed this was more effective and efficient than slashing, because it was much more suited to the verb *attack*. It brought the horse soldier into quicker contact with the enemy. Because the standard American army curved saber was intended for slashing, not stabbing, Patton boldly suggested adopting a straight blade to facilitate attacking with the point.

Patton's paper was circulated to the army adjutant general, who passed it through channels. It was subsequently published in a military journal, which drew considerable attention, and Patton mounted a minor campaign to get the official army saber changed. Assigned to temporary duty in the Office of the Chief of Staff, Patton was in contact with the most senior officers in the army. Early in 1913, Secretary of War Stimson, through the Army Chief of Staff, directed the Army Chief of Ordnance to manufacture 20,000 new cavalry swords according to the design drawn up by Second Lieutenant George S. Patton Jr. The U.S. Army Saber, M–1913, was born. Still in use, it is familiarly called the "Patton sword."

Patton loved swordsmanship and, even as late as 1913, genuinely believed there was still an important role for the sword in modern combat. He published a widely read article on the history of the sword in warfare in the *Cavalry Journal*, carefully drawing from the past lessons for present application. Yet one cannot help feeling that, in his advocacy of the weapon,

Patton was less interested in the sword itself than in exploiting his popular and professional identification with it. The sword was a unique means of gaining renown, and renown was a means of advancing himself. He secured permission from the army to travel at his own expense to France for six weeks of advanced work at Saumur, to perfect his swordsmanship at the hands of Cléry and to carry back to the army's Mounted Service School at Fort Riley, Kansas, the details of Cléry's instructional method.

After returning to the United States, he and Beatrice quickly packed for their move to Fort Riley. In some ways, Kansas would be a sharp comedown after the heady elegance of the capital, but Patton, who was to be a student at the Mounted Service School as well as an instructor in fencing, was given a majestic title the army created especially for him: Master of the Sword. The title was unique in the U.S. Army, and it was certain to draw attention to the young officer who held it. That, of course, was most excellent, but even more appealing to Patton was its romantic ring, suggesting an anachronistic nobility that savored of the age of chivalry. It was a long glance backward from a world on the cusp of a war in which neither swords nor chivalry would find a place. But Patton most certainly would.

CHAPTER 3

In Pursuit of Pancho Villa

ON SEPTEMBER 23, 1913, PATTON REPORTED to the Mounted Service School, Fort Riley, Kansas, to enroll as a student and, simultaneously, as Master of the Sword, to teach his brother cavalrymen the art and science of the saber. Although Patton would emerge early in World War II as a great trainer of men, he did not enjoy teaching swordsmanship to officers who, for the most part, were senior to him and more or less obviously resented instruction from a brash second lieutenant in what they may well have deemed an outmoded skill. He also felt guilty for having torn Beatrice away from the glamour of Fort Myer in exchange for the dusty, dry, dull Midwest of Fort Riley. Although the quarters assigned to him and his family were hardly squalid, they were dreary enough. "You certainly have given up a lot on my account," he admitted to Beatrice.[1]

If Patton was discouraged, he never let his feelings interfere with his work. He studied hard, he taught diligently, and when the Cavalry Board asked him to compose a manual of regulations for the M–1913 sword he himself had designed, he plunged into the work. (Dyslexia notwithstanding, Patton proved to be a skilled writer.) Patton smelled gunpowder in the air in April 1914, when President Woodrow Wilson ordered the occupation of the Mexican port city of Veracruz. To reestablish a friendly democracy in Mexico, Wilson wanted to force out of office General Victoriano Huerta, who had assumed the presidency after the assassination of Francisco Madero the year before. Wilson was pondering military intervention when the detention of a small group of American sailors at Tampico forced his hand. On April 21, with the approval of Congress, Wilson sent a small amphibious party to seize control of the port of Veracruz in order to prevent the landing there of arms and other equipment being transported to Huerta aboard a German ship. After the landing party met stiff resistance, Wilson ordered a larger occupation of the city. Patton prayed for a full-scale war. To his father, on April 19, 1914, he wrote, "If the war is to be short there will be no chance for a man of my rank to make any reputation . . . But should the war last a long time . . . a man with a reputation for personal ability ought to get a good volunteer or malatia [militia] command."[2]

Alas, General Huerta resigned the presidency on July 15, and although the Veracruz occupation continued until November 23, Patton's hopes for a war, short or long, quickly faded. Yet no sooner had these prospects dimmed than all Europe obliged the young second lieutenant by beginning the slaughter of the Great War after Gavrilo Princeps, a consumptive Bosnian-Serb teenager, shot to death the archduke of Austria-Hungary and his wife as they drove through the streets of Sarajevo on June 28, 1914. Like most other Americans, Patton was not quite sure what this obscure European dispute had to do with the United States, but the war quickly exploded, engulfing the European continent. Surely, Patton thought, America would have to get into it sooner or later. And better sooner than later. On November 11, 1914, his twenty-ninth birthday, Patton wrote his papa: "I certainly am aging. . . . I fixed twenty-seven as the age when I should be a brigadier and now I am twenty-nine and not a first Lieutenant." His hair was even thinning. For Beatrice, however, he cast this fact in the rosiest light he could manage: "When I get less hair than I now have I will look like a German duelist."[3]

Master of the Sword or no, the twenty-nine-year-old second lieutenant was deeply frustrated by the dearth of opportunities for glory. For now, to anyone who would listen, he vented his rage against President Woodrow Wilson, who was determined to keep America out of war, even after American lives had been lost when a U-boat torpedoed the British liner *Lusitania*.

Patton's mood was brightened on February 28, 1915, when Beatrice gave birth to a second daughter, Ruth Ellen. But his graduation from the Mounted Service School in June meant that he would return to his regiment, which, he learned, was about to be deployed to the Philippines. Ever since 1898, when the United States acquired the Philippine Islands from Spain as part of the spoils of the Spanish-American War, a tour of duty here was virtually de rigueur for all young army officers. Patton was apprehensive because he knew that, more often than not, the Philippines failed to be a rite of passage and became, in fact, a dead end to an officer's career. Always ready to pull whatever strings he could find, Patton secured 11 days of leave to travel to Washington, where he prevailed on influential friends to get him an alternative assignment. They managed to arrange a transfer to Fort Bliss, in El Paso, Texas, on the Mexican border. To be sure, it was no garden spot and certainly less comfortable than a posting in Manila, but new troubles were brewing between Mexico and the United States, and Patton sensed the possibility of real action at this post.

Mexico was in turmoil. Numerous would-be leaders vied for power, including the brutal Victoriano Huerta and the more moderate Venustiano Carranza. In these struggles, partisans of one leader or the other sometimes crossed the border into the United States to replenish their war chests with cash and goods "liberated" from towns in Texas, New Mexico, and Arizona. Army border garrisons were expected to police the region and prevent or turn back such incursions. Patton's hope was that the police action would soon break into open warfare.

In a matter of months, it would, more or less. But for now, Patton could find no one at Fort Bliss to tell him what he was expected to do.

Eventually, he was informed that there really was nothing for him to do until his regiment arrived. In the meantime, it was suggested that he study for the examination that would qualify him for advancement from second to first lieutenant. He asked for extra time to prepare, and since no one had anything to better occupy him, he was granted the extension. Patton used this time not only to study but, quite shamelessly, to butter up the president of the promotion board by helping him train his polo ponies. Learning that his former Fort Sheridan commander, Captain— now Major—Francis Marshall, was at Fort Bliss on an official visit and was the guest of a promotion board member, Patton wasted no time in calling on Marshall and his host, confident that "Maj. M will blow my horn." [4] No doubt Marshall did, for Patton took the examination and was quickly qualified for promotion. The actual promotion would come on May 23, 1916.

Shortly after he passed his exam, Patton's regiment, the 8th Cavalry, arrived at Fort Bliss. Patton was sent with his troop to Sierra Blanca, a rudimentary Texas border town of perhaps 20 houses plus 1 saloon. It was a town out of a dime novel, populated by cowboys and patrolled by a rugged snowy-haired marshal named Dave Allison, who quickly befriended the young officer. Beyond the few rude streets of the town lay a landscape of desolation, through which Patton led mounted border patrols and, from the saddle, at the trot, hunted jackrabbits. "I like this sort of work," he wrote with satisfaction, "a lot."[5]

Something more exciting than jackrabbits loomed on the horizon on Thanksgiving Eve. While in Sierra Blanca with Troop A of the 8th Cavalry, Patton received a telegram from Fort Bliss warning of an impending raid on the town by some 200 Mexican revolutionary bandits. With all the senior officers out on patrol, Patton was in command. He wrote to his father that he did not believe the "rumor" of a raid, but, in any case, he set about planning how to repel an attack, assigned battle stations to each of the 100 men with him, and ordered everyone to sleep beside their weapons. "I wish they would come. I . . . could give them a nice welcome," he wrote.[6] As Patton had predicted, however, nothing happened.

On Thanksgiving Day, he was ordered to advance against a knot of eighty Mexicans who were reported to have set up camp on the American side of the Rio Grande. He decided to launch a classic attack, with drawn sabers and at dawn, the time of day at which an enemy is most vulnerable. There was little time to relish the prospect of the attack, however. Before Patton led his men out, the troop captain and first lieutenant returned from patrol and ordered the men to leave their sabers in camp. Swordless, the Master of the Sword led the patrol in a tedious 11-hour ride along the Rio Grande, found no Mexicans, then returned to Sierra Blanca. He was soon ordered to return to Fort Bliss, to which Beatrice and the children came for what she planned as a two-month stay. At first appalled by conditions there and terrified by a brutally dusty windstorm, she actually asked her husband to resign his commission. Patton's earliest biographer, Ladislas Farago, described Beatrice as a woman "at her best when the chips were down,"[7] and she proved that now, quickly pulling herself together. Indeed, as she began to explore El Paso, she concluded that it was not so bad after all. She resolved to move herself and her two babies permanently into the less-than-sumptuous on-post housing.

Once the Pattons were settled into their modest house, sister Nita came to visit. Patton introduced her to the senior commander at Fort Bliss, Brigadier General John J. Pershing. Nita Patton was 29, unmarried, unattached, and a figure every bit as imposing as her brother, described by one Pershing biographer as "a tall blonde Amazon."[8] Pershing was a martially handsome 55, having been tragically widowed on August 27, 1915, when fire swept through his family's quarters at the Presidio in San Francisco, killing his wife and three of their daughters while he was on duty in Texas. There was a mutual attraction between Pershing and Nita, who stayed at Fort Bliss longer than she had planned. So far as Patton was concerned, the prospect of a budding romance between his sister and the commanding general was a source of delightful anticipation.

Doroteo Arango, who later called himself Francisco Villa, but became known to the world as Pancho Villa, was the orphaned son of an impoverished field worker. When one of the owners of the estate on which his family labored raped his sister, Pancho Villa killed the man, then fled to the mountains, where he lived out his teen years as a fugitive. He learned the art of survival, and he also discovered that he was possessed of a certain personal magnetism as well as a natural talent for guerrilla warfare. In 1909, he joined Francisco Madero's successful uprising against the brutal dictatorship of Porfirio Díaz. In the process, Villa began to shine too brightly to suit his senior colleagues, and in 1912, he was condemned to death by fellow revolutionary Victoriano Huerta. Madero intervened and sent Villa to prison instead. He escaped, fled to the United States, and, after Madero was assassinated in 1913, returned to Mexico, gathering about himself a band of several thousand, dubbed the División del Norte. Committing himself and his men to the service of Venustiano Carranza, Villa fought against the dictator Huerta, partaking with Carranza in a glorious victory in June 1914.

Shortly after Villa and Carranza rode into Mexico City as the triumphant leaders of the latest revolution, they came to blows, and Villa fled to the mountains of the north with the revolutionary leader Emiliano Zapata. Why he did what he next did has never been satisfactorily explained. Perhaps he resented President Wilson's support of Carranza, once his comrade, now his rival. Perhaps he merely wanted to demonstrate to his fellow countrymen and the world that he, not Carranza, controlled northern Mexico. Whatever his motive, during January 1916, Villa executed 17 American citizens in the Mexican town of Santa Isabel and, on March 9, crossed the border with about 500 "Villistas" to raid Columbus, New Mexico. There he fought with local residents as well as soldiers of the nearby 13th Cavalry. Ten American civilians and 14 U.S. soldiers were killed in the raid, while casualties among Villa's forces were significantly higher, at least 100 dead.

In response to the Columbus outrage, President Wilson ordered Pershing to conduct a "Punitive Expedition" into Mexico with the object of capturing or killing Pancho Villa. This *was* exciting, but Patton now worried that Pershing would not include his regiment, the 8th Cavalry, in the expedition because its colonel was obese and might be judged unfit. To his father, he wrote on March 12, 1916: "There should be a law killing fat colonels on sight."[9] Patton's fears proved well-founded; Pershing chose to leave the 8th behind. In a panic at the thought of being excluded from the action, Patton prevailed on his squadron adjutant personally to recommend him as an aide to Pershing. He also appealed to Major John L. Hines, appointed adjutant general of the Punitive Expedition, and he buttonholed one of the general's regular aides, Lieutenant Martin C. Shallenberger, as well. Then he called on Pershing himself, telling him that he would do anything, no matter how menial, if only he were allowed to join the expedition. Knowing Pershing's distaste for publicity, Patton suggested he could handle newspaper correspondents, something, he said, he was especially good at. (In fact, at the time, he had never before so much as spoken to the press.) Pershing dismissed Patton without giving him his decision. The next morning, however, Patton received a telephone call from the general.

"Lieutenant Patton, how long will it take you to get ready?"

Patton answered that he was already packed. Taken aback, Pershing replied: "I'll be God Damned. You are appointed Aide."[10]

The Punitive Expedition was a large force of two cavalry brigades and a brigade of infantry—ultimately numbering nearly 15,000 men—augmented by the 1st Aero Squadron equipped with a half-dozen rickety Curtiss JN-2 "Jennies," state-of-the-art aircraft for the Army Air Service, but already obsolete by world aeronautical standards. (Although the planes proved highly unreliable, they fascinated Patton, who, in World War II, would pioneer the use of light spotting and reconnaissance aircraft during the Third Army's epic advance across France.)

Over nearly a year, from March 1916 to February 1917, Pershing would lead his men some 400 miles into the rugged eastern foothills of Mexico's Sierra Madres. As an aide, Patton performed the duties of factotum, everything from ensuring the general was well fed to assisting him with inspections; looking after the well-being of his horses, motor vehicles, and troops; and serving as a courier. That last role was a dangerous one, and Patton eagerly embraced it. In April, he volunteered to deliver a message to the 11th Cavalry, which had advanced to the south and was currently—somewhere. It was, Patton wrote, "almost a needle in a haystack." Seeing him off, Pershing shook Patton's hand and cautioned: "'Be careful, there are lots of Villiastas.' Then still holding my hand he said, 'But remember, Patton, if you don't deliver that message don't come back.'"[11] The message, of course, was delivered.

Frustrated by the expedition's failure even to catch sight of Pancho Villa, much less catch him, General Pershing decided to target some of Villa's key subordinates, the most important of whom was General Julio Cárdenas. Patton begged Pershing to give him an opportunity to participate in the manhunt, and he was temporarily attached to Troop C, 13th Cavalry. Learning that Cárdenas was apparently living on a ranch near San Miguelito, Patton and part of Troop C rode out in mid-April. They did not find the general, but they did locate his wife and baby, as well as his uncle. In a letter to his father written on April 17, Patton noted that the "uncle was a very brave man and nearly died before he would tell me anything." Clearly, Patton and his men had tortured Cárdenas's uncle in an effort to extract the general's whereabouts. Just as clearly, they had been unsuccessful. As Patton noted in his diary, "Tried to get information out of uncle. Failed."[12]

The next month, on May 14, Pershing dispatched Patton on a foraging expedition, to buy corn from Mexican farmers. Patton and his party of 10 soldiers, 2 civilian scouts, and 2 civilian drivers set out in three automobiles. They stopped at two villages, Coyote and Salsito, and made the necessary purchases. Then Patton continued on to Rubio, where he spotted a group of 60 very rough-looking Mexicans, whom one of his scouts, an ex-Villista himself, identified as associates of Villa and Cárdenas. This suggested to Patton that Cárdenas was nearby, and he and his men drove the six miles north to San Miguelito and the same hacienda in which he had earlier found the general's uncle, wife, and baby. Several times during his life, Patton described what happened next.[13]

About a mile and a half south of the house the ground is lower than the house. And one cannot be seen until topping this rise. As soon as I came over this, I made my car go at full speed and went on past the house . . . four men were seen skinning a cow in the front. One of these men ran to the house and at once returned and went on with his work. I stopped my car northwest of the house and the other two [cars] southwest of it. I jumped out carrying my rifle in my left hand [and] hurried around to the big arched door leading into the patio. . . . I rounded the comer and walked about half way to the gate. When I was fifteen yards from the gate three armed men dashed out on horseback, and started around the southeast corner.

So schooled was I not to shoot, that I merely drew my pistol and waited to see what would happen. . . . When they got to the corner they saw my men coming that way and turned back and all three shot at me. One bullet threw gravel on me. I fired back with my new [ivory-handled] pistol five times. Then my men came around the corner and started to shoot. I did not know who was in the house. There were a lot of windows only a few feet from our right side. Just as I got around the corner three bullets hit about seven feet from the ground and put adobe [chips] all over me.

Patton had deployed his small force carefully, so that all exits from the house were covered.

I reloaded my pistol and started back when I saw a man on a horse come right in front of me. I started to shoot at him but remembered that Dave Allison had always said to shoot at the horse of an escaping man and I did so, and broke the horse's hip. He fell on his rider and as it was only about ten yards, we all hit him. He crumpled up.

During this gun battle, another Villista who ran out of the hacienda very nearly made good his escape, but Patton and some of his men sent a hail of bullets after him. He, too, fell dead.

Two down, but Patton needed to know just how many Villistas were left in and about the hacienda. He climbed onto the roof of the building to get a better look. As he stepped out onto the dirt roof, it gave way, with Patton falling through and coming to a stop, wedged in at the armpits. Patton quickly struggled out of the hole. In the meantime, one of his scouts shot and killed another escaping Villista.

During the entire adventure, Patton noted, the four men who had been skinning the cow continued to go about their work, completely ignoring the mayhem. Patton now ordered the roundup of these four, and he and three soldiers each seized one as a human shield while they searched the interior of the hacienda. The hate-narrowed eyes of Cárdenas's mother and wife (who held her baby daughter in her arms) followed the men. Cautiously opening a heavy wooden door, Patton found a number of wizened old women, cowering in prayer.

In all, three Mexicans had been killed in the "Battle of San Miguelito." One of the cow skinners identified one of those slain as Julio Cárdenas himself. The others were a Villista captain and a private.

Patton ordered the three corpses to be strapped across the hoods of each of the detachment's three automobiles, like trophy stags. Ready to leave, Patton suddenly saw a band of perhaps 50 Villistas approaching at the gallop. Shots were exchanged, and the vastly outnumbered Americans lead-footed their accelerator pedals and rumbled down the road to Rubio. (Or as Patton sardonically put it: "We withdrew gracefully.") As a precaution, Patton directed one of his men to cut the telegraph wires along the road to prevent word of the shoot-out from reaching the town before their arrival. After passing through at high speed, the party did not stop until it had reached Pershing's headquarters. There Patton was mobbed by news correspondents, who were starving for a story in what had become a long and monotonous Mexican sojourn, as dry as the surrounding desert. Headlines trumpeted Patton's name, and, even better, official army dispatches mentioned him repeatedly.

George S. Patton Jr. was now a national hero—at least for a few weeks. In the longer term, the Punitive Expedition had more important consequences for him. Patton's automobile trip to San Miguelito was, in fact, the very first time a United States Army unit had been transported into battle by motorized vehicles. In his assault on the Cárdenas hacienda, Patton, who would champion the tank in World War I and would be the foremost American exponent of mobile warfare in World War II, had, more or less inadvertently, pioneered mechanized combat. Even more important, the San Miguelito exchange—and indeed the entire Punitive Expedition—created a genuine bond between Patton and Pershing. Patton saw in Pershing the ideal general, the mold from which all others should be struck. Not only did he have a firm grasp of strategy and tactics, he issued crystal-clear orders, he demanded absolute discipline, he earned and returned absolute loyalty, and, while he never lost the big picture, neither did he miss the most minute detail. Added to all of this, he *looked* the part. He was, every inch of him, a commanding officer. Patton watched, admired, and learned. He was more determined than ever that he, too, would become a general— a general just like John J. Pershing.

But San Miguelito proved to be the high point of the Punitive Expedition. Wanting to avoid a major international crisis, President Wilson ordered Pershing to withdraw to within 150 miles of the U.S.-Mexican border, and, from that point on, boredom set in. On May 18, Patton recorded in his diary, "I did absolutely nothing but take a bath." On the next day: "Terrible wind all day. No one did anything."[14] And so it went, day after dreary day.

Second Lieutenant Patton was at last officially advanced to first lieutenant on May 23, 1916, and he spent a good deal of idle time writing to his family, including encouraging letters to Papa, who had decided to run for the U.S. Senate. In August, Patton accompanied Pershing back to Columbus, New Mexico, for a few days of vacation. Beatrice met her husband there, and Nita was on hand to greet Pershing. Everyone began to assume that, despite the difference in age, the two would wed. As Patton put it to Beatrice, "Nita may rank us yet."[15]

Patton soon returned to headquarters in Mexico, where, early in October, he met with a bizarre accident. While writing a report in his tent, his gasoline-fed lamp exploded, sending flames across his face and hair. "I ran out side and put my self out," he later explained to Beatrice.[16] The burns were serious, and they were painful, but Patton suffered neither permanent scars nor was his eyesight damaged. He was granted sick leave, met Beatrice in Columbus, then traveled by train to his boyhood home at Lake Vineyard and, in Los Angeles, was treated by Dr. Billy Wills, an uncle by marriage. His sick leave made it possible for him to be at Papa's side when he learned that he had been very soundly defeated by his Republican senatorial opponent.

As for General Pershing, Patton had clearly and deeply impressed a very important man; however, he had done so in more ways than he intended. Pershing would demonstrate his high regard for Patton by bringing him into his circle almost immediately after the United States entered the Great War. Before this even, however, in an October 16, 1916, letter to the convalescing Patton, Pershing not only wished him a rapid recovery, but felt moved to issue a warning against the dangers of self-absorption: "[D]o not be too insistent upon your own personal views. You must remember that when we enter the army we do so with the full knowledge that our first duty is toward our government, entirely regardless of our own views under any given circumstances."[17]As much as he learned and would yet learn from the example of General Pershing, Patton probably never took these words to heart. Certainly he never found himself capable of putting them into practice.

CHAPTER 4

The Great War
and the New Weapon

GEORGE S. PATTON JR. HAD EARNED A MEASURE of fame in the vain pursuit of Pancho Villa, fame as seductive as it was short-lived, but he had also endured more than a measure of boredom. This was not the war Patton longed for, but there was the inestimable career benefit of entry into the orbit of John J. Pershing. Having earned in Mexico the second star of a major general, Pershing was on his way up. Patton continued to serve as his acting aide until Pershing succeeded Major General Frederick Funston as chief of the Southern Department and left for his new headquarters in San Antonio. Patton stayed in El Paso with his cavalry regiment and was given command of a cavalry troop. He also easily passed his promotion examination, which put him in line for captain. Nor did it hurt Patton's prospects that Pershing and Nita continued to grow closer. Marriage seemed likely, even imminent.

At the end of the Punitive Expedition, Patton's prospects were bright. Then they became brighter still. On April 6, 1917, just two months after Patton returned from Mexico, President Wilson, reelected to a second term on the campaign slogan "He Kept Us Out of War," decided that the United States could no longer endure Germany's assaults on its rights as a neutral. U-boat attacks on British liners carrying American passengers (including the sinking of the *Lusitania* on May 7, 1915) and the revelation of the infamous Zimmermann Telegram, in which the German government proposed to Mexico an anti-American military alliance, as well as the growing perception that German imperial aggression represented an enduring threat to democracy itself, moved the president to ask Congress for a declaration of war against Germany and the other "Central Powers."

Yet the first Patton to try to get into the war was not George, but Papa. Hoping to find a worthwhile government appointment, he boarded a train bound for Washington. With him were his wife and daughter Nita. Because of Nita, they stopped in San Antonio to call on Pershing, only to discover that the War Department had just summoned him to the capital. All four took the same train the rest of the way to Washington.

At the War Department, Pershing received orders to organize a division, assume command of it, then take it to France as America's first contribution to the Allied war effort. Pershing quickly drew up a list of officers, including Patton, he wanted for his staff. But before orders could even be cut, the War Department greatly expanded Pershing's assignment. He would not lead a mere division to France, he would lead the entire "American Expeditionary Force" and command every single soldier the nation sent to Europe. At the same time, Pershing learned that the War Department was about to detail Patton to Front Royal, Virginia, to purchase horses for the army. It is a measure of the general's regard for Patton that he personally saw to it that the order was rescinded and then directed the adjutant general on May 18 to send Patton a telegram, ordering him to report to him, Pershing, in Washington. The responsibility that had suddenly fallen to Pershing was awesome indeed. The army of 1916, from which the Punitive Expedition had been drawn, consisted of about 133,000 officers and men, and its high command occupied itself not with plans for major warfare, but with such issues as Patton's new saber design and the new manual that accompanied it. Now, through a combination of conscription and patriotic enlistment, the army would grow explosively to 4.5 million men by November 1918. Some 2 million of these soldiers would be sent to Europe under Pershing's direct command.

Patton's focus was how best to exploit his great good fortune to be a member of Pershing's inner circle. It would take months to send the whole army to Europe, but he, George Patton, having been promoted to captain on May 15, would be going "over there" almost immediately as part of the very first wave of Yanks. Papa was not so lucky. No one had a job for him in Washington, so he, his wife, and Nita returned to California, where Nita divided her time between volunteer war work and writing long letters to Pershing. Patton was one of just 60 officers and a mix of 120 enlisted soldiers and a handful of civilian clerks who embarked with their general for Liverpool aboard the liner *Baltic* on May 28.

The *Baltic* docked at Liverpool on June 8. From there, Pershing and his staff entrained for London and were welcomed at Euston Station by the American ambassador and others. Pershing was sumptuously accommodated in the luxury of the Savoy Hotel, while Patton and 67 men assigned to his command were sent to quarters in, of all places, the Tower of London. On June 13, Pershing and his staff left London for Paris. Patton took no pleasure in the celebrated City of Light, because there his war instantly bogged down, becoming a tedious matter of managing orderlies, looking after guards, and dispatching drivers.

It was July before Pershing even approached the actual front and took Captain Patton with him as his aide-de-camp. With Pershing, Patton inspected a contingent of newly arrived American troops training at St. Dizier. To Patton, the officers seemed lazy and the troops sloppy. The sight of these indifferent officers pretending to lead halfhearted half-soldiers must have seemed to Patton a vindication of his hard riding of West Point underclassmen during his brief stint as cadet second corporal. Here were the consequences of failing to be "too damn military."

Another, equally significant epiphany was to come. By September, Pershing felt that he had trained a sufficient force at last to begin combat deployment. It was decided to put the first Americans in the relatively quiet Lorraine sector, and so, on September 1, Pershing moved his headquarters and staff from Paris to Chaumont. This small city quickly became a complex of training camps and military specialty schools, through which the growing stream of Americans soon passed. In addition to continuing his service as one of Pershing's aides-de-camp, Patton was appointed post adjutant on September 13, charged with commanding the 250-man headquarters company and a motor pool of about 90 automobiles. It was not a satisfying assignment, and a cranky Patton rode his men hard, insisting on absolute efficiency and the flawless observance of discipline, soldierly appearance, and military courtesy. Whatever his men thought of this, Pershing was greatly impressed, and because it was certain that the Chaumont headquarters was going to grow both quickly and extensively, Patton was now in a perfect position for a larger command and a rapid promotion to major.

Proximity to the inner circle, rapid promotion—on the face of it, these were just what Patton had always hoped for. But, increasingly, he hated it all. Perhaps contemplating the antiaircraft guns over which he had command—but which never had to be fired—he confessed to Beatrice that he was "darned sick of my job" and that "I would trade jobs with almost any one for any thing."[1]

So he started looking precisely for "any thing," and what he soon found was a new, ugly, and utterly unproven weapon the British called the "tank." When Colonel LeRoy Eltinge happened to ask him if he wanted to be a tank officer, Patton found himself answering yes. Then, after the fact, he talked the matter over with another officer, Colonel Frank McCoy, "who advised me to write a letter asking that in the event of Tanks being organized that my name be considered. I did so." In this almost casual way, George S. Patton Jr. arrived at the service branch with which his name would be most intimately connected. He wrote to Pershing, presenting himself as qualified for tanks because their use was "analogous to the duty performed by cavalry in normal wars" and "I am a cavalryman." Moreover, "I have always had a Troop which shot well so think that I am a good instructor in fire. It is stated that accurate fire is very necessary to good use of tanks." Additionally, Patton cited his experience with gasoline engines and the use and repair of "Gas Automobiles," his fluency in French ("so I could get information from the French Direct"), and his aggressive spirit and willingness to take chances. He closed by reminding Pershing of the shootout at San Miguelito: "I believe that I am the only American who has ever made an attack in a motor vehicle."[2]

As an American tank service had yet to be inaugurated, Pershing held off responding directly to Patton's letter, but instead asked him whether, after promotion to major (which would come on January 23, 1918), he wanted to continue on staff or command an infantry battalion. Patton responded instantly: he wanted to be with troops.

In mid-October, Patton began to feel ill. Examining himself in the mirror, he noticed that his complexion had turned to yellow, and he promptly reported to the base hospital, where he was diagnosed with "jaundice catarrhal." He was put into the same room as Colonel Fox Conner, who was recovering from surgery for "stoppage of the bowel." A fine officer who was an early influence on Pershing as well as George C. Marshall and Dwight D. Eisenhower, Conner advised Patton to forget about tanks and try to become an infantry major. Patton agreed, but the very next night Colonel Eltinge came to visit, told him that an American tank school was going to be started at Langres on November 15, and asked Patton "would I take it. Inspite of my resolution to the contrary I said yes. But I kept discussing it pro and con with Col. F. Conner and again decided on Infantry."[3] Patton left the hospital on November 3 and when he was ordered on November 10 to take charge of the tank school, he worried that he had made the wrong decision. Almost immediately, however, he reconciled himself to what he now deemed his "destiny." Besides, the really important thing was not whether he had a command in infantry or tanks, but that he was no longer tied to Pershing's coattails. Association with the commander of the American Expeditionary Force (AEF) had brought him a long way, but the time had come, Patton decided, for him to be seen making it on his own.

As if to lend a hand to destiny, Patton mentally tallied the advantages of getting into tanks. First was exclusivity. The infantry had lots of majors.

Patton would be the one and only major in tanks. Second was the civility of it all. Infantry in World War I was all about cold days and miserable nights in muddy trenches. Tankers fought only during attacks. In between these actions, they lived in the comfort of their warm, dry headquarters. (Patton loved to fight. He did not much care for getting dirty.) Finally: it was just possible that tanks might actually work. Few thought so at the time. They were loud, clumsy looking, and mechanically unreliable. In principle, however, they were able to traverse trenches, mow down barbed wire, and shuck off rifle and machine-gun fire while delivering artillery and machine-gun fire in return. These abilities gave them what the deadlocked trench fighters sorely lacked—mobility. The tank might just be the answer to a stalemate on the Western Front that had endured since 1914. At least, that is what it all meant in principle. "Of course," Patton wrote to Papa on November 6, 1917, "there is about a fifty percent chance that [the tanks] wont work at all but if they do they will work like hell." And he went on to outline what he called "the golden dream":

1st. I will run the [tank] school. 2. Then they will organize a battalion. I will command it. 3. Then if I make good and the T[anks] do and the war lasts I will get the first [tank] regiment. 4. With the same "IF" as before they will make a brigade and I will get the star [of a brigadier general].

"Also," Patton added, "the T. will be a great drawing card in the papers and illustrated magazines." There was yet another advantage. Although the tanks themselves had a high casualty rate of 25 percent, the casualty rate among tank crews was about 7.5 percent "which is much lower than the Dough boys. Also in the tanks you are not apt to be wounded. You either get blown to bitts by a direct hit or you are not touched." [4]

Before he opened the American tank school, Patton spent two weeks at the French tank school near Compiégne to cram into his head everything he could about how tanks worked and what they could and could not do. Unlike the British heavy tanks, which were essentially slow self-propelled guns, the light French tanks were rather like the mechanized equivalent of the mounted knight: mobile, armored, and deadly. He fell in love with the machines. At this time, from November 20 to December 5, 1917, while Patton was at Compiégne, the Battle of Cambrai was fought. It was the first time tanks had been used in battle in a major way. Nearly 500 British machines led infantry in an advance of more than seven miles over just four hours, a spectacular achievement in a trench war that typically measured progress in yards gained by spilling gallons of blood. However, before the battle was over, German counterattacks pushed the British back to their original lines. For Patton, the tanks had proved themselves. Now all that was needed was a commander capable of using them properly, of leading them with fearless aggression and ensuring that follow-up attacks would break through the holes the tanks had punched in the enemy's defensive lines.

Patton was not the only officer who attended to the lessons of Cambrai. Immediately after the battle, the new tank service was inundated with incoming applications for transfer. Patton, the first of what he now believed would be a new breed of soldier, congratulated himself on having made the right decision after all. Then, at the very height of his exhilaration, he suddenly confessed to Beatrice that he was "in quite a 'Funk.'" On the verge of opening the tank school, he suffered a crisis of confidence that recalled his first year at West Point and anticipated the bouts of despair and depression he would suffer between the two world wars. The job, he wrote, "is huge for every thing must be created and there is nothing to start with nothing but me that is."[5]

It was no exaggeration. Although a senior officer, Colonel Samuel D. Rockenbach, was named chief of the entire Tank Service (also called the Tank Corps) and had charge of American tankers training to operate the heavy British vehicles, Patton was expected, single-handedly, to create a force of Americans adept at operating the light French tanks. On December 15, 1917, he recorded in his diary: "This is [my] last day as staff officer. Now I rise or fall on my own."[6]

+≥━═≤+

The location chosen for the American tank school was perfectly suited to Patton's profound sense of history. Langres had once been a Roman

Legion camp and, centuries later, a medieval fortress. Although Rockenbach was his boss, Patton had superior technical and tactical knowledge and quickly persuaded the conservative colonel to do most things his way. He was also quick to impose his will on the 24 Coast Artillery Corps officers who were his first students. For them, lesson number one had nothing to do with tanks and everything to do with soldierly appearance and discipline. Patton was determined that those assigned to him would be good soldiers and good tankers—in precisely that order. Although this attitude harked back to his days as a cadet corporal, his concept of discipline had significantly matured. Discipline was not something to be achieved in and for itself, but was, Patton believed, essential to saving lives in combat because it was the means of ensuring "instant, cheerful, unhesitating obedience" to orders. Moreover, Patton never demanded top performance from his soldiers without giving them something commensurate in return. He ensured that comfortable quarters and hot meals were waiting for each of his new arrivals as they came, from the first two dozen to the increasing numbers that followed. From the beginning, Patton wanted his soldiers to be the best, and, as he saw it, that obligated him to ensure that they were treated as the best. This combination of demanding the utmost and giving the utmost in return created a special bond between Patton and the men he commanded.

Strong willed though he was, Patton also knew when to be politically savvy with his seniors. At Langres, he understood that most of the army was either contemptuous of the new weapon or felt threatened by it. In speaking to senior officers about tanks, he always defined and described their role as subordinate to infantry, a support and adjunct to the all-important business of the foot soldier. If he had a vision of eventually molding the Tank Corps into an autonomous service arm, he kept it to himself and instead concentrated on getting even the most tradition-bound of infantry officers to appreciate the potential of the new, loud, ungainly weapon.

Anxious as he was to get into the field, Patton took time out to attend the Army General Staff College in Langres. He longed for adventure and glory, but he considered himself, first and foremost, a professional soldier. The experience at the college put him into contact with the likes of George

C. Marshall and Adna Romanza Chaffee Jr., both of whom would go on to top positions in the army's high command, and Patton himself continued to advance, gaining rapid wartime promotion to lieutenant colonel on April 3, 1918, after having been a major for just three months.

On August 20, 1918, while he was attending a lecture at the Army General Staff College, Patton was handed a note summoning him to Colonel Rockenbach's office. The American army was about to mount its first big independent offensive of the war, against the St. Mihiel salient. A great German pocket bulging into the Allied lines, the St. Mihiel salient had been, since 1914, the object of one unsuccessful and costly Allied attack after another. Now, at last, the Americans would be given a crack at it—and the tanks were to be a part of the assault.

On August 24, Patton officially organized the 304th Tank Brigade (also called the 1st Tank Brigade). The French delivered some 225 light tanks to equip two American battalions. Of this number, Patton's brigade received 144 tanks. Before they arrived, Patton made meticulous preparations. Not only did he plot out every detail of the expected delivery and reception of the tanks, from their unloading at the rail head to their deployment to the front, but he set out on a hazardous reconnaissance patrol to assess the German lines and also to personally confirm that the ground on no-man's land was firm enough to support the vehicles.

As is typical in war, after the plans had been carefully laid, higher command made major changes in what it wanted. Undaunted, Patton personally reconnoitered the new ground set for the attack, efficiently drew up a new set of battle plans, and saw to it that everything necessary, including some 10,000 gallons of gasoline, was delivered to the newly selected point of departure. On September 11, the day before the operation was to start, Patton spoke to his troops. Even this early in his command career, his message reads as vintage Patton. It is one of attack, advance, and attack. Use the tanks as if they were the ancient warrior's dogs of war:

> No tank is to be surrendered or abandoned to the enemy. If you are left alone in the midst of the enemy keep shooting. If your gun is disabled use your pistols and squash the enemy with your tracks. By quick changes of direction cut them with the tail of the

tank. If your motor is stalled and your gun broken . . . You hang on, help will come . . .

You are the first American tanks [in combat]. You must establish the fact that AMERICAN TANKS DO NOT SURRENDER . . . As long as one tank is able to move it must go forward. Its presence will save the lives of hundreds of infantry and kill many Germans. Finally This is our BIG CHANCE; WHAT WE HAVE WORKED FOR . . . MAKE IT WORTH WHILE. [7]

Patton and his tanks were part of an enormous offensive involving 550,000 U.S. soldiers and 110,000 French troops. As Pershing planned the operation, the French were to keep the Germans occupied from the west, while American units attacked northward from the south and also eastward from the western face of the salient. The object was to pinch off the bulge from three directions. The tanks supported the Americans attacking from the south. A French tank battalion supported the right of the infantry attack, while Patton's tanks (which also included a French battalion placed under his command) supported the left. Patton assigned Captain (later Colonel) Sereno Brett to use the tanks assigned to him to lead the infantry of the 1st Division. The French battalion that was under Patton was to follow the infantry. Another contingent of American tanks, assigned by Patton to Captain Ranulf Compton, was to follow behind the 42nd Infantry Division, then pass through its ranks, and take the lead. It was a sound plan, and Patton had great faith in Brett. He was less sure of Compton, so he decided to remain closer to him during the assault.

The attack on September 12, was preceded by a four-hour artillery barrage, then stepped off at 5:00 A.M. By 6:10, Patton was positioned at a hilltop observation post, from which he could watch the action. Twenty minutes later, however, seeing some of the tanks bog down in muddy trenches, Patton walked two miles to personally attend to their extrication. This accomplished, he did not return to his command post on the hill, but, with his staff and on foot, he pressed forward with the advance. This practice would become a Patton trademark. He always led from the front. When he was told, at 9:15, that some tanks were caught in bad ground, he advanced to them in company with another officer and three runners.

Shells burst all around them. The natural impulse, of course, was to duck. Patton fought the impulse, condemning it as "the futility of dodging fate."[8] He also noticed that he was the only officer in the vanguard of the attack who had not removed the shoulder straps, which bore the oakleaf emblems of his field-grade rank. To be sure, a badge of rank made an irresistible target for sharpshooters, but Patton wanted his soldiers to see that he was unafraid to be a target.

Patton kept walking forward, always under shelling. When he encountered Brigadier General Douglas MacArthur standing on a little hill, he joined him. The "creeping barrage came along toward us," Patton later wrote. "I think each one wanted to leave, but each hated to say so, so we let it come over us. We stood and talked but neither was much interested in what the other said."[9]

From this hill, Patton moved—always forward—to another, from which he saw German troops retreating behind the village of Essey. With the town ripe for the plucking, Patton ordered five of Compton's tanks to roll into the village. When a French soldier turned the tanks back because, he said, the village was being bombarded too heavily, Patton personally intervened, ordering the tanks to continue forward while he preceded them on foot, across the bridge leading into the village. As he stepped foot on the bridge, it occurred to Patton that the structure might be rigged with explosives, but he led the tanks across anyway.

After Essey fell to Patton, he ordered the tanks to move ahead another two miles to Pannes. Just short of this village, however, all but one tank ran out of gas. Without tanks to lead them and provide cover, the accompanying infantry balked. Patton approached the one tank that still had fuel and ordered the sergeant to lead the reluctant infantry in. When the sergeant hesitated, Patton, under fire from the village, hopped onto the outside of the tank to spur him forward. Patton rode the machine all the way through Pannes, leaping off into a shell hole for cover only after enemy fire had become intense enough to chisel the paint from the side of the tank. Realizing then that the infantry lagged some 300 yards behind him, Patton crawled out of the shell hole and dodged fire all the way *back* to the foot soldiers. He confronted the unit's commander and told him to advance behind the tank up ahead. When the commander refused, Patton ran back to the tank and rapped on the back door with the heavy cane that American and British officers carried into the field. The sergeant emerged, and Patton ordered him to turn around and go back. The mission, he well knew, was to support the infantry, even if that meant moving backward. However, when another four tanks appeared, fully fueled, Patton ordered them to advance, on their own, through Pannes and into Beney, the next town. Patton followed on foot as the town fell to the Americans.

Satisfied that Compton's battalion was performing admirably, Patton walked over to Brett's tanks, which he found stuck in the village of Nonsard, out of gas. As a commander, Patton's most basic belief was to do whatever needed doing when it needed doing, and what needed doing now was refueling. Therefore, he walked all the way back to the rear, ordered gas to be transported to Nonsard, then reported to corps headquarters that all of the tank units had attained their objectives and, in fact, more. Having somewhat outrun the infantry, they withdrew by night a short distance to the infantry line.

After the first day of battle, only two tanks had been lost to artillery fire. Engine failure claimed three more and broken tracks another two. Forty became stuck in trenches, and 30 were idled by lack of fuel. Eighty American and 25 French tanks fought the next day. When the battle was over, the resulting advance was significant, the Germans were in full retreat, and the St. Mihiel salient, which had endured since the very first year of the war, existed no more. U.S. forces took 150,000 German prisoners. German resistance in Patton's sector had not been heavy, but Patton had demonstrated both the effectiveness of tanks and his effectiveness as a commander. As for that ride he took atop a tank, the newspapers gobbled it up as the exploit quickly found its way into official reports.

＊━━＊

Colonel Rockenbach did not approve of Patton's leaving his command post to advance personally with the attack, but a letter of congratulations addressed to him from General Pershing prompted the colonel to change his tune. He praised both Patton and his command, then quickly sent them into battle again, 60 miles to the north, to a position just west of Verdun to support I Corps in the Meuse-Argonne Offensive.

If there was anything Patton desperately feared, it was that the war would end before he had fought more of it. Without waiting for the Americans officially to relieve the French in the attack zone assigned to him, Patton donned a borrowed French uniform, advanced to the front lines, and, as he had done in preparation for St. Mihiel, reconnoitered the ground on which his tanks would operate. He then planned an especially aggressive attack in which his tanks would make a hard, sharply focused thrust over rough terrain through the very well defended German lines, which were some 12 miles deep. Once through these, the tanks were to spearhead a pursuit of the retreating Germans. Patton would have 140 tanks to work with.

Per standard procedure, the attack was preceded by "artillery preparation," in this case a massive, steady barrage that began at 2:30 on the morning of September 26. The early-morning mist served to conceal the tanks from the enemy, but it also rendered Patton's observation post useless. Although he knew Rockenbach would not approve of his doing so, he left the observation post with two officers and a dozen or so runners to see, close up, what was happening. As soldiers have done since the invention of gunpowder, he followed the sound of the guns and soon discovered that the tanks had made good progress, advancing some five miles. However, at about 9:00 A.M., in the hamlet of Cheppy, Patton ran into a contingent of panic-stricken soldiers making for the rear under heavy enemy fire. Exercising personal command, he stopped them, rounded them up, rallied them, and led them forward behind the advancing tanks. Then he noticed that a number of the tanks were stalled in trenches. He dispatched some men to get them moving, but, as he watched, the tanks remained motionless. Once again, Patton went forward to take charge. He quickly discovered the problem: the men would start to dig the tanks out, only to scatter for cover whenever they heard an incoming shell or a burst of machine-gun fire.

Patton's bedrock article of faith was that soldiers have a tremendous capacity to be led, by which he meant to be led by example. After hastily organizing more effective work parties, Patton personally unstrapped shovels from the stuck tanks, making a point of exposing himself to the enemy fire, which ricocheted off the tanks. He distributed the shovels, and when a man continued to balk under fire, he hit him in his helmeted head with one. Five tanks were soon on the move again, whereupon Patton raised his walking stick, circled it slowly above his head, and shouted to the infantry behind him: "Let's go get them. Who is with me?"

So they advanced. As they crested a rise, they were greeted by intense machine-gun fire. Everyone hit the deck. Patton later confessed to a "great desire to run." Trembling with fear, he thought suddenly "of my progenitors and seemed to see them in a cloud over the German lines looking at me." The vision filled him with calm, and he found himself "saying aloud, 'It is time for another Patton to die.'" Then, much louder, he called to those around him: "Let's go."

A half dozen troops were gathered about him. One after another, they were cut down. Patton's orderly, Joe Angelo, called to his commander: "We are alone." Patton replied: "Come on anyway."[10]

That is when a round dug into his left thigh, drilled through flesh and muscle, and exited near his rectum. Patton went down. Angelo pulled him into a shell hole, cut his trousers, and tightly bandaged the hemorrhaging wound. Once Angelo had stanched the flow, Patton ordered him to run toward some approaching tanks and direct their fire against the enemy machine guns. After Angelo had done this and returned, Patton was approached by a sergeant. He instructed the man to find Brett, tell him about his wound, and tell him that he had to take command. He ordered the sergeant not to send anyone to take care of him, because the firing was too intense. Turning now to Angelo again, he gave orders for him to point out more targets for the advancing tanks. When a medic came by, Patton motioned for him to change his bandage, but then sent him on to continue tending to other wounded. More than an hour passed before the enemy fire had been suppressed sufficiently to allow three stretcher bearers to approach. Carried two miles to an ambulance, Patton ordered the vehicle to stop at division headquarters so that he could make his report *before* being taken to the evacuation hospital.

Even before Patton was transferred from that hospital to a base hospital near Dijon, the newspapers were reporting how he had led a battle while bleeding in a shell hole. Wounded on September 30, he was promoted to colonel (with Rockenbach's enthusiastic endorsement) on October 17 and was not released from the hospital until October 28, his wound having healed satisfactorily. His tankers, trained by him, continued to fight in the Meuse-Argonne campaign through the middle of the month.

Patton returned to the tank brigade at Bourg, issued on his arrival one of his trademark orders enforcing military appearance and deportment, then set about drawing up recommendations for the decoration of the Meuse-Argonne tank heroes. While he was still in the hospital, he had written to Beatrice: "Peace looks possible, but I rather hope not for I would like to have a few more fights."[11] He would not get them, however, not in this war. On his thirty-third birthday, November 11, 1918, the guns fell silent in an armistice that would bring to the world a peace as welcome as it was all too brief and, to Patton, one that proved both hateful and far too long.

CHAPTER 5

At War with Peace

THE EPIC EXPLOITS AND LEGENDARY FOIBLES of Patton in World War II overshadow his extraordinary achievements during the briefer and more limited compass of World War I. In combat, he simultaneously proved the viability of the tank as a weapon and tested the effectiveness of the doctrine and tactics he had formulated and taught just months, weeks, and even days before. He showed himself to be an efficient and charismatic leader of troops. And he was recognized—he entered the war as a captain and came out a colonel. He was decorated—for his wound, there would be a Purple Heart (though the award was delayed for more than a decade—not uncommon during the post–World War I bureaucratic backlog). For his leadership of the tank school and in the field, he received the Distinguished Service Medal. For his personal courage, he was awarded the Distinguished Service Cross. Patton's achievements were real. His decorations were real. The war had been real. But there was another reality: the peacetime army. On his return to the States, Patton soon found himself wallowing in it.

After the armistice, the nation was not just war weary, it was utterly satiated with violent death and wanted no more of sacrifice, no matter how noble. As President Wilson labored in Paris to remake the postwar world and ensure that the United States would be a controlling force in it, a growing majority of Americans turned their backs on Europe, retreating into what the Republican candidate for president promised: "a return to normalcy." Portly, handsome, benign, dimwitted, and utterly pliable, Warren Gamaliel Harding was elected in 1920, told the American people that they need have nothing to do with the airy idealism of the League of Nations, and, in effect, announced his intention to do exactly what his Republican handlers had put him into the White House to do: make sure America just minded its own business. Because a nation minding its own business had no need of a big army, the military services set about dismantling themselves. By June 1920, an army of 4.5 million had been reduced to an authorized strength of 280,000 men and by 1922 stood at about 140,000. Now, at age 33, Patton feared that this might have been "his" war, his only war.

It was hardly enough. Patton left France on March 2, 1919 and arrived in Brooklyn on the seventeenth. He was briefly assigned to Camp Meade, Maryland, then was transferred to temporary duty in Washington. His promised Distinguished Service Medal finally came through in June, he returned to Camp Meade in the fall, and on June 30, 1920, like so many other officers rapidly promoted overseas in what was known as the National Army, he reverted to his prewar Regular Army rank of captain. One day later, however, he was promoted to major.

He worked now as a staff officer and cordially hated the duty. Good staff officers are vital to the operation of a modern army, because they serve as the middle layer between headquarters command and the commanders in the field, ensuring that high-command decisions are implemented by the front-line commanders. But George S. Patton Jr. had no desire to be a "middle layer." Staff officers did not get medals.

In the American army between the wars, men, money, and machines were in short supply. Time, however, was ample, and Patton used it systematically to review his own combat experience and everything else he had seen and heard during the war. He wrote technical papers and gave speeches at the General Staff College. In this work, he came to one very important and consequential conclusion concerning tank doctrine: it was a mistake to tie the tank to infantry. During the war, he himself had preached the subordination of the tank to the foot soldier, but his own combat experience had taught him that it was folly to slow a machine to the pace of a man. Better to set the tanks free, allow them to punch through enemy lines and wreak havoc clear through to the enemy's rear positions, creating not only a front-line breach but demoralized chaos in the rear, which a massive follow-on infantry attack could then exploit. Unknown to Patton, German military thinkers, even in defeat, were already beginning to pursue precisely this line of thought. The end product, in the case of the German army, would be called blitzkrieg—"lightning war"—and it would set Europe afire. Patton's writings prepared American military planners to understand blitzkrieg when it came, and thus the United States was able to enter World War II with a viable armored force and the doctrine by which to guide its deployment.

Yet this important insight aside, Patton never blossomed into a theorist. His technical papers were invariably pragmatic, practical, and limited in scope. He read voraciously, collecting from his brother officers in French and British units the training documents they used and gorging himself on their after-action reports, always looking for ways to use tanks most effectively in the future. He also pored over the texts of citations for bravery issued during the war. His purpose was to analyze and distill the very nature of heroism. He knew that by studying the movements and results of combat, he could learn to make the most of mechanized warfare. By examining official accounts of heroic behavior, perhaps he also thought that he could learn how to *create* heroism itself.

During his temporary duty assignment in Washington in the spring of 1919, Patton was named to a board tasked with writing a comprehensive manual for tank operations, and he served on a committee charged with making recommendations for improving the tanks themselves. In the course of his committee work, Patton met J. Walter Christie, a former technician with the U.S. Army Ordnance Department and now a race-car builder, driver, and all-round inventor. Patton and his former subordinate, Sereno Brett, were among a group that traveled to Hoboken, New Jersey, to look at Christie's M1919, a tank that could reach 60 miles per hour, climb a two-and-a-half-foot wall, and leap a seven-foot-wide ditch. Patton and the others were impressed, and Patton personally championed the Christie design at the War Department. By 1924, however, interwar funding cutbacks ended the department's involvement in developing the M1919 into a viable weapon. Nevertheless, it is likely (though no documentary evidence exists) that Patton continued personally to help finance Christie's ongoing work with his own money. Whether this is true or not, Patton was instrumental in developing mechanical concepts that would figure prominently in the American army's tracked armored vehicles of World War II, including the amphibious tanks that played vital roles in operations from the beaches of Normandy to the islands of the Pacific.

Yet even working with Christie, whose company Patton enjoyed and whom he greatly admired, could not take the place of fighting in war— war, "the only place where a man really lives."[1] Patton worried that he was growing fat and lazy. He complained of having difficulty waking up in the morning. His malaise may have been aggravated somewhat by news about Pershing and Nita. The couple had been separated during the war, then were briefly reunited in London after the armistice. Now Patton learned that the relationship had been broken off. Whether the decision to end the affair was mutual is not known, but the facts are that Pershing never saw Nita again, he remained a single widower, and she lived the rest of her life as an unmarried woman.

Patton threw himself passionately into polo, the closest thing he could find to combat, and, like many another man prematurely entering a midlife crisis, he bought himself a powerful car. It was a Pierce Arrow, as costly as it was beautiful (I "believe in enjoying myself between wars," Patton remarked[2]), and he set out in it to visit Joe Angelo, the faithful orderly who had saved his life at the Meuse-Argonne.

In addition to the technical papers he wrote in the months after his return from France, Patton also delivered a lecture to junior officers titled

"The Obligation of Being an Officer." The man who was quite literally involved in the nuts and bolts of the latest, most advanced military weapon spoke of today's army officers as "the modern representatives of the demigods and heroes of antiquity," standing at the head of "a line of men whose acts of valor, self-sacrifice and of service have been the theme of song and story since long before recorded history began." His speech rose to a pitch of romantic eloquence—"Our calling is most ancient and like all other old things it has amassed through the ages certain customs and traditions which decorate and ennoble it"—only to penetrate abruptly to the hard bedrock of starkest reality: these customs and traditions "render beautiful the otherwise prosaic occupation of being professional men-at-arms: killers."[3] The fiercest of American warriors who had fought before Patton—Grant, Sherman, and Nathan Bedford Forrest—were willing to face the reality, but Patton embraced both reality and, unapologetically, the romance of his calling.

The National Defense Act of 1920 left little room for romantics in the military. The strength of the army was capped at 280,000, and tanks were permanently attached, by force of the new law, to the infantry, where their development was sure to remain stunted as an auxiliary to combat. At Camp Meade, Patton had met another new apostle of the tank, junior to himself, Major Dwight David Eisenhower, West Point Class of 1915. Although Eisenhower (to his consternation) had been assigned to stateside training duty during the war and had not served overseas, Patton recognized in him a superb and energetic officer, a kindred spirit, and the two established a warm friendship. In the months before the cost-cutting measures mandated by the National Defense Act were implemented, the pair avidly discussed the promising future of tanks. But after the budgetary axe fell, both Ike and Patton left the grossly underfunded Tank Corps, which now seemed a dead end for any U.S. Army career.

On September 30, 1920, Patton officially relinquished command of the 304th Tank Brigade and, on October 3, returned to the cavalry as commanding officer, 3rd Squadron, 3rd Cavalry, Fort Myer, Virginia. It was not war, to be sure, but it was one of the best places for a career army officer to spend time between wars. Patton and Beatrice picked up the thread of Washington high society where they had dropped it back in 1913, when they left Fort Myer for Fort Riley, Kansas.

In 1923, Patton attended the Field Officers Course at the Cavalry School at Fort Riley. Beatrice and her daughters stayed with her parents in Massachusetts, where, on Christmas Eve 1923, she gave birth to a son, whom she named George Smith Patton IV. Patton continued his professional education at the Command and General Staff College at Fort Leavenworth, graduating in the top quarter of the class of 1924. This earned him a temporary appointment to the General Staff Corps in Boston, where he could be with Beatrice and their children. More important, the assignment was a prestigious one reserved for the most promising soon-to-be-senior officers. In March 1925, Patton was reassigned to the army's Hawaiian Division at Schofield Barracks, Honolulu, as G–1 (officer in charge of personnel) and G–2 (officer in charge of intelligence). Beatrice, who was still recovering from the difficult birth of George, remained in Massachusetts with the children. For obvious reasons, assignment to a tropical paradise was a plum posting, and Patton made the most of it. The climate was such that he could ride and play polo virtually every day of the year, which not only satisfied Patton's appetite for violent exercise and warlike sport, but brought him into contact with the moneyed American aristocracy of the islands. For Patton, a military commander was an officer *and* a gentleman, and that meant someone who was welcome at the highest and most exclusive levels of society.

During this period, Patton conducted a lively correspondence with Eisenhower, to whom he generously sent his full set of "Leavenworth notes" when Ike enrolled after him at the Command and General Staff College. The two wrote back and forth on the nature of combat, command, and Patton's favorite subject, courage. Patton wrote that courage was the product of leadership and that it was the commander's job to transform mere soldiers into heroes. The soldiers would not become heroes on their own. Whatever Eisenhower thought about this theory, he avidly studied Patton's notes and ended up graduating from the college number one in his class. Patton congratulated Ike, but was quick to credit his notes for his friend's success.

By the end of 1925, Beatrice and the children joined Patton in Hawaii, and the next year he added the responsibilities of G–3 to his Hawaiian Department portfolio. Director of plans and training, G–3 was the only General Staff post Patton truly relished, one from which he could make himself heard on doctrine, strategy, and tactics. Yet in this post, Patton, now 41 years old, behaved much as he had when he was a West Point second corporal. He became "too damned military," riding subordinate and fellow officers mercilessly for every error or questionable judgment. Within months, G–3 was taken from him. To this demotion was added the blow of Papa's death, in June 1927, from the combined ravages of tuberculosis and cirrhosis of the liver. Patton was "absolutely undone" by the telegram announcing his father's death, and he displayed what even Beatrice called "almost unreasonable grief."[4] When his mother, Ruth Wilson, died the following year, Patton seems not to have been profoundly affected; however, he later expressed regret that neither she nor his Papa would live to see him truly prove himself as a soldier.

Despite taking G–3 from him, Patton's commanding officers consistently rated him an outstanding officer, although one noted that he was "invaluable in war . . . but a disturbing element in time of peace."[5] Patton took this as high praise, but doubtless it was not intended that way. In any case, it was an uncannily perceptive appraisal.

In May, soon after he lost G–3, Patton was transferred to the Office of the Chief of Cavalry in Washington, D.C. It was yet another staff job, but it also put him front and center in the great debate of the interwar American cavalry: How far should mechanization go? In the war between the horse and the machine, which should win? It was a wrenching issue for Patton, who loved horses and honored the traditions of the cavalry. His heart was with the animals and the men who rode them into battle, but his head was increasingly with the machines. Moreover, he believed that an infantry monopoly on armor would squeeze the cavalry ultimately into irrelevance. By the beginning of the 1930s, Patton found himself cajoling his fellow cavalrymen into opening their minds to the new machines. He told them that only cavalrymen could use light tanks the way they should be used— as the mechanized equivalent of horses, for mobility over rough terrain. He argued that the tank was here to stay and that if cavalry did not get control of the new weapon, cavalry would be permanently sidelined. But just as he began to prevail on his colleagues, Congress, laboring in the throes of the Great Depression, pulled the purse strings tighter. A short-lived experiment called the "Mechanized Force," combining personnel from the cavalry, infantry, and artillery branches to operate tanks, armored cars, and other vehicles, ended just months after it had begun. Salvaging what he could with the shoestring budget he had, Army Chief of Staff Douglas MacArthur ordered all three service arms to continue experimenting with mechanization as best they could. This meant that the infantry kept its handful of tanks active, and the cavalry did the same with its few armored scout cars. But equipment was so scarce that meaningful unit maneuvers could not be conducted.

Patton left the Office of the Chief of Cavalry during the summer of 1931, then took time off with his wife and children at Green Meadows, the grand home Beatrice had purchased for them on the banks of the Ipswich River in South Hamilton, Massachusetts. In September, he enrolled in the Army War College, at the time based in Washington. Only the most outstanding officers were selected for this, the army's ultimate institution of higher learning. Patton emerged from the college a "Distinguished Graduate" in June 1932. His growing academic distinction, as well as his unflagging passion for books, demonstrates that the adult Patton had come to terms with his dyslexia. However, he was never entirely free of the disability. Throughout his career, Patton made it his practice either to speak spontaneously or to learn the text of his speeches by heart. Reading a full-length speech aloud in public still presented too many chances for embarrassing failure.

In July, Patton was assigned as executive officer of 3rd Cavalry, at Fort Myer. Three weeks into his new job, he found himself embroiled in the first of several ugly episodes that would mar and even threaten his career. America's veterans of the Great War were entitled by law to a cash payment—a so-called bonus—payable in 1945. The problem was that, by 1932, the Great Depression had put many veterans out of work. A grassroots veterans' movement developed to demand from Congress immediate payment of the bonuses, and, in May, 15,000 to 20,000 "Bonus Marchers" descended on Washington in a demonstration designed to shame the legislators into releasing the bonus money. The members of the "Bonus Army," which included Patton's heroic orderly Joe Angelo, camped in the city and just outside of it, at Anacostia Flats, Maryland. Although the House of Representatives passed a bonus bill on June 15, the Senate voted it down. By then, the Anacostia Flats camp had grown into a sprawling array of tents, crates, and shacks, a squalid "Hooverville" (as similar Depression-era shanty towns were dubbed) skulking in the shadow of the Capitol dome.

On July 28, after the Senate rejected the bonus bill, rioting broke out in the city. President Herbert Hoover ordered Douglas MacArthur to clear the marchers from Pennsylvania Avenue and the downtown area, but not to cross into the Anacostia camp. MacArthur ordered the 3rd Cavalry to ride into the city and await the 16th Infantry. As executive officer, Patton was not expected to lead men in riot duty, but the promise of action was too great a lure. He rode at the head of 217 men and 14 officers. While the regiment waited behind the White House, Patton rode out alone along Pennsylvania Avenue to assess the situation. He was cheered by some of the thousands of Bonus Marchers who lined the street. They recognized him from newspaper photographs that had appeared during World War I and even into the 1930s. Others jeered and hooted. Whether they recognized George S. Patton or not, they knew the uniform of a high-ranking officer when they saw one.

At about 4:00 P.M. the 3rd Cavalry and 16th Infantry formed up, and the cavalry led the infantry down Pennsylvania Avenue. It was not a pretty picture: helmeted, armed with carbines and drawn sabers, a cavalry unit of the United States Army was acting against former soldiers of that same army on a principal street of the capital of the world's oldest democracy. In response to agitation from the crowd, Patton and his men cleared the way by menacing rowdy Bonus Marchers with the very sabers their executive officer had designed. Those who refused to move were struck on the rump with the flat of the weapon. Patton personally administered several such blows. The avenue was quickly cleared.

This accomplished, MacArthur personally ordered Patton to cross the Anacostia River and clear the Flats. It was a violation of the president's direct instructions, but MacArthur, fearing that "Bolshevik" elements among the marchers would foment a full-scale insurrection, refused to accept the chief executive's order. Accordingly, Patton and the Third Cavalry cleared the Hooverville on the Flats. In the process, some tents and shanties caught fire. The cause of the conflagration has never been determined, but the Bonus Marchers believed it had been set as part of the army's deliberate assault.

The government's ugly response to the Bonus Marchers forever stained Herbert Hoover's already troubled presidency. For his part, MacArthur was wholly unapologetic, claiming he had done what he did to protect the city and the government. Patton was not so sure. The idea of marching against former soldiers, including some he may have led in battle and one, Joe Angelo, who had saved his life, was "most distasteful."[6] Nevertheless, Patton believed with MacArthur that an insurrection was imminent, and he later defended his actions by claiming that they saved lives and property. As for the public, many Americans would long remember the image of a spit-and-polish United States military officer lashing out with his saber at unarmed men who had served their country and were now jobless, hungry, and unable to support their families.

Except for the Bonus March incident, the Great Depression hardly touched the Pattons. Indeed, throughout his three-year tour of duty at Fort Myer, Patton led the life of a country squire, playing polo and riding to the hounds—and doing both with a reckless abandon that dared injury or death. Promoted to lieutenant colonel in the Regular Army on March 1, 1934, Patton was transferred to the Hawaiian Department once again, as G–2, in spring 1935. The same hunger for dangerous adventure that drove him to ride so hard and so recklessly prompted him to sail to his Hawaiian post from Los Angeles aboard his new yacht. Acting as skipper and navigator, commanding an amateur crew, and with Beatrice a passenger, Patton set out on May 7 and arrived in Honolulu on June 8. (The children would arrive later by regular passenger liner.)

The sailing had been exhilarating, but, once he arrived at his new post, the exhilaration quickly faded. Patton was G–2, intelligence officer, a position he did not much care for. This time, even the tropical surroundings did little to make him feel good about turning 50 with no new war in sight. He began drinking to excess. His ardor for Beatrice cooled suddenly and deeply, and he earned a reputation as a local ladies man. To his wife, he made little secret of his liaisons, and if she pressed the matter, he became by turns sullen and even verbally abusive. In truth, the affairs generally meant little to him—with the exception of a relationship that developed between him and his niece Jean Gordon, the beautiful dark-haired daughter of Beatrice's older half-sister and a close friend of the Pattons' own daughter, Ruth Ellen. Jean was 21 years old when she apparently fell in love with Patton.

One of Patton's regular assignments during this period was to purchase horses for the army. He relished the duty, and he often took family members along on buying trips. Beatrice, Ruth Ellen, and Jean Gordon were to accompany him to the big island of Hawaii, where he was to purchase mounts from Alfred Carter, who ran the 500,000-acre Parker Ranch. Beatrice fell ill before the trip, and Ruth Ellen decided to stay home to look after her mother. Patton and Jean traveled alone together, and a passionate affair reportedly developed. Ruth Ellen and a few others who knew both Jean and Patton subsequently denied any romance. Jean, they said, loved Patton as an uncle, and he, in turn, loved her as a niece or even a daughter. But, in later years, Patton boasted of the affair, and it is certain that Beatrice believed the two were intimately involved.

The grim fact was that life in the Patton household had become, more often than not, sordid, and on at least one occasion, Patton took the sordidness outside the family. During the Inter-Island Polo Championship in August 1935, Patton exploded at Walter Dillingham, a local manufacturing magnate and captain of the Oahu team, which was playing against the army team, captained by Patton. Dillingham collided with Patton, who cursed him as "an old son of a bitch," then continued: "I'll run you right down Front Street." It was behavior not befitting what Patton deemed himself to be: an officer *and* a gentleman. As soon as the chukker ended, his commanding officer, Hugh Drum, relieved Patton of his captaincy and barred him from continuing to play. Only a protest to Drum by Dillingham and the captain of the Maui team restored Patton. They would not play, they said, if "George" did not return to the field.[7]

On June 12, 1937, Patton, Beatrice, and their son George sailed the family yacht from Honolulu back to Los Angeles, arriving on July 12. They sold the craft, then traveled to their Massachusetts home for an extended leave. During this time, while Patton was out riding with Beatrice, her horse kicked him in the leg, fracturing it in two places. The injury laid Patton up for six months, during which time he developed phlebitis—a blood clot condition—which nearly killed him. Even after he was out of immediate danger, there were serious questions about his ability to resume active duty. In 1938, army physicians decided to assign him to limited administrative duty for a time in the Academic Department of the Cavalry School at Fort Riley, Kansas. It turned out to be a salubrious assignment and a much-needed tonic for Patton's physical as well as emotional health.

CHAPTER 6

Restless Mentor

AFTER SIX MONTHS OF LIGHT DUTY, HIS LEG fully recovered, Patton was promoted to regular army colonel and, on July 24, given command of the 5th Cavalry at Fort Clark. For the middle-age trooper, it was a kind of second youth or, at least, a return to the Wild West range riding he had enjoyed at the Sierra Blanca outpost during the Punitive Expedition of 1916–1917. Not only was Patton able to enjoy roughing it in the saddle, he quickly established connections with the Texas equivalent of Washington's social elite: the prosperous ranchers in the countryside surrounding Fort Clark. He was as happy as he could be—in the absence of a war.

Patton had a reputation not only as one of the army's ablest and most "colorful" officers, but also, quite possibly, thanks to his marriage with Beatrice, as its wealthiest. And that aspect of his notoriety was about to cost him. Colonel Jonathan Wainwright, who would earn grim fame in the coming war as the commander of doomed Bataan, was going broke as commanding officer of Fort Myer. The army's showplace installation, which most officers considered a plum assignment, made inordinate social demands on senior commanders, who were expected to finance endless entertainment expenses from their own pockets. Wainwright's pockets were empty, and he requested a transfer. The army turned to what it knew were the deep pockets of Patton. In December, Major General John Herr personally called at the Patton home to tell him that he was being reassigned to Fort Myer. Patton had enjoyed Fort Myer, but the *real* army, he felt, was at places like Fort Clark. To Herr he could only reply Yes, sir, but to Beatrice he vented his wrathful disappointment. "You and your money have ruined my career," he snapped at her, and the two argued bitterly as they packed for the trip east.[1]

The Fort Riley and Fort Clark interlude had been a tonic to the Pattons' often turbulent marriage. Reassignment to Fort Myer brought not only a return of discontent, but an intensification of it. Dark as Patton's mood was, the posting adjacent to Washington, D.C., hardly "ruined" his career. On the contrary, it gave Patton an opportunity to come within the orbit of George C. Marshall, who, in the spring of 1939, became the acting chief of staff, the army's senior officer. Patton and Marshall were both stationed at Fort Myer, and when Marshall's on-post house was being repaired and repainted, Patton invited him to share his family's house for the duration of the work. Marshall accepted the invitation, but it was certainly Patton's record as a leader of troops, not his hospitality, that moved Marshall to ensure his eligibility for promotion to brigadier general. Eligibility, however, was one thing, and actual promotion another. Commanding a cavalry regiment was a colonel's job. As along as that job was his, Patton would remain a colonel, and as long as peace prevailed, commanding a regiment would probably be his job. Then, on September 1, 1939, two momentous events occurred. George C. Marshall was permanently and formally elevated to Army Chief of Staff, and, after counterfeiting a Polish assault on a German border radio transmitter, the armies of Adolf Hitler invaded Poland, beginning a new world war.

Patton must have scented blood. He also must have felt a certain grim vindication in the spectacle of the German blitzkrieg through Poland, the kind of fast, highly mobile, unremittingly aggressive warfare he, as a tank pioneer, had advocated, in which masses of armor punched through the enemy's front-line defenses, then wreaked havoc in the rear as infantry broadened the assault into an overwhelming general attack. Yet far from feeling himself at the center of power in Fort Myer, Patton feared that he had been sidelined in a primarily ceremonial and social role. Nevertheless, under Marshall, the army prepared for war, and Patton continued to curry the chief's favor. When news came of the chief of staff's promotion to full general, Patton purchased a double set of four sterling silver stars from a New York jeweler and had them delivered to Marshall. Never one to succumb to such blandishments, Marshall was nonetheless gracious in his reply of thanks: "I will wear these stars with satisfaction and honor to the Army."[2] Patton need not have cajoled the chief in this fashion. Marshall had taken note of Patton as early as the end of World War I and had begun thinking of him for command of an armored division or corps if another war ever developed. As was Marshall's way, he just did not tell Patton about it.

In the spring of 1940, Patton served as an umpire in the Third Army war games in Louisiana. What he saw confirmed what he already knew: cavalry did not stand a chance against a mechanized force. With other officers, including armor commander and highly placed champion of mechanized warfare Adna R. Chaffee Jr., Patton secretly met in the basement of an Alexandria, Louisiana, high school. These so-called basement conspirators, all advocates of armor, sought a quiet, secluded place, free from the listening ears and prying eyes of tradition-bound infantry and cavalry commanders, to set about formulating their recommendation that the army create an independent an autonomous armored force. General Marshall received the recommendation and, without consulting anyone else, approved it. He assigned Chaffee—as commander of the 7th Mechanized Brigade, the army's senior tank officer—to command the new "Armored Force," and Chaffee not only created the 1st and 2nd Armored Divisions, but is credited with laying the foundation of U.S. armored doctrine as well as combined arms doctrine: the coordinated employment of armor, infantry, and artillery. The credit is well deserved, but we can only guess what Patton had contributed to Chaffee's thinking in that high school basement, for no record of the meeting was kept. That Chaffee thought highly of Patton is beyond dispute. He put him at the head of a list of officers he wanted to command a brigade within one of his armored divisions. Accordingly, on July 26, 1940, Patton reported to 2nd Armored Division at Fort Benning, Georgia, where he assumed command of the division's 2nd Armored Brigade.

As usual, he found the officers and men of his new command in urgent need of remolding in his own military image. Through a program of drill, discipline, and the inculcation of pride, he began making Patton-style soldiers of them all. Then he worked on making them tankers. On October 2, Patton finally received his first star and was now a brigadier general in command of a brigade. The very next month, he was assigned as acting commanding general of the entire 2nd Armored Division and, on April 4, 1941, he was promoted to major general, assigned just days later as permanent commanding general of the division.

Cutting his customarily picturesque military figure while forging a model division, Patton drew much recognition. Chaffee's growing illness—he would die of cancer in the summer of 1941—forced him to step down as commander of what was now designated I Armored Corps. This put the spotlight squarely on Patton, and he did not squander the attention he received. Under the watchful gaze of superiors and subordinates, Patton gave a bravura performance as a commander of boundless dash and limitless energy. He also addressed two critically urgent military problems: how to achieve the highest possible degree of speed and mobility in an armored force and how to transform civilians swept up by the nation's first peacetime draft into soldiers capable of modern armored warfare.

The first problem was chiefly a matter of organization, and Patton contributed to the evolution of the armored division by streamlining it. As originally conceived, the armored division was bloated and unwieldy. Patton began its transformation into a highly flexible unit consisting (in its final World War II incarnation) of three combat commands, which could work independently or in close coordination, depending on immediate need. The second problem yielded to a more mystical solution, and it was on the basis of this that the Patton legend crystallized and that he became one of the most compelling personalities of World War II.

George S. Patton Jr. was among the greatest trainers of troops in American military history. A superficial look at what Patton taught his soldiers is limited to an emphasis on discipline, military courtesy, military appearance, physical conditioning, unremitting drill, and so on. To be sure, all of these elements were important to Patton and occupied a prominent place in his training regimen, but the catalyst in the Patton training formula was his physical presence. He brought to his command a profound blend of military romanticism and realism and a genuine vision of effective leadership, which he conveyed in part through colorful lectures but mostly through constant modeling of the behavior and performance of every officer and every enlisted man. His limitless energy was part but never purely showmanship. A commander's duty, he believed, was to be everywhere. As he had walked among his advancing tanks on the battlefields of World War I France, so he now circulated among his troops as they trained. He corrected them mercilessly, but also usefully, practically, and when someone showed improvement or achieved excellence, he was generous, prompt, and public with his praise. He made himself conspicuous, driving among his division's tanks in one that had its turret specially painted in bold stripes of red, white, and blue plus a broad stripe of cavalry yellow, the army's traditional symbol of mobility. The Jeep he used not only bore a red-and-white two-star placard in front and back, but also was equipped with a piercing siren and klaxon horn, which would announce his approach long before his actual presence.

Perhaps no modern American military commander has been more haunted by personal demons than Patton—a combination of impulsiveness, reckless personal behavior, feelings of worthlessness, and outright depression—yet before the officers and men of his command he never allowed himself to appear as anything other than supremely self-confident and confident of each of them. Beset by myriad doubts, Patton never allowed his subordinates to doubt him or themselves. His message was never *we must succeed* but always *we will succeed.* Imbued, however imperfectly, with a consciousness of his own destiny, Patton strove to inoculate everyone else with a similar sense. When he spoke of combat, he spoke viscerally, of blood and guts, but he also emphasized that blood and guts had to be mastered by intellect and put into the service of the great new weapon they now possessed: the tank.

As Patton extolled the virtues of the tank to his troops, he also tirelessly promoted the weapon to the public, to the press, and to politicians. Already a virtuoso in the art of personal showmanship, Patton demonstrated commensurate mastery of the public arena by staging, as an army exercise in December 1940, a mass movement of some 1,000 tanks, halftracks, and other vehicles from Columbus, Georgia, to Panama City, Florida, and back. This 400-mile round trip Patton advertised as the longest movement ever made by an armored division. To complete the blitzkrieg effect, he choreographed aircraft overflights with the caravan. Prior to the exercise, Patton mounted a publicity campaign to ensure an audience all along the route. His object was to build morale by letting his troops think of themselves as celebrities and, simultaneously, to impress civilian America with the awesome power of the tank. By getting the public to buy in to armor, Patton reasoned, he could gain stronger, more enduring support for the still-emerging service arm.

The Columbus-to-Panama City exercise drew plenty of publicity, and Patton took the opportunity to promote himself in the papers as a daring commander who "would never order men to do anything . . . that he wouldn't do himself."[3] The demonstration went so well that, in January of the next year, Patton mounted a parade of the entire division, 1,300 vehicles in all, which thundered through the streets of Columbus to the cadence of a march composed by none other than Beatrice Patton, an amateur musician.

The hard training and the publicity paid off in recognition from higher command. Even conservative officers had to admit that armor may well have come of age. The Columbus-to-Panama City circuit had been a grand spectacle, which is precisely what Patton had wanted, but it also presented a serious practical problem. What was grand in peacetime made for an inviting target in war. Even a relatively fast-moving convoy was highly vulnerable to air attack. Furthermore, driving 1,000 tanks and assorted vehicles down a public highway in the sleepy American South was very different from driving an armored division under fire in a foreign country during war. Patton needed a way to visualize the movements of a huge mechanized force and to keep his tanks from becoming sitting ducks for enemy aircraft. How to get the big picture? How to understand the point of view of an enemy pilot? Patton purchased a light plane, took flying lessons, and, at age 55, earned a pilot's license. During exercises, he flew over and over his tanks, looking for better ways to manage the flow of traffic and to protect the vehicles from air attack. Every lesson learned was distilled from practical experiment. A by-product of his flying observations was insight into a combat role for light, or "liaison," aircraft as the eyes of armor and the artillery. An observer or even a commander could survey the battle situation from the air and, using two-way voice radio, direct complex tank movements in real time. Thanks in part to Patton's early experiments, the light aircraft spotter mission would figure importantly in World War II combat.

Not all of Patton's pioneering ideas for the armored corps were accepted. Because tankers were practitioners of war's cutting-edge technology, Patton wanted to dress them in a uniform that was utilitarian and strikingly modern in appearance, and that conveyed elite status. He personally designed a uniform of green gabardine featuring a tightly tailored abbreviated tunic with a row of brass or white metal buttons running diagonally down the front from the right shoulder to the middle front of the hem. The trousers were thickly padded and amply supplied with all manner of pockets. Topping off the ensemble was a gold football helmet. In many ways, the uniform was very practical: the dark green material hid oil stains, the padding and the football helmet protected the tankers in the close metal quarters of rough-riding tanks, and the multiple pockets were essential in an environment in which loose objects readily became missiles. But overall the look was ridiculous, and the same newspapers that had reported enthusiastically on the convoy, the parade, and the leadership of George S. Patton now mocked him as "the Green Hornet." Needless to say, Patton's uniform design was rejected by the army.

In the spring of 1941, the United States was still officially neutral, and most Americans remained eager to stay out of the war. Nevertheless, President Roosevelt steered steadily closer to outright alliance with Winston Churchill's Britain, trading 50 obsolescent destroyers for leases on British bases in the Western Hemisphere, pledging America's industrial might as the "arsenal of democracy," and, in March 1941, signing the Lend-Lease Act, which authorized the president to supply arms and material to any nation whose defense he deemed vital to American interests. Moreover, the peacetime draft had been under way since September 1940, and the tiny interwar army had already rapidly expanded to about 1.5 million men on the eve of Pearl Harbor. In this climate, Lesley J. McNair, who had charge of the army's combat training, announced the first of what would be a series of three massive maneuvers—war games—the biggest and most realistic the army had ever conducted.

Patton saw war games as an extraordinary opportunity to achieve three objectives: (1) to perfect the training of his men; (2) to create, test, modify, and hone armored tactics and doctrine—mechanized warfare was, after all, a new kind of warfare; (3) simply to win. For Patton, war games were an arena second only to actual combat in which he could demonstrate his personal prowess as a warrior and, somewhat secondarily, demonstrate the effectiveness of mechanized armor as a weapon of modern war. He was exhilarated, but also scared—not of failure (that, he knew, was not his destiny) but of being chosen, once again, as an umpire rather than as a participant.

In the lead-up to the maneuvers, Patton put aside his fears and prepared his men. He stressed three things. First, all eyes would be on the tanks. The army had plenty of old-line officers drooling at the prospect of the failure of the newfangled mechanized service. The maneuvers were make or break, a one-time opportunity to prove the value of the tank. Second, Patton hammered away at the theme of aggressive mobility. The entire division was to keep moving with a "desperate determination to go forward," always attacking, but never pausing to attack, and always striking against weakness while blowing past strength. The tanks were not to stop. When one objective was attained, Patton admonished, "do not say 'I have done enough,' keep on, see what else you can do to raise the devil with the enemy." The third point he stressed in preparation for the maneuvers was the creation of an elite identity. Under Patton's command, the 2nd Armored Division dubbed itself "Hell on Wheels" and proudly accepted the role and identity of "blitz troopers," the scourge of the battlefield. For Patton, creating a proud unit identity was as indispensable as the tanks themselves.[4]

The maneuvers took place in Tennessee in June 1941, and, to his great relief, Patton was assigned to lead the 2nd Division. There was some initial fumbling in deployment of the division's 12,000 troops, but once the action got under way in earnest, Patton was fully its master and drove his forces with relentless speed and efficiency, executing in a mere nine hours an exercise that had been scheduled for two-day completion. He basked briefly in both the professional and public praise his performance had garnered and made no secret of being driven by a hunger for glory won in battle. As for flamboyance, that was simply part and parcel of being a great commander. To officers who took pains to make themselves inconspicuous on the field by donning the drab uniform of an ordinary G.I., Patton would cite the example of Lord Nelson, who strode the deck of HMS *Victory*, under fire, wearing the full dress uniform of a Royal Navy admiral, ribbons, medals, cocked hat, and all. Glory, yes, Patton acknowledged, but never vainglory. He regarded genuine glory as bounty to be shared, and he was always generous in assigning credit to the men of his command. Among his favorite maxims, which he often repeated, was "The soldier is the army."[5] Not the plan, not the equipment, and not even the commanding general. Personal glory was important, but it was important precisely in proportion to its being more than merely personal.

For Patton, leadership was never simply about making plans and giving orders. It was about transforming oneself into a symbol, a kind of totem or talisman with which the group identified and, indeed, in which the group invested and merged their individual identities. The men of the 2nd Armored Division were nicknamed Hell on Wheels, but mostly they referred to themselves as "Patton's men."

No sooner were the Tennessee maneuvers completed than Patton began planning for the even bigger war games to be staged across a vast area of Louisiana and Texas during September 1941. These were, and they remain today, the most ambitious maneuvers in the history of the United States Army. Four hundred thousand troops were engaged in a "war" between the Red Army and the Blue. In Phase I of the maneuvers, Patton found himself on the losing side as part of Lieutenant General Benjamin Lear's Red Army. In Phase II, his 2nd Armored Division was assigned to the Blue Army, which was commanded by the brilliant Lieutenant General

Walter Krueger (whose chief of staff was Patton's old friend, Dwight D. Eisenhower). This time, Patton was at the point of a bold attack against the Red Army flank and led a spectacular 400-mile end run around the enemy so that he could strike Shreveport (which the Red Army was defending) from the rear. The movement was audacious and fully exploited the mobility of a mechanized force. Adding to the audacity of the attack was Patton's refusal to do the conventional thing by waiting for all his massive forces to arrive at the point of the attack. Deeming surprise the overriding objective, he attacked with what he had when he had it. This was a Patton trademark. War is not about perfection, which is timeless, it is about opportunity, which is chained to time. The best, Patton frequently said, is the enemy of the good. It is always better to execute a good plan violently and immediately than it is to sacrifice fleeting opportunity by waiting for perfection.

Not only did Patton win, he won the kind of victory that could be achieved only with tanks. There were plenty of congratulations to go around, but also some cries of foul from officers on the losing side. To make his end run, Patton briefly led the 2nd Division outside of the designated maneuver area, and when he ran out of gas he paid local filling stations to refuel his thirsty vehicles. Rumor had it that the cash was Patton's own, and he never denied the rumor. Nor did Patton argue with those who protested that he had broken the rules. He merely responded that winning was ultimately the only rule in war. General Marshall and the rest of the senior command agreed. The Louisiana maneuvers made Patton the star of American armor.

These maneuvers were quickly followed in October and November by maneuvers in the Carolinas, in which Patton and his men not only performed brilliantly but even captured the commander of the opposing army, Hugh Drum, who had been Patton's commanding officer during his tour in Hawaii and whom Patton resented for having nearly ejected him from the Inter-Island Polo Championship in 1935 because of ungentlemanly behavior. Best of all, the culminating phase of the maneuvers was personally witnessed by Chief of Staff George Marshall, who came away more impressed than ever by Patton's performance.

Patton knew that, as a result of the three sets of war games, he was most advantageously positioned to get an important command once America finally entered the war. He assumed that, as was the case in World War I, he would be among the first to go overseas, and the December 7, 1941, attack on Pearl Harbor gave him hope, which seemed perfectly justified when Marshall elevated Patton, on January 15, 1942, to command of I Armored Corps. Now he awaited his marching orders.

He did not have to wait long. In February, Patton was assigned to create and command a desert training center. Marshall and the other army planners knew that the first fighting would be against the dreaded German Afrika Korps under the brilliant Field Marshal Erwin Rommel in the deserts of North Africa. They also knew that, aside from police actions against Indians and Pancho Villa, the United States Army had never fought in such an environment, let alone with tanks. Patton had to locate a site for a large desert training area, had to put it together, then had to train America's first generation of desert warriors. It was an urgently important assignment, but Patton, who craved combat, was profoundly disappointed by it. Orders, however, were orders, and, in March, Patton flew a Piper Cub over an extensive area of California, Nevada, and Arizona, looking for a large, uninhabited tract of desert that simulated conditions in North Africa. Ultimately, he settled on 16,200 square miles of desolation adjacent to the California hamlet of Indio, some 200 miles east of Los Angeles. After surveying the site from the air, Patton and a small party ranged over it on horseback. Officially the United States Army Desert Training Center (today called the National Training Center), the installation was dubbed "Little Libya," and offered sand, cactus, rocks, rattlers, and midday temperatures pushing 130 degrees in the summer with winter nights that plunged near or even below freezing.

It was a hard place, and that is exactly what Patton wanted. There was plenty of room for realistic maneuver and live-fire exercises, and the harsh conditions would test machines as well as men. Instead of barracks, everyone, including the commanding general, would live in tents. There would be no electricity, no running water, no hot water, no heat. There would be daily conditioning runs: one mile in 10 minutes. There would be marching: eight miles in 2 hours. Patton made it as hard as possible, because he wanted it to be as real as possible. Making it real would build effective desert soldiers and save lives.

Patton formally arrived at Indio on April 10. Training commenced within a week. However much he longed to be fighting overseas, Patton threw his heart, soul, and intellect into the work at hand. As always, he commanded in the field. Although he had an observation post atop a hill that his men called King's Throne, he rarely stayed there for long, preferring to move about among his troops and tanks, traveling by Jeep, tank, half-track, and light plane. Patton saw his mission as twofold: he had to train and harden his men—some 60,000 would pass through Indio during his tenure, which began in April and ended in July of 1942—and he also had to formulate desert tank doctrine. He experimented extensively with tank formations, and he developed specifications for a new vehicle, the tank retriever, which was specifically designed to recover damaged or broken-down tanks from the field, under fire. He also innovated the use of light aircraft not just for reconnaissance, but as a command platform from which the commander could issue real-time movement orders by voice radio. Above all, he put everything up for discussion. Once an order was issued, Patton expected obedience born of perfect discipline. But up to the moment of the order, he wanted to hear all sides on each important issue. The Desert Training Center became the focus of lively discussion and debate, in which Patton listened, argued, and questioned. From these debates, Patton harvested whatever ideas seemed most promising, and he sent them on to higher headquarters, with a request that they be circulated for further comment.

Despite his commitment to the work at Indio, Patton continually reminded his two commanding officers, Lesley McNair and Jacob Devers, that he wanted to fight. These men, like Marshall, knew from World War I experience that Patton was highly effective in combat, but they were also convinced that, as a great trainer and motivator as well as the army's foremost exponent of tank warfare, Patton was more useful building an armored force and doctrine than on the field. It was July 1942 before Patton received a summons to Washington to receive a combat assignment at last. On the thirtieth of the month, the very day of his departure from the Desert Training Center, he wrote a summary of lessons learned. Today such "lessons learned" summaries are standard procedure in the military and exist in abundance. Patton drew up his summary on his own initiative, believing that those who would be assigned to fight in the desert would find it useful. He wrote:

> Formation and material are of very secondary importance compared to discipline, the ability to shoot rapidly and accurately with the proper weapon at the proper target, and the irresistible desire to close with the enemy with the purpose of killing and destroying him.

He further advised commanding from the air in a liaison plane via two-way radio, and he closed, pithily, with: "Sitting on a tank watching the show is fatuous—killing wins wars."[6]

Patton had been in such a hurry to leave that he did not have the time to assemble his men for a formal farewell. He wrote to Major General Alvan Gillem, the officer who replaced him at Indio, with a request that he publish to the men a message he enclosed. What he wrote was vintage Patton:

> Soldiers: Owing to circumstances beyond my control, I left you so hastily that I was unable to speak to you personally. However, I would be lacking in gratitude if, even at this late date, I failed to tell you of my sincere appreciation of the magnificent conduct of each and everyone of you whom I had the honor to command.
>
> Having shared your labors, I know the extreme difficulties under which we worked and I know also how splendidly and self-sacrificingly you did your full duty.
>
> I thank you and congratulate you—it was an unparalleled honor to have commanded such men.[7]

Now, in Washington, he was told that he would command the Western Task Force in an operation code named Torch. His mission was to invade North Africa.

CHAPTER 7

From African Defeat
to African Victory

PATTON ARRIVED IN WASHINGTON ON JULY 30 and was quickly briefed on Operation Torch, the proposed invasion of North Africa. He put together a small staff of officers and set himself up in an office in the Munitions Building on Constitution Avenue, where he and his staff spent the next several days poring over maps, preliminary plans, and reports on climate, terrain, and other conditions. Then, on August 5, Patton flew to the London headquarters of Dwight D. Eisenhower, whom General Marshall had chosen over 366 more senior officers, among them Patton himself, to assume the role of commander of the European Theater of Operations and Allied commander for Torch.

Ike was thrilled to see him, for Patton brimmed with all the confidence, energy, and eagerness for battle that Eisenhower, under the present circumstances, wished he had. Not only was he buried under the myriad details of a highly complex amphibious operation spread out across the Atlantic shore of Morocco and the Mediterranean shore of Algeria, he lacked faith in the very idea of Operation Torch. The United States entered World War II because the Japanese attacked Pearl Harbor. The American people wanted, first and foremost, to avenge that "sneak attack," but President Roosevelt and his senior military planners agreed with Winston Churchill that the first order of business had to be dealing with Hitler and Mussolini in Europe. Where the military commanders and the political leaders parted company, however, was in how to go about this. Like most of their uniformed colleagues, Generals Marshall and Eisenhower favored a rapid buildup of American and British forces in England for an invasion of France across the English Channel. Having barely recovered from the catastrophes of Dunkirk and Dieppe, both premature actions on the Continent, Prime Minister Churchill argued that the Allies were not ready for a cross-channel invasion and that the only viable alternative was to begin by invading Europe through what he called its "soft underbelly." His idea was to defeat the Germans and Italians in North Africa, then leap off to landings in Sicily and then mainland Italy and elsewhere in Mediterranean Europe. This strategy, Churchill argued, would draw off German forces from the Eastern Front, giving Stalin's Red Army some immediate relief. In the meantime, preparations could continue for a later cross-channel invasion. Both Marshall and Eisenhower objected that this indirect approach would sacrifice valuable time and resources. President Roosevelt, however, believed that building up to a cross-channel invasion would take time, and he wanted to get America into the fighting as soon as possible. Good soldiers that they were, Marshall and Eisenhower followed orders and prepared for Torch.

After a long night of conversation with Eisenhower, Patton noted in his diary that we "both feel that the operation is bad and is mostly political. However, we are told to do it and intend to succeed or die in the attempt." Yet where Eisenhower's response to Torch emphasized the near impossibility of its success, Patton fell back on the innate fatalism born of his sense of personal destiny: in the worst case, Operation Torch would be "an impossible show . . . but, with a little luck it can be done at a high price . . . and it might be a cinch."[1]

In fact, it is by no means certain that Patton was displeased with the plan. For all his aggressiveness, he never favored the simple head-on approach, what the maverick cold war-era air force fighter pilot and military theorist John Boyd famously derided as the army's customary "hi-diddle-diddle-right-up-the-middle" mind-set. Instead, Patton frequently spoke of "holding the enemy by the nose . . . and kicking him in the pants." He intended this as tactical advice—use part of your forces to hold the enemy at the front with fire while moving the rest of your forces around his flank—rather than as strategic philosophy, but it is quite likely that Patton saw a value in Torch that Eisenhower and even Marshall did not see. In a grand strategic sense, much as Churchill suggested, the soft underbelly approach could serve to hold the enemy by the nose and thereby give a later attack from the west, from across the English Channel, a better chance of succeeding. In any case, Patton was just happy to get into a fight—any fight, even if it was in North Africa and not across the English Channel.[2]

Nevertheless, Patton's initial euphoria quickly ebbed, not because of the plan, but because of the personalities responsible for its execution. He was disappointed—and jealous—that Eisenhower chose Mark Clark, a major general with eight years less experience than Patton, as his deputy commander for the operation. Patton feared Clark might get in his way and be "too intrusive." But he also began to doubt Eisenhower himself: "Ike is not as rugged mentally as I thought; he vacillates and is not a realist." Moreover, he was disturbed by what he saw as the undue deference the American officers paid to their British counterparts. "It is very noticeable," he recorded in his diary on August 11, "that most of the American officers here are pro-British, even Ike . . . I am not, repeat not, pro-British."[3]

Outside the pages of his diary, however, Patton did not complain, but worked hard and cooperatively with Eisenhower and Clark to plan the operation. The deeper they got into it, the more dubious the project seemed. Both Eisenhower and Clark worried that the odds were stacked too high against success, and Patton went so far as to quantify the matter, calculating that the actual odds were "52 to 48 against us." In contrast to the other men, however, he favored going on. "I feel," he noted in his diary, "that we should fight . . . I feel that I am the only true gambler in the whole outfit." Always, Patton's controlling imperative was action, however imperfect: "We must do something now," he wrote.[4]

After three weeks of meeting and planning in London, Patton returned to Washington. There he hammered out with the navy the details of the landings. The pessimism of the naval officers greatly aggravated Patton, who frequently exploded in fits of frustration. Despite this, by September 24, Patton had completed his portion of the plan and confided to his diary that he now felt "very calm and contented." Even though the operation could be "a very desperate venture . . . I have a feeling we will win."[5]

Operation Torch would consist of three major landings. The Eastern and Central Task Forces, which would sail from Britain, would land at Algiers and Oran, respectively; the Western Task Force, under Patton, would sail from the States and land near Casablanca. Patton subdivided the Western Task Force into three task groups. His trusted friend Lucian Truscott would land near Mehdia and take Port Lyautey. The other two groups, commanded by Jonathan W. Anderson and Ernest N. Harmon, would land at Fédala and Safi, then converge on the city of Casablanca, which they would capture.

On October 20, Patton wrote a series of sentimental valedictory letters, directing that they be posted only after the invasion had begun. He wrote to his childhood nurse, Mary Scally, who now lived with his sister Nita: "When Nita gives you this letter, I will either be dead or not. If I am, please put on a good Irish wake." To Mrs. Francis C. Marshall, the widow of his first company commander at Fort Sheridan, he wrote to express his conviction "that whatever success I have attained, I owe largely to the influence of you and the General." To André W. Brewster, a fellow member of Pershing's World War I staff, he wrote: "Before starting on the Second World War I wish to bid goodbye to one of the men who in the First War did so much for me." To James G. Harbord, who had been Pershing's chief of staff, he wrote that he had "been one of the chief inspirations of my military life." To his brother-in-law Frederick Ayer, Patton expressed gratitude and admiration. He explained that his task would be "about as desperate a venture as has ever been undertaken by any force in the world's history," and he enclosed a sealed letter for Beatrice, to be given to her only "if I am definitely reported dead." He allowed that this "all sounds very gloomy, but it is not really so bad. All my life I have wanted to lead a lot of men in a desperate battle; I am going to do it."[6]

On October 24 at 8:10 A.M., Patton sailed from Norfolk, Virginia, with 24,000 men in 100 ships. He passed the long voyage in exercising, writing in his diary, and reading the Koran, which he found both "good" and "interesting." The quickest way to prepare himself for combat in the Islamic world was to discover something of its very soul. Patton also spent time "giving everyone a simplified directive of war. Use steamroller strategy; that is, make up your mind on course and direction of action, and stick to it. But in tactics, do not steamroller. Attack weakness. Hold them by the nose and kick them in the pants."[7]

In the days leading up to the landings, the weather along the North African coast was miserable, but, on the morning of November 8, it cleared as if by a miracle. Patton took this as a providential sign and an indication that he was to be permitted to fulfill his destiny by fighting this battle. The landings were resisted by Vichy French forces, but the beachheads were quickly secured. Algiers fell to the Americans on the first day, and the fighting there stopped. Fresh Allied units, mostly British, followed the first wave at Algiers and advanced on Bizerte and Tunis in Tunisia. From his headquarters within the Gibraltar rock, Eisenhower dispatched Mark Clark to negotiate a wide-ranging North African armistice with Vichy admiral Jean Darlan. In the meantime, fighting was sharp at Oran and lasted two days. As for Patton's sector in Morocco, the French offered stiff resistance, but the landings proceeded briskly nevertheless. Ernest Harmon's task group pinned down the garrison at Marrakech while Truscott's group took the vital Port Lyautey airfield. The principal landing was at Fédala, which fell to Anderson's troops by 8 A.M. At that point, Patton was supposed to disembark from the *Augusta*. His personal gear had been stowed in a landing craft, and he was about to board it, when he paused to ask his orderly, Sergeant George Meeks, to first retrieve from the craft his trademark ivory-handled revolver. Meeks did so, and Patton took a moment to strap it on just as seven French cruisers opened fire on the landing fleet. *Augusta*'s guns replied. The fierce muzzle blast from the great cruiser's rear turret blew the landing craft off its davits and to bits. By pausing to get his favorite revolver and strap it on, Patton had saved his life.

Doubtless gratified by so remarkable a manifestation of what he believed was his providential good fortune, Patton was nevertheless frustrated that he now could not leave the ship until after noon. In a foul mood as he finally came ashore about 1:30, he was appalled by the spectacle of soldiers digging foxholes. To dig a foxhole, Patton always said, was to dig a grave. The object was to *advance,* not to *dig in,* and he wasted no time in personally motivating his troops with curses, kicks, and encouragement. Very quickly they left off digging foxholes and went about the business of securing the beachhead and commencing the inland advance.

Although the combat troops now performed well, the unloading of supplies and equipment was sluggish. Early the next morning, Patton again took personal charge, and the logistical problems disappeared. With this matter settled, Patton returned to the *Augusta* to persuade Admiral Hewitt to move his transports closer to the shore, so that unloading and reinforcement could be handled even faster. Whether it was giving orders to enlisted G.I.'s or cajoling a senior admiral, Patton believed in the persuasive power of personal contact face-to-face.

From the *Augusta,* he returned to the scene of battle, sent his staff to set up headquarters at Fédala, and advanced on Casablanca with his combat troops. As the Americans approached, the French surrendered the city on November 11, Patton's birthday. He met with the French officers at his headquarters in the Hotel Miramar at Fédala, having ordered his deputy commander, Geoffrey Keyes, to welcome the delegation with a guard of honor. The Frenchmen were ceremoniously escorted to the hotel's smoking room, where Patton congratulated the officers on the gallantry of their troops. He well understood the importance of self-respect and honor among military men, and he also understood that even the Vichy French were hardly wholehearted in their commitment to the Axis. The enemy officers with whom he was dealing now were potential allies. His task, however, went beyond ceremony. He carried with him two versions of an armistice agreement, both prepared and authorized in Washington. One version assumed token French resistance and provided lenient terms. The other assumed fierce and stubborn resistance and called for the dissolution and disarming of all French forces. What had actually happened on the beaches fell somewhere between token and stubborn resistance. Moreover, General Auguste Noguès explained that disbanding the French forces would result in violent unrest among the Arabs, Jews, and Berbers, perhaps even civil insurrection. Assuming authority beyond his official instructions, Patton delayed concluding a formal armistice and instead proposed a gentlemen's agreement by which the French vowed not to hinder the Americans in their contest against the Axis, prisoners of war would be immediately exchanged, and the French troops would retain their arms but remain, for the present, in barracks, pending final word from General Eisenhower. This settled, Patton offered everyone present champagne and proposed a toast to the "happy termination of a fratricidal strife" and "the resumption of the age-old friendship between France and America."[8]

Patton's invasion of Morocco was a triumph and elevated him to the status of national hero. Yet it was Mark Clark that the army immediately rewarded with the third star of a lieutenant general. Patton was intensely jealous of the dashing, handsome, and considerably younger man. He choked back his bitterness as he sent Clark his "sincere congratulations on your promotion and also on the magnificent work you have been doing in connection with the operation."[9]

To add to his misery, having taken Morocco, Patton was now sidelined there. Longing to join the battle then under way in Tunisia, he was instead occupied with overseeing the conversion of Casablanca into a major American military base, hardening and training incoming troops, and serving as military administrator of a government putatively run by a sultan, French general Noguès, and French admiral Darlan. He trusted French officers to manage French troops guarding roads and bridges, manning antiaircraft installations, and generally serving to discourage invasion from Spanish Morocco. A stable Morocco meant that American troops would be free to devote their full attention to fighting the Axis.

On November 30, when Clark telephoned with a request that he fly to Algiers, Patton had a flash of hope, but after supper with Eisenhower and Clark, a phone call came for Ike from Washington via Gibraltar. Eisenhower hung up the receiver and turned to Clark: "Well, Wayne, you get the

Fifth Army." To Beatrice, Patton wrote on December 2: "Some times I think that a nice clean death . . . would be the easiest way out."[10]

As Patton stewed, his resentments simmered. He wrote in his diary that Clark was one of the "glamour boys [who] have no knowledge of men or war," and he complained that Eisenhower was no longer really "commanding" because he always yielded to the British, in depressing contrast to World War I's General Pershing, who had always put American interests first. The comparison between Eisenhower and Pershing became even more invidious when Patton was tapped to host the Casablanca Conference between FDR, Churchill, and their respective military advisers in January 1943. His dark mood notwithstanding, Patton was a gracious, entertaining, impressive, and efficient host, whose razor-sharp troops made a great impression on everyone. To each compliment, however, Patton gave the same response: *I'd rather be fighting.* Then he heard that the Casablanca conferees had decided to make the next attack in Tunisia primarily a British show, with the United States II Corps under British command. "Shades of J. J. Pershing," he wrote in disgust. "We have sold our birthright."[11]

One product of the Casablanca Conference did excite Patton. Churchill and Roosevelt definitively agreed to invade Sicily after Tunisia had been conquered. This came as a blow to Marshall and Eisenhower, who had hoped to turn directly to the cross-channel invasion after North Africa, but Patton was thrilled. Not only would this invasion certainly get him back into the fight, it appealed to his sense of history. To jump off from North Africa to the conquest of Sicily would be to follow in the footsteps of Hannibal, Scipio Africanus, and Belisarius, the great generals of the ancient world. Of course, what FDR, Churchill, and, for the moment, even Patton glided over was the fact that Tunisia had to be conquered first. In this, the American army was about to learn a very hard and very bitter lesson.

It was one thing to achieve victory against the Vichy French, quite another to prevail against the German forces of Field Marshal Erwin Rommel. On February 14, 1943, the American 1st Armored Division under Orlando Ward was mauled and withdrew, along with Free French forces, 50 miles to the Western Dorsale, the mountains near the Tunisian-Algerian border. Like Patton himself, Rommel was a believer in relentless attack, and, seeing an opportunity to push the Allies out of Tunisia altogether, he attacked next at the Sbiba and Kasserine passes in an engagement known as the Battle of Kasserine Pass. Rommel very nearly broke through, but chronically beset by logistical problems, unable to maneuver adequately in the rough terrain, and menaced by a buildup of Allied reinforcements, he was forced to break off the offensive on February 22 and withdraw to his formidable redoubt known as the Mareth Line.

Yet Rommel had succeeded in doing plenty of damage. Lloyd Fredendall, commanding the U.S. II Corps, had been woefully outgeneraled. More than 3,000 of his troops were killed or wounded, and another 3,700 were taken prisoner. Equipment losses were heavy, including 200 tanks. Bad as all this was, far worse was the effect on American morale. In this, the first direct American encounter with the Germans, the United States Army was not merely defeated, it was humiliated. A shiver of panic shot through the American home front. As for the British, alarm and disgust ran high. Tommies and officers alike began slyly referring to their American allies as "our Italians," a cutting reference to the notoriously inept service Mussolini's army rendered to the Germans.

Removed from battle, Patton writhed in his Casablanca seat. Such a blow to the pride of the American army, his army, was agony. That his own son-in-law, John Waters, the husband of his eldest daughter, Bea, was now a prisoner of war added to the pain. Patton felt both neglected and useless. Then, on March 4, he picked up a telephone message from Eisenhower ordering him to leave the next day for extended field duty. He flew to Algiers, where Ike was waiting for him at the airfield. Ike was relieving Fredendall and giving Patton temporary command of II Corps. His mission was to transform the corps from a defeated army into a victorious one or, as Eisenhower put it in a formal memorandum of March 6, to effect "the rehabilitation of all American forces under your command." In his memorandum, he made clear that Patton was "taking over a difficult task. . . . But I know you can do it and your success there is going to have far-reaching effects. . . ." He also reminded Patton of having spoken to him "about personal recklessness. Your personal courage is something you do not have to prove to me, and I want you as Corps Commander—not as a casualty."[12]

British general Sir Harold Alexander briefed Patton on the role of the II Corps, which, he said, was to support British forces under General Bernard

Law Montgomery by threatening the Axis flank. Patton did not relish a supporting role, and he was distressed not only that it would inhibit him personally, but that it would not allow sufficient scope of action for the American army to redeem itself after the failure at Kasserine Pass. But Patton accepted that Alexander was in command, and he bit his tongue.

Patton formally replaced Fredendall on March 6 and contemplated the sloppy, demoralized, unsoldierly command the general had left to him. The soldier is the army. Plans, equipment, commanders, all are necessary, but without hard, disciplined soldiers, there could be no army, and without an army, there could be no victory. His orders were to take II Corps into action in 10 days' time. That gave him little more than a week to transform a beaten rabble into a force of warriors absolutely determined to win.

What he did became one of the legends of the United States Army. As usual, he was everywhere, speeding about in a siren-equipped scout car accompanied by a motorcycle escort. He demanded that the officers and men of II Corps look and behave like soldiers. He ordered everyone to wear clean, pressed uniforms, complete with neckties, leggings, and helmets. He established rigorous schedules and requirements for every activity, no matter how mundane. He insisted on the strict observance of all military courtesies, including the salute. (It is said that anyone in the army could instantly recognize a "Patton man" by the sharpness of his salute.) He had his troops carefully overhaul all weapons. He instituted a strict schedule of monetary fines for the slightest infractions. The men grumbled, but they soon began to see themselves as soldiers: *Patton's men.* While he saw to the minutiae of the troops' discipline, he also delivered talk after personal talk, exhorting his men to fierce, aggressive action. He did not want them to die for their country, he said, but to kill for it.

Even as he demanded the utmost from II Corps, he moved heaven and earth to see that its personnel were the best-equipped and best-fed men in the U.S. Army. Even as he set the bar higher and higher, demanding more and more, he continually assured his men that they would be worthy, they would succeed, they would win. Many men hated him, but no one ignored him, and everyone, even the grumblers, was excited by what he had to say.

In the meantime, he found that he had an old comrade, Omar Bradley, to deal with. Although Ike had expressed total confidence in Patton, he sent Bradley to Patton as his personal "representative." Patton took this to mean spy, and he responded by securing Eisenhower's approval to appoint Bradley his deputy commander. Once the transformation of II Corps had been completed, Patton would go on to continue planning Operation Husky, as the Sicily invasion was called, and Bradley would assume command of the corps.

Patton was promoted to lieutenant general on March 12. On March 17, a II Corps division under Terry Allen took the village of Gafsa, the first objective Alexander had assigned the corps, then advanced toward the second objective, Gabès, along the way achieving a fine victory at the Battle of El Guettar. Here Allen's division checked the advance of a German and an Italian panzer force, not once but twice. In contrast to the demoralized chaos of Kasserine Pass, the American troops fought bravely and efficiently, destroying 30 Axis tanks and driving the enemy from the field. The victory was well publicized and, on the home front, did much to exorcize the shame of Kasserine.

Less impressive was Orlando Ward's performance at Maknassy Pass, the third of Alexander's prescribed objectives. Bogged down in mud, Ward was at a loss. Patton, who did not believe a commander should allow himself to be defeated by mud or any other natural circumstance, ultimately relieved Ward.

In contrast to his command in France during World War I, Patton could not be everywhere at once on the battlefield. El Guettar and the Maknassy Pass were simply too far apart, and although he made frequent front-line inspections, Patton had to spend most of his time at his headquarters, between the widely dispersed divisions. It was yet another frustration.

At length, as Montgomery finally forced the German tanks out of the Mareth Line, Alexander ordered Patton to pull out of stubborn Maknassy and attack down the road toward Gabès with the object of harrying the German retreat from Mareth. Patton was resentful of the condescending tone of Alexander's orders, which were so detailed as to leave nothing to Patton's discretion. Hadn't the American army proven itself at El Guettar? Nevertheless, Patton took the assignment and put together what he hoped would be another brilliant victory. In fact, the assault, under C. C. Benson, made little progress. This Patton ascribed in part to an absence of close air support from the Allied air forces, which were under the command of Alexander's own air officer. When, on April 1, Patton's aide, Captain Dick Jenson, the son of a family friend and a young man of whom Patton was very fond, was killed in an air attack on the general's headquarters, Patton complained that "total lack of air cover . . . has allowed German air force to operate at will." Air Vice Marshal Arthur Coningham responded angrily and insultingly that Patton was using the air force to excuse his own failures on the ground. Patton, in turn, demanded a public apology for this slander. Seeking to avoid an ugly breach in the alliance, three air force generals were dispatched to Patton's headquarters to assure him that air support was forthcoming. As they spoke, the headquarters came under air attack again, and a portion of the ceiling collapsed around Patton and the air force officers. Fortunately, everyone escaped unharmed, but Patton could have said nothing that would have made his case more eloquently.

"How in hell did you manage to stage that?" someone was heard to ask.

"I'll be damned if I know," Patton replied, "but if I could find the sons of bitches who flew those planes, I'd mail each one of them a medal."[13]

Following this, Coningham agreed to send a cable retracting his remarks and closing the matter. For his part, Patton returned to the struggle on the Gabès plain. Benson was still making little headway there, so Patton visited him in his headquarters. He told Benson to keep his units moving until he either found a fight or ended up in the sea, then both men drove out to the units in the vanguard. Finding the tanks halted at the edge of a minefield, Patton, preceded by a Jeep and a scout car, drove through the mines himself, leading Benson's tanks safely through them. It was an extreme instance of leadership by example, and it demonstrated precisely the kind of reckless courage Eisenhower had warned Patton to avoid. In any case, the gesture had not been worth the risk. By the time Benson's tanks were rolling again, the bulk of the Axis troops had already moved on, evading any attempt to engage them.

Although disappointed by the action at Gabès, Patton felt that the victory at El Guettar was sufficient proof of II Corp's rehabilitation. Alexander was about to commence what he intended as the final operation in Tunisia. When Patton learned that Alexander did not intend to include II

Corps in it, he protested to Alexander as well as to Eisenhower. He had given back to the unit its self-esteem and its honor, and he insisted that II Corps be given a fitting role in the culmination of the Tunisian campaign. Once Patton had secured a promise that the American army would indeed be represented in the final operation, he turned over command of the corps to Bradley and returned to his headquarters in Casablanca.

As he resumed work on plans for Operation Husky, he received congratulations from Marshall—"You have done a fine job and have justified our confidence in you"—and from Eisenhower: "I hope that you . . . personally will accept my sincere congratulations upon the outstanding example of leadership you have given us all." In the privacy of his diary, Patton, who always craved recognition and praise from others, seemed to suggest that he had now moved beyond this need: "As I gain in experience, I do not think more of myself but less of others. Men, even so-called great men, are wonderfully weak and timid. They are too damned polite. War is very simple, direct, and ruthless. It takes a simple, direct, and ruthless man to wage war." Then, looking at the words he had just written, Patton wrote: "Some times I wonder if I will have to laugh at myself for writing things like the above." He must have lifted his pen from the paper and paused before adding: "But I think not."[14]

Young George Patton (left) in 1897, with his friend Hancock Banning in San Marino, California. (Virginia Military Institute Archives)

(left) *Patton as a VMI cadet in 1903–1904, before he transferred to West Point. (Virginia Military Institute Archives)*

(right) *The wedding portrait of George S. Patton Jr. and Beatrice Ayer, 1910. (Virginia Military Institute Archives)*

(above) *Lieutenant Colonel Patton in France during World War I, summer of 1918, standing in front of a French Renault light tank. (Patton Museum of Cavalry and Armor, Fort Knox, Kentucky)*

(left) *Patton with General Henry E. Mitchell at a Middleburg, Virginia, hunt, during the 1930s. (Virginia Military Institute Archives)*

(above) *With President Franklin D. Roosevelt in Casablanca, North Africa, January 17, 1943. (Patton Museum of Cavalry and Armor, Fort Knox, Kentucky)*

(below) *Patton discusses the capture of Palermo with his staff, July 23, 1943. (Patton Museum of Cavalry and Armor, Fort Knox, Kentucky)*

(left) *George S. Patton, conqueror of Sicily, August 1943. (Virginia Military Institute Archives)*

(below) *Patton, commanding general, Third U.S. Army, inspects troops of the 2ⁿᵈ Division in Armagh, Northern Ireland, April 1, 1944. (Patton Museum of Cavalry and Armor, Fort Knox, Kentucky)*

Patton (center) confers with General Hugh J. Gaffey (seated) and Colonel M. C. Helfers of the 5th Division, August 26, 1944, during Patton's expansion of Operation Cobra. (Virginia Military Institute Archives)

Patton with staff and other officers outside his headquarters in Etain, France, during a visit by Dwight David Eisenhower on September 30, 1944 (Patton Museum of Cavalry and Armor, Fort Knox, Kentucky)

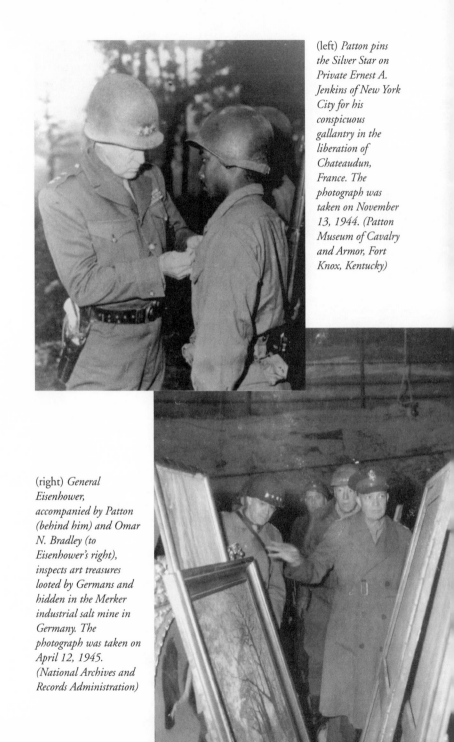

(left) *Patton pins the Silver Star on Private Ernest A. Jenkins of New York City for his conspicuous gallantry in the liberation of Chateaudun, France. The photograph was taken on November 13, 1944. (Patton Museum of Cavalry and Armor, Fort Knox, Kentucky)*

(right) *General Eisenhower, accompanied by Patton (behind him) and Omar N. Bradley (to Eisenhower's right), inspects art treasures looted by Germans and hidden in the Merker industrial salt mine in Germany. The photograph was taken on April 12, 1945. (National Archives and Records Administration)*

(above) *The original caption for this 1945 post-VE Day photograph reads, "This is the brass that did it. Seated are [William Hood] Simpson, Patton (as if you didn't know), [Carl A. "Tooey" Spaatz], Ike himself, Bradley, [Courtney H.] Hodges and [Leonard T.] Gerow. Standing are [Ralph] Stearley, [Hoyt] Vandenberg, [Walter Bedell] Smith, [Otto P.] Weyland and [Richard E.] Nugent." (National Archives and Records Administration)*

(left) *George S. Patton, Jr., General, U.S.A., May 1945. (Patton Museum of Cavalry and Armor, Fort Knox, Kentucky)*

CHAPTER 8

Conqueror of Sicily

AS ORIGINALLY DRAWN UP IN WASHINGTON AND LONDON, far from the scene of the proposed action, the plan for Operation Husky, the invasion of Sicily, was admirably straightforward. The British Eighth Army (designated the Eastern Task Force), under Bernard Law Montgomery, would land around Catania on the eastern shore of Sicily, and the I Armored Corps (the Western Task Force), commanded by Patton, would land near Palermo on the northern shore. The two task forces were to secure these major port cities, which would enable an orderly buildup of additional troops as the task forces drove along the eastern and northern coastal roads to link up at Messina on the northeastern tip of the island. In this way, not only would Sicily be conquered, but the Allied armies would end up in an ideal position from which to launch an invasion of the Italian mainland.

The broad, slashing strokes of this unadorned plan greatly appealed to Patton. Montgomery, however, saw it very differently. To him, it was as an egregious example of "penny-packet" warfare because the plan divided the assault forces, spreading them out over some 600 miles of Sicilian coastline. Montgomery feared that Husky would suffer the fate of the early assaults in Tunisia, which General Sir Claude Auchinleck had conducted in similarly piecemeal fashion. The plan was, he pronounced, "a dog's breakfast," and his criticism led to three months of tortured wrangling among the British themselves and between the British and the Americans. Patton, who must have recognized that the others regarded him as a fighter, a field commander and tactician, not a strategist, mostly stayed out of the debate, which reached a three-hour anticlimax in a meeting of April 29, 1943. Tempers flared and, as Patton wrote to Beatrice afterward, "It ended in stalemate. It was one hell of a performance. War by committee."[1]

Then, three days later, it was all suddenly resolved.

On May 2, Montgomery strode into Allied headquarters, Algiers, asked for Eisenhower's chief of staff, Walter Bedell Smith—universally called Beetle or Beadle—and was told he was in the lavatory. Montgomery walked into the lavatory, cornered Beadle Smith, and took him to a mirror hanging over the sink. He breathed on the mirror and, with his finger, outlined the inverted triangle of Sicily. He then traced a plan in which his Eighth Army landed at two locations on the northeast corner of Sicily on either side of Messina while Patton's I Armored Corps (to be redesignated the Seventh U.S. Army once it landed) would make three landings below Montgomery along the eastern coast at Gela, Scoglitti, and Licata for the sole purpose of supporting Montgomery's assault.

In an Algerian men's room, Montgomery succeeded in doing what three months of conference-room debate had failed to do: formulate an acceptable plan for the invasion of Sicily. Patton hardly relished being cast in the shadow of Montgomery, and wrote in his diary, "The U.S. is getting gypped," then he reminded himself that "the thing I must do is retain my SELF-CONFIDENCE. I have greater ability than these other people and it comes from, for lack of a better word, what we must call greatness of soul based on a belief—an unshakable belief—in my destiny." For Patton, that destiny meant that "The U.S. must win—not as an ally, but as a conqueror." To his staff, he allowed himself a rare expression of disgust with Eisenhower, complaining that Montgomery's dominance of Operation Husky is "what you get when your Commander-in-Chief ceases to be an American and becomes an Ally."[2]

To his field officers at all levels, Patton expressed neither discontent nor doubt. Instead, on June 5, he issued a letter of instructions in which he distilled into aphorisms some of his most memorable war-fighting principles:

There is only one sort of discipline—perfect discipline. . . .

Discipline must be a habit so ingrained that it is stronger than the excitement of battle or the fear of death. . . .

Officers who fail to correct errors or to praise excellence are valueless in peace and dangerous misfits in war.

Officers must assert themselves by example and by voice. . . .

There is only one tactical principle which is not subject to change. It is: "To use the means at hand to inflict the maximum amount of wounds, death, and destruction on the enemy in the minimum amount of time."

Never attack [enemy] strength [but rather his weakness]. . . .

Casualties vary directly with the time you are exposed to effective fire. . . . Rapidity of attack shortens the time of exposure. . . .

If you cannot see the enemy . . . shoot at the place he is most likely to be. . . .

Battles are won by frightening the enemy. Fear is induced by inflicting death and wounds on him. Death and wounds are produced by fire. Fire from the rear is more deadly and three times more effective than fire from the front. . . .

Few men are killed by bayonets, but many are scared by them. Having the bayonet fixed makes our men want to close. Only the threat to close will defeat a determined enemy. . . .

Never take counsel of your fears. The enemy is more worried than you are. . . .

A good solution applied with vigor *now* is better than a perfect solution ten minutes later. . . .

IN CASE OF DOUBT, ATTACK![3]

To the 90,000 men he led in the initial landings, Patton published a message as he sailed with them from Algiers: "We are indeed honored in having been selected [for] . . . this new and greater attack against the Axis. . . . When we land we will meet German and Italian soldiers whom it is our honor and privilege to attack and destroy." He admonished his men to "keep punching," warning that "in landing operations, retreat is impossible. To surrender is as ignoble as it is foolish. . . . No man is beaten until he thinks he is. . . . The glory of American arms, the honor of our country, the future of the whole world rests in your individual hands. See to it that you are worthy of this great trust."[4] There was, of course, no hint in this message of Patton's feeling of "being gypped." For one thing, that is not what a general tells men about to go into battle, and, for another, Patton was already thinking about how he would follow orders by supporting Montgomery's attack, but also, in the process, not merely upstage him, but steal the whole show.

The landings took place before dawn on July 10, 1943. Montgomery met little initial resistance, quickly seized Syracuse, then was pinned down outside of Augusta, a dozen miles up the coast. The landing of Patton's troops was hampered by fierce winds and high waves; however, naval artillery bombardment performed magnificently against enemy shore batteries, and the combined fire of the first American ground forces ashore and the naval batteries drove back German and Italian resistance at Gela. That resistance was renewed, and fiercely, on the following day, just as Patton and his staff were coming ashore. Attired in a freshly pressed uniform, complete with necktie and polished riding boots, exploding shells hitting the water not 30 yards away, Patton waded through the surf at 9:30 A.M. and proceeded directly to Gela to pay a visit on a fighting officer he greatly admired, Lieutenant Colonel William Darby, commander of the famed Rangers. Just as

Patton entered Gela, German and Italian troops launched an assault. Patton was thrilled to find himself thrust into the front lines, and, as he always did in such situations, he strode among the troops, offering himself as a target, shouting encouragement, giving personal commands, exhorting the men to "Kill every one of the goddamn bastards," and even lending a hand in laying (aiming) mortars.[5]

After he was satisfied that the enemy had been repulsed, Patton continued down the coastal road to the position commanded by Terry de la Mesa Allen, one of Patton's most colorful subordinates. After arranging with Allen and subordinate commanders Theodore Roosevelt Jr. and Hugh J. Gaffey to attack on the following day, he drove back to Gela, where he again deliberately exposed himself to aerial bombardment as well as ground fire in order to inspire the men on shore. "I earned my pay," he noted in his diary.[6]

In North Africa, Patton had discovered that the British not only habitually underrated the fighting ability of the American army, but also underestimated the great speed with which it was capable of moving, especially under his command. He decided to exploit this misconception to his advantage in the Sicily operation. Unknown to Montgomery, Patton had come ashore having decided to race, and beat him, to Messina.

After some delay, Montgomery finally took Augusta and began his advance to Catania along the route to Messina. Encountering very strong resistance, however, he decided to deploy his forces not only on the coastal road, which the battle plan had assigned to him, but on the inland road as well, which had been reserved for Patton's forces. With the inland road suddenly (and, as he saw it, unfairly) appropriated, Patton could not proceed with his drive to Messina and, once again, found himself relegated to protecting Montgomery's flank and rear. But instead of raging against Montgomery for violating the rules of engagement, Patton decided to make a change of his own and take Palermo, distant from Messina on the island's northwest coast. There was no pressing strategic reason to take this objective at that time, but Patton knew that capturing the capital city of Sicily would score headlines as well as glory for the American army, not to mention for himself. Understandably fearful of being denied permission to take Palermo, Patton asked Alexander for authorization to take Agrigento and Porto Empidocle, more modest objectives next to one another on the south-central coast. Somewhat reluctantly, Alexander agreed. Patton then assigned the highly reliable Lucian Truscott to take Agrigento and instructed Omar Bradley, commanding II Corps, to yield the inland road to Montgomery then to attack to the north.

In the meantime, General Alexander issued an explicit order that Patton's Seventh Army was to do nothing more than guard Montgomery's rear. Patton flew back to North Africa on July 17 to lodge a personal protest with Alexander for this humiliating public order. With Montgomery now embarrassingly bogged down along both the inland and coastal roads, Patton felt emboldened to reveal to Alexander his plan to take Palermo. Embarrassed at having impugned the valor of an ally, Alexander hastily agreed.

Patton wasted no time. On his return to Sicily, he quickly formed a Provisional Corps, assigned it to his deputy commander, Major General Geoffrey Keyes, and ordered him to make an all-out effort to take Palermo. In just 72 hours, Keyes's Provisional Corps covered 100 mountainous miles, mostly on foot. Truscott had rigorously trained the 3rd Division (which formed a major part of the corps assigned to Keyes) to march at the rate of five miles per hour instead of the army's prescribed three. This celebrated "Truscott trot" helped get Keyes to Palermo on July 21, and the city quickly fell to him. Patton toured Palermo on the twenty-third, then returned to Agrigento on the following day. There he made sure that the press got an earful of how the *American* army had killed or wounded 6,000 Italian troops and captured 44,000 more in a glorious campaign that had seized the very heart of Sicily. Contrary to what some of his detractors claimed, Patton assiduously avoided taking personal credit for the conquest. It had been the work of General Keyes, he scrupulously told reporters. Indeed, the night before he was to take Palermo, Keyes called on Patton to invite him to enter the city first. "You took it," Patton replied. "You enter and I will enter it after you."[7] There was never any question that Patton craved glory, but not just for himself; he craved it for his command and, ultimately, for the entire United States Army.

The triumph was not without its controversies, two of which contributed to the ever-growing Patton myth. To begin with, General

Alexander had apparently regretted the blanket permission he gave for the assault on Palermo and, on July 19, had sent an order sharply curtailing Patton's mission brief. Popular legend holds that Patton ignored the order, complaining that it was garbled in transmission. In fact, it was his chief of staff, Hobart "Hap" Gay, who intercepted the order, withheld it from his boss (as he knew Patton would want him to), let the limiting part of the order get lost in a desktop paper shuffle, then, after much delay, found the order and complained that it had been garbled in transmission. By the time it was retransmitted, of course, Palermo had fallen.[8]

The second incident took place on or about July 22. Near Licata, one of Patton's armor columns ground to a halt at a bottleneck on a one-way bridge. In his typical fashion, Patton personally inspected the situation and discovered that the tanks and other vehicles were being exposed to enemy fire, including aerial strafing, because a pair of balky mules pulling a Sicilian farmer's cart refused to budge. While the farmer and others cajoled and pleaded with the animals, Patton pulled out his revolver, shot each mule in the head, and then had both pushed off the bridge, still hitched to the cart. When the driver protested, the general admitted in a letter to his wife that he ended the dispute by breaking his walking stick over him. Patton (he explained to Beatrice) refused to have "human rights . . . exalted over victory."[9]

Once Palermo was his, Patton turned his full attention to resuming the race to Messina. He met with Alexander and Montgomery on July 25 to hammer out troop dispositions. Montgomery was stymied on the Catania plain and also on the western path around Mount Etna; therefore, Patton was given permission to use both the northern coastal road and the parallel inland road to attempt a push toward Messina. He made no secret that he intended to defeat the Germans and Italians as well as Bernard Montgomery and his Eighth British Army. To his commander of the U.S. 45th Division, Troy Middleton, Patton wrote on July 28: "This is a horse race, in which the prestige of the U.S. Army is at stake. We must take Messina before the British. Please use your best efforts to facilitate the success of our race."[10]

But no horse race was ever run through rugged mountains stubbornly defended by German and Italian troops. Outnumbered and cut off from supply and reinforcement, the defenders knew that Sicily would fall, but they intended to make the island's conquest as costly as possible, and they worked to buy ample time for the evacuation of Axis troops onto the mainland. Patton was not so intent on winning his horse race that he neglected the objective of destroying the enemy. From a reluctant navy, the general wheedled as many landing craft as it thought it could spare, and then looked for a way to make an end run to the northern shore of Sicily in order to disrupt the Axis withdrawal. He was frustrated, however, that he could get sufficient craft to transport only about 1,500 men, too small a force to survive an Axis counterattack. Patton's fighting instincts urged him to stage the assault, but he did not want to sacrifice a battalion for nothing. He debated with himself until, at last, on August 8, he decided to gamble and mounted the operation. By the time his men waded ashore at Santo Stefano on the north coast, the enemy was gone.

But the landings had given Patton an idea. On August 10, he decided to land another force in order to speed up the taking of Messina. Both Lucian Truscott and Omar Bradley objected. A more conservative and safer ground attack alone would, sooner or later, take Messina, they pointed out, whereas an amphibious operation was both risky and unnecessary. The idea of risking men for the sake of a "horse race" did not appeal to them. Patton listened, but insisted that the landings would take place. Truscott replied with an unenthusiastic "Alright, if you order it," to which Patton responded: "I do."

Concerned about Truscott's reluctance, Patton paid a call on him at his command post. There he saw "Truscott . . . walking up and down, holding a map and looking futile. I said, 'General Truscott, if your conscience will not let you conduct this operation, I will relieve you and put someone in command who will.'" Truscott replied: "General, it is your privilege to reduce me whenever you want to."

> I said, "I don't want to. I got you the DSM [Distinguished Service Medal] and recommended you for a major general, but your own ability really gained both honors. You are too old an athlete to believe it is possible to postpone a match."

He said, "You are an old enough athlete to know that sometimes they are postponed."

I said, "This one won't be. The ships have already started."

Truscott then explained the grounds of his reluctance: "This is a war of defile, and there is a bottleneck delaying me in getting my guns up to support the infantry. They—the infantry—will be too far west to help the landing." He was afraid of being defeated in detail during a necessarily piecemeal landing on difficult terrain. Patton dismissed these concerns by citing Frederick the Great: "L'audace, toujours l'audace!" He continued: "I know you will win and if there is a bottleneck, you should be there and not here."

Audacity, always audacity. It was vintage Patton. But Patton always went beyond mere words, and, true to form, he dramatically demonstrated his absolute faith in Truscott. "I told him I had complete confidence in him, and, to show it, was going home to bed." With that, Patton left.

"On the way back alone I worried a little, but feel I was right. I thought of Grant and Nelson and felt O.K. That is the value of history." He followed up on his gesture of faith (as he noted in his diary on August 11) by "not going to the front today as I feel it would show lack of confidence in Truscott, and it is necessary to maintain the self-respect of generals in order to get the best out of them."[11]

Truscott's men took heavy casualties, but they succeeded in pushing the Axis troops back. If Patton could have obtained more landing craft, he would have been able to cut off and capture or kill a substantial number of enemy forces. But, acting on his principle that it is better to attack with what you have, even if it is less than perfect, Patton made the hard-fought landing a success. By acting on another principle, attacking sooner rather than later, he cost the enemy more casualties. It is true that Truscott's losses were also significant, but destroying the enemy here and now, Patton felt, would avoid even greater losses later. "I have a sixth sense in war as I used to have in fencing . . . I am willing to take chances," he noted in a letter to Beatrice on August 11.[12]

Again overriding the objections of Truscott and Bradley, Patton ordered a third landing on August 16. This one turned out to be superfluous, however, as Truscott's 3rd Division was already marching into

Messina when the third landing commenced. The city fell by 10:00 P.M.; 40,000 Germans and 70,000 Italians had withdrawn to the mainland, along with 10,000 vehicles and 47 tanks. Patton did not dwell on the fact that a large portion of the enemy army had survived intact. Instead, at 10:00 A.M. on August 17, he rode out to a high ridge overlooking the city and surveyed his conquest. Rounding up a crew of war correspondents and photographers—"What in hell are you all standing around for?"—he drove into town, even as fire from Axis units now based on the mainland lobbed the occasional shell onto or near the road. British units had entered the city hours after the Americans early on the morning of the seventeenth. When Patton himself arrived, a British officer approached him, saluted, and extended his hand. As the two men shook hands, the officer said: "It was a jolly good race. I congratulate you."[13]

In terms of military history, the Allied invasion of Sicily was only a partial success. Just as the German blitzkrieg of France in 1940 had fallen short of achieving ultimate devastation when British and French troops were allowed to escape across the English Channel from Dunkirk, so the Allied failure to prevent thousands of Axis troops from evacuating Sicily reduced the magnitude and meaning of the victory in this campaign. Yet this failure did not deter Patton from writing to his cousin Arvin H. Brown that his "campaign . . . will . . . go down in history as a damn near perfect example of how to wage war." Nor did he hesitate in praising his soldiers and defining for them the magnitude of their victory. In General Order Number 18, issued on August 22, 1943, and addressed to the "Soldiers of the Seventh Army," he wrote: "Born at sea, baptized in blood, and crowned with victory, in the course of thirty-eight days of incessant battle and unceasing labor, you have added a glorious chapter to the history of war." Instead of dwelling on the Axis troops who got away, Patton precisely tallied the Seventh Army's bag: "you have killed or captured 113,350 enemy troops. You have destroyed 265 of his tanks, 2324 vehicles, and 1162 large guns . . . . But your victory has a significance above and beyond its physical aspect—you have destroyed the prestige of the enemy."[14]

ed and skill you have shown in the Sicilian operation." Even Gen-
rshall, always parsimonious with praise, wrote to tell Patton that he
ne a grand job of leadership and your corps and division com-
s and their people have made Americans very proud of their army
fident of the future." This was a man who, Patton believed, under-
e significance of Palermo and Messina. But perhaps most of all,
elished a message from Bernard Law Montgomery: "The Eighth
warmest congratulations to you and your splendid Army for the
captured Messina and so ended the campaign in Sicily."[1]
Patton, who (despite his claims to the contrary) still craved ap-
as also always acutely uncomfortable resting on his laurels. Anx-
how what the Seventh Army would be assigned to do next, he
no definitive answer. All Alexander would tell him was that the
as to rest and then begin training for operations in terrain similar
Sicily. This suggested to Patton that the outfit had been ear-
a campaign on the Italian mainland. However, Eisenhower in-
m that the Seventh would play no part in Italy. Did that mean
uld form part of the planned cross-Channel invasion force?
was not saying. Then, after weeks of silence, came the blow:
instructed to retain certain essential garrison units and to send
he Seventh Army's personnel and equipment to Mark Clark's

lessina, Ike had personally assured Patton that he would not
in Sicily, which had become a quiet backwater of the war. Yet
rue, why was his army being dismembered beneath him?
, driven by a sense of destiny, yet deeply worried that those
eant to withhold realization of that destiny from him, Patton
me with administrative duties and by visiting the wounded,
did far more frequently than any other senior commander.
appearance was purposely calculated to set him apart from
d, spent as little time as possible in his headquarters and was
along the front lines. He wanted to see the battle for him-
than that, he wanted those fighting the battle to see him.
vacuation hospitals was part of this see-and-be-seen philoso-
ed his presence improved morale. "Inspected all sick and

N

Patton closed the General Order with a sentence of timeless triumph: "Your fame shall never die." Addressed to an army now numbering some 200,000 men, that sentence, he must have thought, applied
above all to himself as conqueror of Sicily. What he was about to discover, however, was that he had yet to conquer the impulses of his own
highly wrought emotions.[15]

CHAPTER

The Slap
'Round t

IN TAKING PALERMO, PATTO
Sicily—not in the sense of ensur
but by making certain that the
seen—or see itself—as subordin
regarded them, Palermo and M
mered out an American army s
be the far harder battles to com

At the end of the Sicily
and enthusiastic approbation"
ration for not only your recer

the spe
eral Ma
had "do
mander
and con
stood th
Patton r
sends its
way you
But
proval, w
ious to k
could get
Seventh w
to that of
marked fo
formed hir
that it wo
Eisenhower
Patton was
the rest of
Fifth Army.
After N
long remain
if this were t
Anxious
above him m
passed the ti
something he
Patton, whose
the men he le
always present
self, but, more
Visiting field e
phy. He believ

wounded," he noted in his diary on August 2. "Pinned on some 40 Purple Hearts on men hurt in air raid. One man was dying and had an oxygen mask on, so I knelt down and pinned the Purple Heart on him, and he seemed to understand although he could not speak." On August 10, at another evacuation hospital, "one boy with a shattered leg said, 'Are you General Patton? I have read all about you.' All seemed glad to see me." But the visits took a heavy emotional toll on Patton, who struggled to maintain his command presence. "One man had the top of his head blown off," Patton noted in an August 6 diary entry, "and they were just waiting for him to die. He was a horrid bloody mess and was not good to look at, or I might develop personal feelings about sending men to battle. That would be fatal for a General."[2]

What Patton dared not acknowledge was that he had long since developed such "personal feelings." On August 3, he learned that General Eisenhower was to award him the Distinguished Service Cross for his "extraordinary heroism" at Gela on July 11. It should have been welcome news, but in a letter to Beatrice, Patton admitted that "I rather feel that I did not deserve it, but wont say so."[3] Later in the day, on his way to visit II Corps, Patton stopped at the 15th Evacuation Hospital near Nicosia. Among the sick and wounded, he encountered Private Charles H. Kuhl, Company L, 26th Infantry Regiment (1st Division). Kuhl did not appear to be wounded.

A report by a senior medical officer, Lieutenant Colonel Perrin H. Long, headed "Mistreatment of Patients in Receiving Tents of the 15th and 93rd Evacuation Hospitals," reveals what happened next:

> [Patton] came to Pvt. Kuhl and asked him what was the matter. The soldier replied, "I guess I can't take it." The General immediately flared up, cursed the soldier, called him all types of a coward, then slapped him across the face with his gloves and finally grabbed the soldier by the scruff of his neck and kicked him out of the tent.

Corpsmen picked Kuhl up and rushed him to a ward tent. "There he was found to have a temperature of 102.2 degrees Fahrenheit and he gave a history of chronic diarrhea for about one month, having at times as high as ten or twelve stools a day. The next day his fever continued and a blood smear was found to be positive for malarial parasites." Patton, of course, had been unaware that Kuhl was sick. That night, he wrote in his diary that he had met "the only arrant coward I have ever seen in this Army." He noted that "Companies should deal with such men, and if they shirk their duty, they should be tried for cowardice and shot."[4]

Those who witnessed the "slapping incident" on August 3 were appalled by the spectacle of a general in necktie, shiny helmet, and shinier boots striking an enlisted man. By any measure, it was a brutal act, and by army regulations, it was a court-martial offense. Yet it also suggests something of the inner struggle within Patton, whose outburst came on the very day he learned that he was to be decorated—undeservedly—for heroism. The troops who were lying, shattered, in 15th Evac—*they* were the real heroes, and their wounds pained Patton, as he pinned medals on the dying.

Private Kuhl was in the wrong place at the wrong time, not only for himself but for Patton as well. To the general, Kuhl may well have seemed the ugly embodiment of his own feelings of guilt over having sent boys to be torn apart in order to advance what many said was a quest for personal glory. Moreover, beginning in his cadet days, when he raised his head above the shooting-range trench in front of the targets during live-fire practice, and then through the Punitive Expedition, World War I, any number of polo matches, and now in World War II, Patton repeatedly defied death as if in a compulsive effort to prove to himself that he was not a coward. Suddenly, as if from ambush, Charles H. Kuhl materialized, appearing to Patton the very embodiment of cowardice, the yellow beast he feared was alive and lurking within himself. Some time after the encounter and with considerable insight, Kuhl observed to reporters that "at the time it happened, [General Patton] was pretty well worn out . . . I think he was suffering a little battle fatigue himself."[5]

Patton, of course, did not think he was suffering from battle fatigue—a condition he did not even believe real—nor did he subject himself to self-analysis. Instead, two days after the encounter with Kuhl, he issued a directive to all Seventh Army commanders summarily and categorically forbidding "battle fatigue":

It has come to my attention that a very small number of soldiers are going to the hospital on the pretext that they are nervously incapable of combat. Such men are cowards and bring discredit on the army and disgrace to their comrades, whom they heartlessly leave to endure the dangers of battle while they, themselves, use the hospital as a means of escape. You will take measures to see that such cases are not sent to the hospital but are dealt with in their units. Those who are not willing to fight will be tried by court-martial for cowardice in the face of the enemy.[6]

Beyond the directive, surprisingly little was made of the August 3 incident. Then, on August 10, Patton toured the 93rd Evacuation Hospital. There he came across Private Paul G. Bennett, C Battery, 17th Field Artillery, II Corps. According to Lieutenant Colonel Long's official report, Bennett had already served four years in the army and had been in II Corps since March.

[He] never had any difficulties until August 6th, when his buddy was wounded. He could not sleep that night and felt nervous. The shells going over him bothered him. The next day he was worried about his buddy and became more nervous. He was sent down to the rear echelon by a battery aid man and there the medical officer gave him some medicine which made him sleep, but still he was nervous and disturbed. On the next day the medical officer ordered him to be evacuated, although the boy begged not to be evacuated because he did not want to leave his unit.

Indeed, he had a fever, was sick, dehydrated, fatigued, confused, and listless. In that condition, despite his protests, he could not be returned to the front.

Patton, who knew nothing of this, looked at Bennett, who, like Kuhl, was unwounded. He asked him what the trouble was. Long relates the exchange:

"It's my nerves," [said Bennett and] began to sob. The General then screamed at him, "What did you say?" The man replied, "It's my nerves, I can't stand the shelling any more." He was still sobbing. The General then yelled at him, "Your nerves, hell; you are just a Goddamned coward, you yellow son of a bitch." He then slapped the man and said, "Shut up that Goddamned crying. I won't have these brave men here who have been shot at seeing a yellow bastard sitting here crying." He then struck the man again, knocking his helmet liner off and into the next tent. He then turned to the admitting officer and yelled, "Don't admit this yellow bastard; there's nothing the matter with him. I won't have the hospitals cluttered up with these sons of bitches who haven't got the guts to fight." He then turned to the man again, who was managing to sit at attention though shaking all over and said, "You're going back to the front lines and you may get shot and killed, but you're going to fight. If you don't, I'll stand you up against a wall and have a firing squad kill you on purpose. In fact," he said, reaching for his pistol, "I ought to shoot you myself, you Goddamned whimpering coward." As he left the tent, the General was still yelling back to the receiving officer to "send that yellow son of a bitch back to the front line."[7]

Again, those who witnessed the outburst saw an act of almost incomprehensible brutality. What actually occurred, however, was an episode of raw emotion. Patton resumed touring the tent wards, but he kept talking about Bennett and was on the verge of tears himself when he was heard to say "I can't help it, but it makes my blood boil to think of a yellow bastard being babied." He clearly saw cowardice as an infectious disease (to which, doubtless, he was as vulnerable as anyone): "I wont have those cowardly bastards hanging around our hospitals," Patton said to the hospital commander, Colonel Donald E. Currier. "We'll probably have to shoot them some time anyway, or we'll raise a breed of morons."[8]

It was the second incident, coming as it did just days after the first, that motivated the medical officer to send a report through army medical channels to Omar Bradley, who was now commanding officer of II Corps. Doubtless out of loyalty to Patton and a sense of his importance to the war, Bradley did nothing more than lock the report in his safe. But the medical officers also sent a report directly to Eisenhower, who received it on August 16. The very next day, Ike wrote Patton what Patton himself described as "a very nasty letter," in which he pulled no punches: "if there is a very considerable element of truth in the allegations . . . I must so seriously question your good judgment and your self discipline as to raise serious doubts in my mind as to your future usefulness." However, Eisenhower took pains to make it clear that the incident had not been entered into the records of Allied Headquarters. He did not want to bring Patton up on official charges, and when Demaree Bess, a correspondent for the *Saturday Evening Post,* and other reporters heard about the incident, they complied with Eisenhower's request to bury the story because, Ike explained, the American war effort could not afford to lose Patton.[9]

Contrary to some accounts, Eisenhower did not order Patton to make a round of apologies for his outburst. Patton himself decided that such amends were necessary, albeit mainly to placate his commander: "I hate to make Ike mad when it is my earnest study to please him," he wrote in his diary on August 20. Patton made his first apologies to the doctors and nurses of the hospitals involved, then to Kuhl and Bennett personally and in private (he insisted on their shaking hands with him), and, in September, to a body of troops assembled for a USO show. Each time, he spoke sincerely, if defensively, insisting that while his method had been, beyond question, wrong, his motive had been unimpeachable. To the group of doctors and nurses, he even told a story about a World War I friend who had lost his nerve in battle and subsequently committed suicide. Patton suggested that, had someone slapped sense into him in a timely manner, his life might have been saved. As for Kuhl and Bennett, Patton explained that he was urgently trying to return them to an understanding of "their obligation as men and soldiers." When he addressed the large assembly of troops in September, Patton offered humor. "I thought I would stand here," he said as he took the stage, "and let you see what a son of a bitch looks like and whether I am as big a son of a bitch as you think I am."[10]

The troops ate it up. But Patton remained in the doghouse.

Clark, not he, was leading the Fifth Army on the Italian mainland. Bradley, not he, had been chosen by Eisenhower to organize an army for the cross-channel invasion. Patton remained on Sicily overseeing the dismemberment of the Seventh Army. Soon his entire command, nothing more than a headquarters and antiaircraft batteries, consisted of just 5,000 men, down from 200,000.

The newspapers, which had been filled with stories about Patton, now rarely mentioned him. Only in German headquarters was the name of Patton constantly in the air. What was he doing? What army and operation would he lead next? When would his attack come? He was one of the few Allied officers the German generals truly feared, not only for his consummate skill on the field, but because they saw clearly what he was: a warrior.

Eisenhower made good use of Patton's reputation—among the Germans. Knowing that the Germans would hear about it all, he sent Patton on high-profile trips to Algiers, Tunis, Corsica, Cairo, Jerusalem, and Malta, all places from which Allied operations were plausible. By using Patton as a decoy to keep the enemy guessing, the Allies sought to force the Germans to spread themselves thin and to waste effort and resources moving from one place to the next. It was a useful role, playing decoy, even as it was utterly humiliating.

The weeks and then the months passed. Suddenly, late in November 1943, during a Sunday-evening radio broadcast from Washington, the popular columnist Drew Pearson made the slapping incidents public. Earlier in the year, Patton had been a media hero. Then he faded from the headlines, only to reemerge, in the wake of the broadcast, demonized as the darkest of villains and nastiest of bullies, the very kind of tyrant the Allied armies were fighting against. All the worse for Patton, Pearson leveled his criticism against Eisenhower as well, for having failed to issue an official reprimand. Sensitive to public sentiment, senators and congressmen clamored for Patton's dismissal, some freely comparing him to Adolf Hitler. Secretary of War Stimson asked Eisenhower for a full report. A man of lesser character than Eisenhower might have been tempted to seek relief by turning against Patton and yielding to the public and political demand for the general's head on a platter. Instead, he defended Patton on the basis of his record and explained that the personal, nonofficial form of reprimand had been intended to preserve a highly effective fighting commander, a leader whose skill, courage, and efficiency were not

Patton closed the General Order with a sentence of timeless triumph: "Your fame shall never die." Addressed to an army now numbering some 200,000 men, that sentence, he must have thought, applied above all to himself as conqueror of Sicily. What he was about to discover, however, was that he had yet to conquer the impulses of his own highly wrought emotions.[15]

CHAPTER 9

The Slap Heard
'Round the World

IN TAKING PALERMO, PATTON TURNED THE TIDE of the Battle of Sicily—not in the sense of ensuring victory against the Axis on the island, but by making certain that the United States Army would no longer be seen—or see itself—as subordinate to the army of Great Britain. As Patton regarded them, Palermo and Messina were the forges on which he hammered out an American army strong enough to fight what he knew would be the far harder battles to come on the European mainland.

At the end of the Sicily campaign, FDR personally sent his "thanks and enthusiastic approbation" and General Alexander his "sincerest admiration for not only your recent great feat of arms in taking Messina, but for the speed and skill you have shown in the Sicilian operation." Even General Marshall, always parsimonious with praise, wrote to tell Patton that he had "done a grand job of leadership and your corps and division commanders and their people have made Americans very proud of their army and confident of the future." This was a man who, Patton believed, understood the significance of Palermo and Messina. But perhaps most of all, Patton relished a message from Bernard Law Montgomery: "The Eighth sends its warmest congratulations to you and your splendid Army for the way you captured Messina and so ended the campaign in Sicily."[1]

But Patton, who (despite his claims to the contrary) still craved approval, was also always acutely uncomfortable resting on his laurels. Anxious to know what the Seventh Army would be assigned to do next, he could get no definitive answer. All Alexander would tell him was that the Seventh was to rest and then begin training for operations in terrain similar to that of Sicily. This suggested to Patton that the outfit had been earmarked for a campaign on the Italian mainland. However, Eisenhower informed him that the Seventh would play no part in Italy. Did that mean that it would form part of the planned cross-Channel invasion force? Eisenhower was not saying. Then, after weeks of silence, came the blow: Patton was instructed to retain certain essential garrison units and to send the rest of the Seventh Army's personnel and equipment to Mark Clark's Fifth Army.

After Messina, Ike had personally assured Patton that he would not long remain in Sicily, which had become a quiet backwater of the war. Yet if this were true, why was his army being dismembered beneath him?

Anxious, driven by a sense of destiny, yet deeply worried that those above him meant to withhold realization of that destiny from him, Patton passed the time with administrative duties and by visiting the wounded, something he did far more frequently than any other senior commander. Patton, whose appearance was purposely calculated to set him apart from the men he led, spent as little time as possible in his headquarters and was always present along the front lines. He wanted to see the battle for himself, but, more than that, he wanted those fighting the battle to see him. Visiting field evacuation hospitals was part of this see-and-be-seen philosophy. He believed his presence improved morale. "Inspected all sick and wounded," he noted in his diary on August 2. "Pinned on some 40 Purple Hearts on men hurt in air raid. One man was dying and had an oxygen mask on, so I knelt down and pinned the Purple Heart on him, and he seemed to understand although he could not speak." On August 10, at another evacuation hospital, "one boy with a shattered leg said, 'Are you General Patton? I have read all about you.' All seemed glad to see me." But the visits took a heavy emotional toll on Patton, who struggled to maintain his command presence. "One man had the top of his head blown off," Patton noted in an August 6 diary entry, "and they were just waiting for him to die. He was a horrid bloody mess and was not good to look at, or I might develop personal feelings about sending men to battle. That would be fatal for a General."[2]

What Patton dared not acknowledge was that he had long since developed such "personal feelings." On August 3, he learned that General Eisenhower was to award him the Distinguished Service Cross for his "extraordinary heroism" at Gela on July 11. It should have been welcome news, but in a letter to Beatrice, Patton admitted that "I rather feel that I did not deserve it, but wont say so."[3] Later in the day, on his way to visit II Corps, Patton stopped at the 15th Evacuation Hospital near Nicosia. Among the sick and wounded, he encountered Private Charles H. Kuhl, Company L, 26th Infantry Regiment (1st Division). Kuhl did not appear to be wounded.

A report by a senior medical officer, Lieutenant Colonel Perrin H. Long, headed "Mistreatment of Patients in Receiving Tents of the 15th and 93rd Evacuation Hospitals," reveals what happened next:

> [Patton] came to Pvt. Kuhl and asked him what was the matter. The soldier replied, "I guess I can't take it." The General immediately flared up, cursed the soldier, called him all types of a coward, then slapped him across the face with his gloves and finally grabbed the soldier by the scruff of his neck and kicked him out of the tent.

Corpsmen picked Kuhl up and rushed him to a ward tent. "There he was found to have a temperature of 102.2 degrees Fahrenheit and he gave a history of chronic diarrhea for about one month, having at times as high as ten or twelve stools a day. The next day his fever continued and a blood smear was found to be positive for malarial parasites." Patton, of course, had been unaware that Kuhl was sick. That night, he wrote in his diary that he had met "the only arrant coward I have ever seen in this Army." He noted that "Companies should deal with such men, and if they shirk their duty, they should be tried for cowardice and shot."[4]

Those who witnessed the "slapping incident" on August 3 were appalled by the spectacle of a general in necktie, shiny helmet, and shinier boots striking an enlisted man. By any measure, it was a brutal act, and by army regulations, it was a court-martial offense. Yet it also suggests something of the inner struggle within Patton, whose outburst came on the very day he learned that he was to be decorated—undeservedly—for heroism. The troops who were lying, shattered, in 15th Evac—*they* were the real heroes, and their wounds pained Patton, as he pinned medals on the dying.

Private Kuhl was in the wrong place at the wrong time, not only for himself but for Patton as well. To the general, Kuhl may well have seemed the ugly embodiment of his own feelings of guilt over having sent boys to be torn apart in order to advance what many said was a quest for personal glory. Moreover, beginning in his cadet days, when he raised his head above the shooting-range trench in front of the targets during live-fire practice, and then through the Punitive Expedition, World War I, any number of polo matches, and now in World War II, Patton repeatedly defied death as if in a compulsive effort to prove to himself that he was not a coward. Suddenly, as if from ambush, Charles H. Kuhl materialized, appearing to Patton the very embodiment of cowardice, the yellow beast he feared was alive and lurking within himself. Some time after the encounter and with considerable insight, Kuhl observed to reporters that "at the time it happened, [General Patton] was pretty well worn out . . . I think he was suffering a little battle fatigue himself."[5]

Patton, of course, did not think he was suffering from battle fatigue—a condition he did not even believe real—nor did he subject himself to self-analysis. Instead, two days after the encounter with Kuhl, he issued a directive to all Seventh Army commanders summarily and categorically forbidding "battle fatigue":

It has come to my attention that a very small number of soldiers are going to the hospital on the pretext that they are nervously incapable of combat. Such men are cowards and bring discredit on the army and disgrace to their comrades, whom they heartlessly leave to endure the dangers of battle while they, themselves, use the hospital as a means of escape. You will take measures to see that such cases are not sent to the hospital but are dealt with in their units. Those who are not willing to fight will be tried by court-martial for cowardice in the face of the enemy.[6]

Beyond the directive, surprisingly little was made of the August 3 incident. Then, on August 10, Patton toured the 93rd Evacuation Hospital. There he came across Private Paul G. Bennett, C Battery, 17th Field Artillery, II Corps. According to Lieutenant Colonel Long's official report, Bennett had already served four years in the army and had been in II Corps since March.

[He] never had any difficulties until August 6th, when his buddy was wounded. He could not sleep that night and felt nervous. The shells going over him bothered him. The next day he was worried about his buddy and became more nervous. He was sent down to the rear echelon by a battery aid man and there the medical officer gave him some medicine which made him sleep, but still he was nervous and disturbed. On the next day the medical officer ordered him to be evacuated, although the boy begged not to be evacuated because he did not want to leave his unit.

Indeed, he had a fever, was sick, dehydrated, fatigued, confused, and listless. In that condition, despite his protests, he could not be returned to the front.

Patton, who knew nothing of this, looked at Bennett, who, like Kuhl, was unwounded. He asked him what the trouble was. Long relates the exchange:

"It's my nerves," [said Bennett and] began to sob. The General then screamed at him, "What did you say?" The man replied, "It's my nerves, I can't stand the shelling any more." He was still sobbing. The General then yelled at him, "Your nerves, hell; you are just a Goddamned coward, you yellow son of a bitch." He then slapped the man and said, "Shut up that Goddamned crying. I won't have these brave men here who have been shot at seeing a yellow bastard sitting here crying." He then struck the man again, knocking his helmet liner off and into the next tent. He then turned to the admitting officer and yelled, "Don't admit this yellow bastard; there's nothing the matter with him. I won't have the hospitals cluttered up with these sons of bitches who haven't got the guts to fight." He then turned to the man again, who was managing to sit at attention though shaking all over and said, "You're going back to the front lines and you may get shot and killed, but you're going to fight. If you don't, I'll stand you up against a wall and have a firing squad kill you on purpose. In fact," he said, reaching for his pistol, "I ought to shoot you myself, you Goddamned whimpering coward." As he left the tent, the General was still yelling back to the receiving officer to "send that yellow son of a bitch back to the front line."[7]

Again, those who witnessed the outburst saw an act of almost incomprehensible brutality. What actually occurred, however, was an episode of raw emotion. Patton resumed touring the tent wards, but he kept talking about Bennett and was on the verge of tears himself when he was heard to say "I can't help it, but it makes my blood boil to think of a yellow bastard being babied." He clearly saw cowardice as an infectious disease (to which, doubtless, he was as vulnerable as anyone): "I wont have those cowardly bastards hanging around our hospitals," Patton said to the hospital commander, Colonel Donald E. Currier. "We'll probably have to shoot them some time anyway, or we'll raise a breed of morons."[8]

It was the second incident, coming as it did just days after the first, that motivated the medical officer to send a report through army medical channels to Omar Bradley, who was now commanding officer of II Corps. Doubtless out of loyalty to Patton and a sense of his importance to the war, Bradley did nothing more than lock the report in his safe. But the medical officers also sent a report directly to Eisenhower, who received it on August 16. The very next day, Ike wrote Patton what Patton himself described as "a very nasty letter," in which he pulled no punches: "if there is a very considerable element of truth in the allegations . . . I must so seriously question your good judgment and your self discipline as to raise serious doubts in my mind as to your future usefulness." However, Eisenhower took pains to make it clear that the incident had not been entered into the records of Allied Headquarters. He did not want to bring Patton up on official charges, and when Demaree Bess, a correspondent for the *Saturday Evening Post,* and other reporters heard about the incident, they complied with Eisenhower's request to bury the story because, Ike explained, the American war effort could not afford to lose Patton.[9]

Contrary to some accounts, Eisenhower did not order Patton to make a round of apologies for his outburst. Patton himself decided that such amends were necessary, albeit mainly to placate his commander: "I hate to make Ike mad when it is my earnest study to please him," he wrote in his diary on August 20. Patton made his first apologies to the doctors and nurses of the hospitals involved, then to Kuhl and Bennett personally and in private (he insisted on their shaking hands with him), and, in September, to a body of troops assembled for a USO show. Each time, he spoke sincerely, if defensively, insisting that while his method had been, beyond question, wrong, his motive had been unimpeachable. To the group of doctors and nurses, he even told a story about a World War I friend who had lost his nerve in battle and subsequently committed suicide. Patton suggested that, had someone slapped sense into him in a timely manner, his life might have been saved. As for Kuhl and Bennett, Patton explained that he was urgently trying to return them to an understanding of "their obligation as men and soldiers." When he addressed the large assembly of troops in September, Patton offered humor. "I thought I would stand here," he said as he took the stage, "and let you see what a son of a bitch looks like and whether I am as big a son of a bitch as you think I am."[10]

The troops ate it up. But Patton remained in the doghouse.

Clark, not he, was leading the Fifth Army on the Italian mainland. Bradley, not he, had been chosen by Eisenhower to organize an army for the cross-channel invasion. Patton remained on Sicily overseeing the dismemberment of the Seventh Army. Soon his entire command, nothing more than a headquarters and antiaircraft batteries, consisted of just 5,000 men, down from 200,000.

The newspapers, which had been filled with stories about Patton, now rarely mentioned him. Only in German headquarters was the name of Patton constantly in the air. What was he doing? What army and operation would he lead next? When would his attack come? He was one of the few Allied officers the German generals truly feared, not only for his consummate skill on the field, but because they saw clearly what he was: a warrior.

Eisenhower made good use of Patton's reputation—among the Germans. Knowing that the Germans would hear about it all, he sent Patton on high-profile trips to Algiers, Tunis, Corsica, Cairo, Jerusalem, and Malta, all places from which Allied operations were plausible. By using Patton as a decoy to keep the enemy guessing, the Allies sought to force the Germans to spread themselves thin and to waste effort and resources moving from one place to the next. It was a useful role, playing decoy, even as it was utterly humiliating.

The weeks and then the months passed. Suddenly, late in November 1943, during a Sunday-evening radio broadcast from Washington, the popular columnist Drew Pearson made the slapping incidents public. Earlier in the year, Patton had been a media hero. Then he faded from the headlines, only to reemerge, in the wake of the broadcast, demonized as the darkest of villains and nastiest of bullies, the very kind of tyrant the Allied armies were fighting against. All the worse for Patton, Pearson leveled his criticism against Eisenhower as well, for having failed to issue an official reprimand. Sensitive to public sentiment, senators and congressmen clamored for Patton's dismissal, some freely comparing him to Adolf Hitler. Secretary of War Stimson asked Eisenhower for a full report. A man of lesser character than Eisenhower might have been tempted to seek relief by turning against Patton and yielding to the public and political demand for the general's head on a platter. Instead, he defended Patton on the basis of his record and explained that the personal, nonofficial form of reprimand had been intended to preserve a highly effective fighting commander, a leader whose skill, courage, and efficiency were not only effective against the enemy, but certainly saved the lives of the soldiers under his command.

Through much of November and into December, the public and political uproar continued, then began to subside. Letters continued to pour into the office of the president and of the secretary of war, but their tenor shifted by the middle of December. Increasingly, they voiced support for Patton and forgiveness for his outburst. Some even suggested a promotion was due. Clearly, given time for reflection, most of the American public realized it wanted one thing above all else—to win the war—and Patton, with all his flaws, was a commander capable of doing just that.

In the wake of the slapping incidents, Ike stood by Patton, but he made it clear that, had General Marshall asked for Patton's relief, he would not have offered an argument. As Patton saw it, the slapping incidents were the reason he was passed over as commander of the American forces in Operation Overlord, the Normandy "D-Day" invasion. The incidents must certainly have reaffirmed in Eisenhower's mind that Bradley, not Patton, was the better choice for the job, but that decision had been made months before the incidents became public knowledge. Eisenhower judged that Patton was a great combat commander, who possessed the rare faculty of always thinking in terms of attack. Yet the very qualities that made him fast and aggressive also created a certain instability and volatility, which, Ike believed, were barely under control. For the overall job of Overlord, from planning, through landings, to initial deployment, the unassuming and even drab Omar Bradley was the safer choice. However, Eisenhower reasoned, once the landings had been accomplished and the beachheads established—once the likelihood of out-and-out disaster had been reduced—Patton was just the man to lead an army in the breakout from the beachhead and the advance into the enemy's heart. Whatever his liabilities, Patton would bring to the invasion the one asset without which it could never in the long run succeed: unremitting drive.

Thus it is a myth that slapping two G.I.'s. cost Patton leadership of Overlord. The truth is that Eisenhower would never have chosen him for the job. But it is also true that, after the Sicily operation, Patton—whom the enemy considered America's most formidable general—was put on the shelf. For 11 months following the capture of Messina, he was not present on the field of battle. Patton's superiors were never quite sure what to do with him in the absence of an ongoing campaign, but the slapping incidents led them to lengthen his hiatus during a critical period in the war. In a very real sense, Patton had become a casualty of war, just as if he had suffered a disabling physical wound. It was the price of carrying within him the emotional equipment that drove him swiftly, daringly, and hungrily in combat and that, at the same time, rendered him vulnerable to the stress of warfare fought with the ceaseless intensity he himself created. The cost to Patton is known: 11 months on the sidelines. The cost to the Allied war effort can only be guessed.

CHAPTER 10

In England

MESSINA FELL TO THE SEVENTH ARMY on August 17, 1943. As of that day, strictly on the basis of his record, George S. Patton Jr. was widely regarded as America's best combat general, the conqueror of Sicily. Even more important in the long run, he had created an effective and victorious army, a splendid example of American military prowess and valor. It is, therefore, difficult to imagine how he felt when most of the Seventh was turned over to Mark Clark and he himself was left as a garrison officer in what had become an obscure corner of the war, facing the all-too-real prospect of being relieved of command altogether.

It was January 1944 before the suspense was at least partially eased. On the twenty-second, Patton was ordered from Sicily to London, where, on the twenty-sixth, he was told that he had been named to command a new force, the Third United States Army. Now the only question was what he would be assigned to do with this outfit. The biggest, greatest, most consequential operation of the war, the invasion of Hitler's Fortress Europe, was being planned—by Eisenhower, Bradley, and others, without Patton. Grateful to be out of Sicily at last, Patton was nevertheless anxious to know just how long he would be staying at his new headquarters in the sleepy little Cheshire town of Knutsford, five hours outside London, as the war continued to swirl about the rest of the world.

Patton wanted nothing so much as an immediate assignment to command an army already in combat; however, there were advantages to building an army from scratch. Although it was true, as he wrote to his wife, that "this thing of imitating God and creating new worlds out of thin air is wearing," Patton did have the opportunity to mold the Third in his image, from the very beginning, instead of merely "rehabilitating" a unit, as he had done in North Africa with II Corps. He immediately requested Jacob L. Devers, now the senior U.S. commander in the Mediterranean theater, to transfer his principal staff officers from the Seventh Army to the Third. Devers obliged, and thus Patton had a staff he knew, trusted, and thoroughly controlled. For their part, his top staff, Hugh Gaffey and Hobart "Hap" Gay (chief and assistant chief of staff, respectively), and his key personal aides, Charles Codman and Alexander Stiller, plus his African-American orderly, Sergeant George Meeks, and his chief medical officer, Charles B. Odom, were fiercely loyal and quite willing to subject themselves to the total control of their boss. Patton considered these men his military family, and since no family is complete without a pet, he also acquired an English bull terrier, which he christened William the Conqueror. To his master's chagrin, however, the dog soon proved itself timid and was especially terrified of bombardment and shell fire. As soon as he discovered this, Patton renamed him Willie. A coward, the dog also behaved with singular rudeness in the presence of women, mounting their legs and pushing his wet nose up their skirts. It is not clear how Patton felt about this, but he doted on the dog because, as he wrote to Beatrice, he "took to me like a duck to water."[1]

With his "family" established at Peover Hall, "a huge house last repaired in 1627 or there abouts,"[2] Patton chose a code name for Third

Army headquarters: Lucky. That portion of headquarters consisting of himself and his key officers was Lucky Forward, while the administrative section was Lucky Rear. Patton's personal code name was Lucky 6. Throughout the war, the size of Third Army would vary from about 100,000 to a peak strength of 437,860 as its final campaign ended on May 8, 1945.

As he had done in his previous commands, Patton began shaping his army by creating "perfect discipline," beginning with the details of spit and polish—impeccably maintained uniforms complete with leggings and neckties (both of which enlisted men detested), observance of every military courtesy, precision in every movement and item of drill—then proceeding to intensive combat training, which Patton personally supervised. As usual, he was rarely in his headquarters and could instead be found regularly out in the field, appearing everywhere officers and men were being trained to do anything at all. To create officers in his image, he lectured frequently and issued a series of letters of instruction, perhaps the most important of which was the first, dated March 6, 1944. In it, his cardinal instruction was to "lead in person" and to take full responsibility for obtaining assigned objectives. Failing this, an officer who is "not dead or severely wounded has not done his full duty." More specifically, commanders as well as staff officers (accustomed to working in the relative safety of a more or less remote headquarters) were to "visit the front daily." There they were to "observe, not to meddle." The leader's "primary mission . . . is to see with your own eyes and be seen by your troops while engaged in personal reconnaissance." At the front, "praise is more valuable than blame," and a good officer provides plenty of positive reinforcement for specific achievements. In addition, a personal presence at the front, Patton wrote, is essential to ensuring the effective execution of orders. Merely issuing an order counted for about 10 percent of a commander's job. "The remaining 90 percent consists in assuring . . . proper and vigorous execution."[3]

Patton explained to his officers that, in battle, it is "always easier for the senior to go up [to the front] than for the junior to come back [to headquarters]." Officers were to visit the wounded frequently and award decorations promptly. Although such instructions required that officers risk their lives and frequently exert themselves, Patton also emphasized the importance of adequate rest. Tired officers were not only inefficient, they tended to judge situations pessimistically and, therefore, failed to act aggressively. Fatigue makes "cowards of us all." There are crises in which "everyone must work all the time, but these emergencies are not frequent." In counseling vigorous effort, Patton did not want officers to exert themselves needlessly. That was another reason for putting command posts as far forward as possible. Such a location would reduce time wasted in driving to and from the front.[4]

As for maps, Patton wrote, they were certainly important, but mainly for the sake of telling a commander where his personal presence was required. Plans should be "simple and flexible," and they should be "made by the people who are going to execute them." Plans should be based on reconnaissance, providing fresh information—"like eggs: the fresher the better." As with plans, so with orders. They should be simple and short. They should tell "what to do, not how." Yet orders should be clear and complete and never keep anyone in the dark. "Warning orders"—advisories in advance of a move or action—were to be issued in good time and to everyone who needed them, including the support branches, such as the medical department, the quartermaster, and so on, as well as the combat branches. If the support units "do not function, you do not fight." Responsibility for supply, Patton admonished, rests equally "on the giver and the taker."[5]

The letter of instruction, which is still read by army officers today, closed with one final admonition: "Courage. DO NOT TAKE COUNSEL OF YOUR FEARS."[6]

Printed aphorisms encapsulated something of the Patton spirit and style, but nothing could compare with the personal presence of this commander. As one young soldier wrote to his family after attending an address by Patton, "we stood transfixed upon his appearance. . . . Not one square inch of flesh [was] not covered with goose pimples. It was one of the greatest thrills I shall ever know. . . . That towering figure impeccably attired froze you in place and electrified the air."[7]

"I can assure you," Patton addressed his troops on this occasion, "that the Third United States Army will be the greatest army in American history. . . . We are going to kill German bastards—I would prefer to skin them alive—but, gentlemen, I fear some of our people at home would accuse me of being too rough." The young soldier wrote that, at this point, the general "slyly smiled. Everyone chuckled enjoyably. He talked on to us for half an hour, literally hypnotizing us with his incomparable, if profane eloquence. When he had finished, you felt as if you had been given a supercharge from some divine source. Here was the man for whom you would go to hell and back."[8]

Yet as the weeks rolled on, Third Army was not going to hell or anywhere else. Although Patton was commanding general of Third Army, he had virtually no role in the ongoing planning or overall direction of Operation Overlord, the upcoming Normandy invasion. Once again he was assigned duty as a decoy, part of an ambitious and comprehensive program of disinformation, which put Patton in charge of a fictitious army group preparing to invade France not by way of Normandy but at Pas de Calais. The most obvious place for an invasion, because it lay directly across Dover on the other side of the English Channel at its narrowest point, Pas de Calais was a gateway that opened onto the most direct route to Germany. Knowing that the German high command would assume that an invasion would arrive there, well up the coast from Normandy, the Allies built a vast decoy force at Dover, up the English coast from where the actual invasion force was being assembled. The decoys included plywood aircraft, inflatable rubber tanks, empty tents, and the shells of buildings, much of it ingeniously designed and fabricated by British and American movie studios, and all accompanied by the appearance of human activity, bogus radio traffic, and phony news stories. Using Patton, the general the Germans were known to most fear and respect, was perhaps the boldest stroke of the grand deception. As German high command saw it, where Patton was, that is where the invasion would come from.

As if decoy work were not disagreeable enough to a man of Patton's temperament, he was also obliged to keep a low profile, so that the press would not pick up too many stories placing him anywhere other than in and about Dover. Toward the end of April, the ladies of Knutsford opened a Welcome Club for American G.I.'s, a place for doughnuts, coffee, and conversation, all in the interest of cementing fellow feeling among allies. Invited to participate in the opening ceremonies, Patton at first declined. It was clear that the Allied sleight-of-hand was working—the entire Fifteenth

German Army had been moved to Pas de Calais—and Patton did not want to risk compromising the deception by revealing himself to be at Knutsford instead of Dover. However, sincerely wishing to maintain good relations with the Third Army's hosts, he finally decided to appear at the ceremony, but not speak. He even purposely arrived 15 minutes late, hoping thereby to avoid most of the proceedings. But the polite ladies of Knutsford waited for him, and, when he arrived, he was welcomed, introduced, and asked to speak. He could not refuse without giving offense, so he took the floor. No one could have predicted what happened next.

Because Patton's brief remarks were unscripted, his own recollection of the speech is the only substantial record that survives. He was mildly witty: "until today, my only experience in welcoming has been to welcome Germans and Italians to the 'Infernal Regions.'" Then he went on to say that he felt "such clubs as this are a very real value, because I believe with Mr. Bernard Shaw, I think it was he, that the British and Americans are two people separated by a common language, and since it is the evident destiny of the British and Americans, and, of course, the Russians, to rule the world, the better we know each other, the better job we will do."[9]

"Innocuous" best describes the occasion and the speech. Patton, therefore, was stunned when, on April 26, army public relations officers were in an uproar. Despite Patton's request for a publicity blackout of the Knutsford event, several newspapers had selectively cited his remarks— quite out of context—some even reporting that he had said that the British and Americans would rule the postwar world, omitting entirely any mention of the Russians. No one much cared about this in Britain— Prime Minister Churchill dismissed it as a tempest in a teacup—but American newspapers printed headlines trumpeting Patton's insult to our gallant Russian allies. Even newspapers that did not object to insulting the Russians complained that the very idea of "ruling the world" was better suited to Hitler and Tojo than to the leader of an army of a democracy. Soon senators and congressmen were once again calling for the general's dismissal.

Patton was both devastated and bewildered. He understood why the slapping incidents had created a scandal, but this? The sin, he protested, was in the reporting, not his remarks.

Eisenhower, who had staunchly defended Patton after the slapping incidents, now wrote to General Marshall that he was "seriously contemplating the most drastic action," sending Patton home. Marshall threw the matter back to Eisenhower, telling him that if he believed Lieutenant General Courtney Hodges (commander of First Army) could lead Third Army as effectively as Patton, he should not hesitate to sacrifice Patton. If, however, he was persuaded that Patton was the best commander for Third Army, Marshall advised bearing "between us . . . the burden of the present unfortunate reaction."[10]

Eisenhower summoned Patton to his headquarters on May 1. As Patton recalled it, Ike began the conversation with "George, you have gotten yourself into a very serious fix." Patton interrupted: "I want to say that your job is more important than mine, so if in trying to save me you are hurting yourself, throw me out." Eisenhower did not respond reassuringly to this gallantry. He bluntly told Patton that he had indeed become a liability and that there was a very serious question about his continuing in command. Patton wrote in his diary that he replied by expressing his willingness to be reduced in rank to colonel, provided that he be allowed to command one of the assault regiments: "this was not a favor but a right." In his recollection of the interview, Eisenhower did not mention this but recalled only that

> in a gesture of almost little-boy contriteness, [Patton] put his head on my shoulder. . . . This caused his helmet to fall off—a gleaming helmet I sometimes thought he wore in bed.
>
> As it rolled across the room I had the rather odd feeling that I was in the middle of a ridiculous situation . . . his helmet bounced across the floor into a corner. I prayed that no one would come in and see the scene. . . . Without apology and without embarrassment, he walked over, picked up his helmet, adjusted it, and said: "Sir, could I now go back to my headquarters?"[11]

Two days after this interview, Eisenhower sent Patton a cable: "I am once more taking the responsibility of retaining you in command in spite of damaging repercussions resulting from a personal indiscretion. I do this solely because of my faith in you as a battle leader and from no other motives." Eisenhower followed up the cable by dispatching his public relations officer, Colonel Justus "Jock" Lawrence, with a message forbidding Patton or his staff from making any public statements until further notice from Eisenhower personally. "Come on, Jock, what did Ike *really* say?" Patton asked. Lawrence answered: "He said that you were not to open your goddamned mouth again publicly until he said you could!"[12]

Patton had been saved once more, this time by the thinnest of margins. Reprieved, he resumed training his army, and he passed the time as he had at most of his previous postings, enjoying the society of the most prominent local families. As D-Day approached and with his troops highly trained and finely tuned, Patton was concerned lest they lose their edge while waiting for action. He therefore toured each unit personally and made more of his famous fighting speeches. By far the most famous was delivered—more than once—during the month or so before the invasion. As usual, Patton did not resort to notes. Several variations of the speech have been handed down by a variety of witnesses who heard it at different times. "As in all my talks," Patton noted in his diary, "I stressed fighting and killing":

> Men, this stuff some sources sling around about America wanting to stay out of the war and not wanting to fight is a lot of baloney! Americans love to fight, traditionally. All real Americans love the sting and clash of battle. America loves a winner. America will not tolerate a loser. Americans despise a coward, Americans play to win. That's why America has never lost and never will lose a war.
>
> You are not all going to die. Only two percent of you, right here today, would be killed in a major battle. Death must not be feared. Death, in time, comes to all of us. And every man is scared in his first action. If he says he's not, he's a Goddam liar. . . . The real hero is the man who fights even though he's scared. . . .
>
> All through your Army careers, you've been bitching about what you call "chicken-shit drill." That, like everything else in the Army, has a definite purpose. That purpose is Instant Obedience to Orders and to create and maintain Constant Alertness! This

must be bred into every soldier. A man must be alert all the time if he expects to stay alive. If not, some German son-of-a-bitch will sneak up behind him with a sock full o' shit! There are four hundred neatly marked graves somewhere in Sicily, all because ONE man went to sleep on his job . . . but they are German graves, because WE caught the bastards asleep! An Army is a team, lives, sleeps, fights, and eats as a team. This individual hero stuff is a lot of horse shit. The bilious bastards who write that kind of stuff for the *Saturday Evening Post* don't know any more about real fighting under fire than they know about fucking!

Every single man in the Army plays a vital role . . . even the guy who boils the water to keep us from getting the G.I. shits!

Remember, men, you don't know I'm here. . . . I'm not supposed to be commanding this Army. . . . Let the first bastards to find out be the Goddam Germans. I want them to look up and howl, "ACH, IT'S THE GODDAM THIRD ARMY AND THAT SON-OF-A-BITCH PATTON AGAIN!"

We want to get this thing over and get the hell out of here, and get at those purple-pissin' Japs!!! The shortest road home is through Berlin and Tokyo! We'll win this war, but we'll win it only by showing the enemy we have more guts than they have or ever will have!

There's one great thing you men can say when it's all over and you're home once more. You can thank God that twenty years from now, when you're sitting around the fireside with your grandson on your knee and he asks you what you did in the war, you won't have to shift him to the other knee, cough, and say, "I shoveled shit in Louisiana."[13]

A minority of those who heard Patton speak were offended by his profanity, but most of his men relished it. Yet what he could not tell the troops whose fighting spirit he was trying to raise and maintain was perhaps the most important thing he knew: that the Third Army would not participate in the D-Day landings. The operation would begin with an airborne assault of paratroops and glider troops, who would disrupt the enemy defenses at key points, then Bradley's First U.S. Army and Sir Miles Dempsey's Second British Army would land on the Normandy beaches. Dempsey was assigned to capture Caen then advance inland and clear the Falaise plain to make way for the First Canadian Army under Henry Crerar. In the meantime, Bradley was to take Cherbourg, then drive south to Avranches. Once Avranches had been secured, Patton's Third Army would land and begin the breakout through Brittany. To be sure, it was a major assignment, but Patton was deeply disappointed that he was not in on the start of it all, leading the initial amphibious assault.

D-Day, June 6, 1944, came and went. In England, Patton could only wait. Jean Gordon, the young woman with whom Patton almost certainly had an affair in Hawaii in 1936, arrived in London at the beginning of July 1944 and was assigned to the Third Army as a Red Cross "doughnut dolly," a volunteer who dispensed doughnuts and coffee to G.I.'s. According to Everett Hughes, one of Eisenhower's logistics officers, Patton told him that the beautiful young woman had been "mine for twelve years." Others who knew Patton, Jean Gordon, or both denied that anything other than an uncle-niece relationship existed between them. Beatrice, however, clearly believed the two were romantically involved. She wrote anxiously to her husband about Jean. He replied on August 3: "We are in the middle of a battle, so don't meet people so don't worry."[14]

In early July, the Third Army was quietly relocated from England to Normandy. Even though the invasion had begun nearly a month earlier, many in the German high command still believed that the principal landings were yet to come, at Pas de Calais and led by Patton. Accordingly, the Germans continued to maintain their entire Fifteenth Army in that sector. Hoping to keep the deception going, Patton remained in England while his army started to move across the channel. Finally, on July 6, exactly one month after D-Day, he and his staff flew across the Channel in a C–47. On landing, his first order of business was to set up a headquarters. But no sooner had he touched down than the secret of his arrival was out. Correspondents as well as ordinary soldiers and sailors mobbed him. Patton rose to the occasion: "I'm proud to be here to fight beside you. Now let's cut the guts out of those Krauts and get the hell to Berlin. And when we get to Berlin"—Patton conspicuously wore his ivory-handled revolver—"I am going to personally shoot that paper-hanging goddamned son of a bitch just like I would a snake." As one naval lieutenant who witnessed his arrival remarked, "When you see General Patton . . . you get the same feeling as when you saw Babe Ruth striding up to the plate. Here's a big guy who's going to kick hell out of something."[15]

But Patton had yet to step up to the plate. Now, even in France, the waiting continued. When word reached Patton of the July 20 attempt to assassinate Hitler, he ran in panic to Bradley's headquarters: "For God's sake, Brad, you've got to get me into this fight before the war is over." On July 22, he wrote to Beatrice: "It is three weeks yesterday since I got here and still no war." Rain, unremitting rain, delayed Operation Cobra, Bradley's plan for breaking out from the deadly hedgerow country and into the open plain beyond it. In his diary, Patton complained about Bradley's timidity, Courtney Hodges's incompetence, and Eisenhower's lack of "the stuff."[16]

On July 24, Bradley attempted to punch through an area between the villages of La Chapelle-Enjuger and Hébécrevon, just north of the main road between Saint-Lô and Coutances.

Allied bombers accidentally dropped ordnance on American front lines, killing or wounding 150 men. But on the next day 1,500 B–17s and B–24s let fall torrents of high explosives precisely on target. This bombardment was followed by medium bombers and fighter bombers dropping napalm. The combined air assault blew a hole in the German line, and the ground forces of Operation Cobra exploded through it. On July 27, Bradley asked Patton to take unofficial command of Troy Middleton's VII Corps and head toward Avranches. After 11 months, he was finally in the war again.

CHAPTER 11

Warrior

BRADLEY'S ORIGINAL PLAN HAD BEEN to put the Third Army—and
Patton—into action after the fall of Avranches, a key port on the Gulf of
St. Malo and the gateway to Brittany. After much heartbreaking and
bloody delay in the treacherous *bocage* (hedgerow country)—countryside
networked by ancient stone walls overgrown with hedges, which presented
formidable obstacles to the advance of men and vehicles alike—the Cobra
breakthrough had been so sudden that it occurred before Avranches could
be taken. It must have given Patton considerable pleasure to be called on to
capture this important objective, even before his entire army had been officially activated in France. Patton mounted one of his trademark hell-on-
wheels advances, using two armored divisions, running side by side, as the
point of a spear aimed at the town. Within three days, Patton's troops were

in Avranches. On the fourth day, they took the bridge at Pontaubault, which gave the American army access to three principal roads, one leading south to the Loire, one leading east to the Seine and Paris, and the other opening onto Brittany and the west. Cobra had possession of the major arteries for breakout into all France.

On August 1, Bradley became commander of the 12th Army Group, which included (as initially constituted) the First Army, under Courtney Hodges, and the Third, under Patton. Nearly two months after it had begun, Patton was fully joining the battle in France. As he saw it, this was his misfortune, but, more objectively, it was actually a stroke of luck, which may well have enhanced the general's subsequent reputation. By the time he came into action, the dreadful rains of June and early July had cleared, and Bradley had finally broken through the crippling hedgerow country. This was precisely the moment highly mobile warfare was most needed and, at the same time, had finally become possible. Now, at the beginning of August, the war in France was just the kind of war Patton had prepared himself and Third Army for and for which he was, by temperament and genius, best suited.

Under orders from Bradley, Patton deployed Troy Middleton with VIII Corps to advance through Brittany, which was rather lightly defended, most of the German force having left Brittany to meet the landings at Normandy. (Remarkably, however, the entire Fifteenth German Army was still up the coast at Pas de Calais, still anticipating more Allied landings. Although Patton's arrival in France was hardly secret any longer, Eisenhower insisted that news stories refrain from mentioning the general's name. He hoped to keep the Germans guessing—and their Fifteenth Army out of the action—as long as possible.) Whereas Patton's Third Army had remarkable freedom of movement, Hodges's First, Dempsey's Second British, and Crerar's First Canadian were stalled in fierce engagements with the stronger German presence to the northeast of Patton's area of operation. Bradley therefore ordered three corps of Third Army to head out of Avranches and advance to the east and the southeast, to the Seine and the Loire, to draw off pressure from the other Allied armies. Simultaneously, Patton sent one armored division via Rennes to take Lorient (on the Bay of Biscay, the south coast of Brittany, some 100 miles from Avranches) and another to take Brest (at the western tip of the Brittany coast, 200 miles away). From the beginning, then, Patton's army operated across a broad swath of France north of the Loire. These sweeping movements were vintage Patton, fostered in the Louisiana and Texas maneuvers, which taught him to think in terms of swift drives over long distances.

Middleton, who unlike Patton was a conventional commander, diverted the division assigned to Brest to attack a German concentration at St. Malo. As mentioned, one of Patton's directives to his officers was that issuing orders constituted 10 percent of a commander's job and seeing to their proper execution the other 90 percent, so Patton followed up on his order concerning Brest, immediately rescinded Middleton's diversion, and ensured that the division drove on to the objective he had assigned. Instead of tying down an armored division at St. Malo, Patton sent an infantry division to lay siege to the town. Fast armor was best reserved for remote objectives, such as Brest, whereas St. Malo, a short distance from Avranches, could be addressed by infantry. Although Patton had responded quickly, there was a price to pay for the delay that Middleton had caused. By the time the armor reached Brest, the city's garrison had been reinforced. Instead of folding rapidly, Brest would not yield until early September. Fighting a war of speed required a high degree of coordination, with every subordinate commander partaking of the chief's unwavering aggressiveness. Conventional commanders, no matter how competent, were weak links who could bring about disproportionately costly delays.

The division Patton had sent breezed through Rennes, but found Lorient very strongly garrisoned. American infantry were deployed around the city, which was thereby cut off, but Lorient did not surrender until the very end of the war.

Patton did not allow himself to become preoccupied with Brest and Lorient. In compliance with Bradley's orders, he sent his XV Corps in a long end run southeast and east around the open end of the German position. Simultaneously, he sent XX Corps to the Loire. Under their aggressive commanders, Wade Haislip and Walton H. Walker, these two corps swept everything out of their way and disrupted German rear-echelon units. Haislip reached Le Mans within a week.

At about this time, German commanders began to realize the magnitude of the Normandy invasion and sought permission from Hitler to withdraw from Normandy altogether. Hitler not only refused permission for a withdrawal, he ordered a counterattack. Thanks to Ultra, the Allies' extraordinary code-breaking operation, the counterattack orders were intercepted. Patton frequently expressed his belief that he possessed what he called a sixth sense in combat, and it was on this, not on any high-tech decrypts, that he placed most of his reliance. However, the Ultra information was sufficiently convincing to prompt him, albeit reluctantly, to halt one of his divisions and retain it defensively near Avranches, ready for movement to nearby Mortain, in case an attack actually materialized. When it did, Patton revised his thinking about Ultra and, from that point on, insisted on daily briefings from Melvin Helfers, his Ultra officer. This was typical Patton—a dyed-in-the-wool cavalryman with a well-nigh mystical belief in his own intuition, he had nevertheless embraced the most modern technology once its value was demonstrated. He had earlier given up horses for tanks, and now he was willing to supplement intuition with advanced cryptanalysis. Thus the division Patton left was available to assist the First U.S. Army when it was attacked at Mortain on August 8. Assuming a defensive posture was anathema to Patton, but he nevertheless deployed his forces in a pattern of deep defense that drew the attackers in and then annihilated them.

Patton, however, regarded Mortain as a sideshow. Acting on orders from Eisenhower and Montgomery, Bradley next ordered Patton to turn Haislip at Le Mans from the east to the north. The idea was to narrow the gap between the Americans and the Canadians at Falaise, through which German units withdrawing from Normandy would have to pass. This would create a situation ideal for a double envelopment, the classic winning strategy Hannibal had used during the Second Punic War at the Battle of Cannae, 216 B.C., which every West Point cadet studied thoroughly. Patton liked the idea of emulating a great general of the ancient world, but, as usual, he wanted to up the ante. He wanted to let both Haislip and Walker drive deeper to the east, perhaps even as far as the Seine, before making the turn north, thereby bagging all the Germans in a very wide area. Predictably, Patton was overruled, and Bradley, Montgomery, and Eisenhower agreed that a safer and more conservative shallow encirclement, hooking at Argentan and Falaise, would take a sufficient bite out the enemy forces. Patton, who must have sighed inwardly, followed orders.

He also followed orders when Bradley, on August 13, instructed him to halt Haislip short of Argentan so that Bradley's army group would not encroach on territory reserved for Montgomery's army group. It was a controversial decision. Fearful that the Germans would attack between Patton and Hodges, hammering at Haislip's exposed flank, Bradley decided to hold Haislip safely back and not release him until Montgomery gave the all-clear and invited him to cross the boundary between the two army groups. In the meantime, the Canadians were delayed in their advance to Falaise. But, unknown to Bradley, the Germans were also suffering a delay. Instead of making good use of the slowdown in the Allied encirclement by immediately moving out through the still-open Agentan-Falaise gap, they were fighting to hold the so-called Falaise pocket while awaiting Hitler's permission to withdraw. And to Hitler, withdrawal was not an option.

Patton, seeing that the Germans were still vulnerable, was itching to move. On August 14, he talked Bradley into allowing part of Haislip's XV Corps as well as Walker's XX Corps and the XII Corps, under Manton Eddy, to move east to destinations along a broad north-south line: Haislip to Dreux, Walker to Chartres, and Eddy to Orléans. The very next day, however, as Patton noted in his diary, Bradley, "suffering from nerves," met with Patton in Patton's headquarters. Worried about a rumor that five panzer divisions were at Argentan, Bradley called for Patton to hold his drive east. "His motto seems to be, 'In case of doubt, halt.'" But Patton managed to persuade Bradley to allow him to continue, and all three corps reached their objectives by the sixteenth. "I wish I were Supreme Commander," Patton scrawled in his diary.[1]

In a run characterized by speed and coordination and employing the advance-attack-advance-and-attack-again formula, Patton consummated the transformation of Bradley's modestly conventional Operation Cobra into a spectacular breakout. Recognizing this, Eisenhower wasted no time in releasing Patton's name to the press, and, immediately, the pages of every paper in the nation were crowded with accounts of how, in just

two weeks, Patton had led a massive advance from the Cotentin penin-
sula, through Normandy, pursuing and encircling thousands of Germans
while liberating a huge expanse of France, from Brest in the west to some
250 miles eastward. To Beatrice, Patton wrote on August 16: "I supposed
you had guessed it. We took Brittany, Nantes, Angers, LeMans, and
Alencon and several other places still secret." He did complain, however,
that what he ungrammatically called "the fear of they" had "stopped us
on what was the best run yet . . . I feel that if [I were] only unaided I
could win this war."[2]

As Patton pushed east, the Seventh U.S. Army, now commanded by
Alexander Patch, together with Free French units invaded the Riviera in
the south of France on August 15. On August 16, Hitler at last gave his
permission for German withdrawal from the Argentan-Falaise pocket, just
as the Canadians finally reached Falaise. Pursuant to Montgomery's request, Bradley ordered Patton to send troops north, beyond Argentan, and
link up with the Canadians, thereby pinching off the pocket. Patton responded quickly, ordering Hugh Gaffey to lead an attack on August 17.
However, Leonard Gerow, commanding V Corps, objected to Gaffey's plan
and delayed the attack until the eighteenth, once again giving the Germans
another precious day to make good their withdrawal. The pocket was not
closed off until August 21. Although some 50,000 Germans became casualties, more than 100,000 exploited the dithering among Allied field commanders and withdrew intact. There would be no decisive double
envelopment of the enemy, no second Cannae.

Patton did not waste time mourning lost opportunities. Instead, he
sent Haislip from Dreux to the Seine. His intention was for Haislip to
cross the river, then proceed downstream to keep the Germans from crossing. If their retreat had not been intercepted at Falaise-Argentan, it could
be blocked at the Seine. But, yet again, higher command intervened, allowing Patton to send just one of Haislip's two divisions across the Seine
on August 19 while the other had to drive downstream along the compar-
ative safety of the near bank. This made Patton's drive less risky but also
far less effective in its ability to cut off the German retreat. The Allied victory at Normandy was thereby diluted. Patton took risks not for the sake
of risk, but to expose his forces to the enemy as decisively and as briefly as

possible. As he saw it, the enemy you fail to kill or capture now, you will have to fight later and closer to his homeland, for which he will fight all the more fiercely.

In a journalistic haste to publicize Patton, the news media erroneously credited the liberation of Paris to him and his Third Army. In truth, the First U.S. Army under Hodges, together with an American infantry division and a French armored division (under Jacques Leclerc), liberated the City of Light on August 25. Patton, during this time, gave Haislip's XV Corps to First Army and, with Walker and Eddy, crossed the Seine southeast of Paris at Melun and Fontainebeau, then crossed the Yonne River at Montereau and Sens. The sheer speed of this advance allowed Patton to secure the key bridges before the Germans could blow them. Patton turned over the bridges at Mantes and Melun to First Army, which was driving north into Belgium. With Third Army, Patton then resumed his eastward drive, taking in quick succession Troyes, Reims, and Chalons. He set his sights on crossing the Moselle River between the old fortress towns of Nancy and Metz, which would put Third Army within just 100 miles of the Rhine. Patton desperately wanted to be the first Allied commander to cross that fabled river.

If the Germans could not stop Patton, Allied logistics could—and did. On the Meuse, at the end of August, Third Army outran its gasoline. Germany lay just beyond reach, its vaunted Siegfried Line, the country's main western defensive wall, was virtually unmanned. Given 400,000 gallons of gasoline, Patton told Bradley, he could be in Germany within two days. "It is terrible to halt," he wrote in his diary on August 30, "even on the Meuse. We should cross the Rhine in the vicinity of Worms, and the faster we do it, the less lives and munitions it will take. No one realizes the terrible value of the 'unforgiving minute' except me."[3] Patton suspected that Bradley, Montgomery, and others envied his show-stealing advance and that they were deliberately withholding gasoline from him. It is true that Eisenhower had decided to divert a significant portion of precious fuel and supplies to Montgomery, who was intent on neutralizing the launch sites from which V–1 buzz bombs and V–2 rockets were being sent to terrorize London and other English cities. Stopping the slaughter of civilians seemed to the supreme Allied commander an important priority, but Patton was not so sure. He argued that, with sufficient gas, he could deliver a decapitating blow to Germany that much faster.

This dispute over priorities aside, the overriding fact was that Allied logistics had not kept pace with the combat forces. Huge quantities of gasoline (and other supplies) were being stockpiled on the coast, but could not be transported inland fast enough or in sufficient quantity. Eventually even the suspicious Patton realized that the problem was less a matter of clashing egos than it was a failure of logistics.

Perhaps Patton could have reconciled himself to this. However, on September 1, he recorded in his diary: "At 0800 we heard on the radio that Ike said Monty [Montgomery] was the greatest living soldier and is now [promoted to] Field Marshal. I then flew up to the Command Post and worked on administrative papers for the rest of the day."[4]

Patton had expanded the modest Operation Cobra into an advance that encompassed the entire French theater. In only a month, he had led the Third Army in the liberation of most of France north of the Loire and had brought that army now within spitting distance of Germany itself. And now Montgomery was being hailed as the greatest living soldier?

Patton, who had achieved so much, found the exhilaration slipping away from him, the elation short-lived. It was not just the personal pain of Montgomery's elevation over him, but the very real loss of momentum in a drive, his drive, that had brought ultimate victory within the Allies' grasp. Everything was changing for the worse. The beautiful, clear, dry weather of summer—ideal attacker's weather—gave way to unseasonably early rains, ice storms, and snow in the fall of 1944. The pause forced on Patton by a shortage of supplies and what he saw as Ike's misplaced sense of priorities, including his maddening adulation of Montgomery, had given the Germans time to man their last-ditch defenses guarding the "West Wall" of the homeland.

Patton was resupplied during the second week in September, and he renewed his drive, but with the grim knowledge that the going would now be much harder and much slower. Nancy fell to him on September 15, and Metz, a fortress both formidable and venerable, was largely neutralized by the middle of November, although the last fort of this fortress complex did not surrender until days before Christmas.

These gains were important, but it was Hodges's First Army, not Patton's Third, that crossed into Germany first, on September 12. Now everyone was eager to breach the Rhine, which was strategically important, to be sure, but even more important psychologically. The Rhine was mythic country for the Germans, the sacred river of the heartland, and to cross it would surely signify to them the beginning of the end. Field Marshal Montgomery came up with Operation Market-Garden, a bold but poorly conceived plan to cross the lower Rhine through Holland. Although the American units involved in the operation attained their objectives, the British units found themselves in an impossible situation and were cut to shreds. Operation Market-Garden ended in an Allied retreat.

Patton was hardly pleased by the failure of Market-Garden, even though it was his rival's brainchild. Third Army was not bogged down—it continued to advance—but it moved slowly, painfully, and at significant cost in blood. By the end of September, the flow of supplies declined again, and Patton was forced to accept what higher command called the "October pause." The idea was to conserve ammunition and other supplies until Montgomery could open the port of Antwerp. There was logic to this. The port of Antwerp would unload supplies much closer to the advancing Allied armies than the ports along the channel. But, as Patton saw it, his supplies were once again being diverted to serve Montgomery's needs. With ammo strictly rationed, Patton was forced to do what he most hated: assume the defensive.

Because he was depressed, Patton assumed that the same low feeling would probably steal over his troops, who, like him, were used to being on the attack. To prevent this, he toured throughout his area, making encouraging speeches and talking personally with small groups of soldiers. He stressed the importance of maintaining morale, which meant getting good food, as many hot meals as possible, and getting mail from home in a timely manner. Patton was always especially concerned to provide daily changes of socks, because he knew that dry socks were the only way to prevent trenchfoot, an infection as disabling as any wound. The soldier, he often said, was the army, and Patton never let his frustration over dealing with higher command distract him from looking after his men. When a reporter asked him if he still thought "the corporal is the most important man in the army," Patton replied: "The private first class."[5]

It was early November before Bradley gave Patton authorization to resume attacking. But unremitting rain, flood, and mud slowed progress to a grim crawl, even as Jacob Devers led elements of the 6th Army Group to positions along the Rhine, from which Patton and the Third were still distant. Between November 8 and December 15, Third Army had advanced no more than 40 miles, inches compared with the summer sweep through France, but they were inches paid for in blood. Grisly and dispiriting as this progress had been, Patton now looked forward to his major attack through the Siegfried Line, thence to the Rhine, and on to attack and take the great city of Frankfurt. He made preparations to move his headquarters east, but instead of feeling exhilarated, as he always did when contemplating a great operation, Patton found himself worried. It was that sixth sense of his. Toward the end of November, he noted in his diary that "First Army is making a terrible mistake in leaving the VIII Corps [under Troy Middleton] static" on the western border of Luxembourg, southeast of a town called Bastogne, "as it is highly probable that the Germans are building up east of them."[6]

Everyone in Allied command had the same maps, but no one except Patton seems to have sensed danger near Bastogne. Bradley's idea was to retain this area as what had been called in World War I a "quiet sector," a place for green units to be introduced "gently" into combat and for war-weary units to get some rest. As for the Germans, their army, to all appearances, was pretty well finished. At least, this is how Patton's fellow generals saw the situation. The enemy, however, saw things very differently, and Patton, who had just slogged through some of the hardest fighting of the war, who had seen and felt the level of resistance the "beaten" German army could still muster, was uncannily capable of seeing the situation through enemy eyes.

CHAPTER 12

90 Degrees to the North

BY DECEMBER 1944, THE ALLIED ARMIES WERE firmly in the grip of what Ike Eisenhower called "victory fever," an affliction Eisenhower knew to be as intoxicating as it was lethal. Patton, however, proved to be immune. He was keenly aware that you are not beaten until you admit defeat—advice he repeatedly gave to his own officers—and that this was as true for the enemy as it was for his own men. On December 16, Hitler launched Operation Autumn Fog, an all-out offensive against Troy Middleton's VIII Corps, First U.S. Army, covering the Ardennes in Luxembourg, near the town of Bastogne. The attackers on that foggy morning surely did not fight like men who believed themselves beaten.

Perhaps it was the effects of victory fever that caused Bradley and others to interpret the assault as a mere "spoiling attack," the military phrase for a "demonstration" or harassment of little consequence. After all, how could the Germans have any real punch left in them? In contrast to Patton, who always positioned his headquarters as far forward as possible, Bradley, at this stage of the war, maintained his headquarters in Luxembourg City, rather far from First Army's main position. He therefore could not see for himself evidence of the German buildup. Moreover, Bradley chose not to inspect the VIII Corps situation personally, and he even decided it was safe to travel to Versailles, where he was scheduled to discuss plans with Eisenhower. The miserable weather during this period made flying impossible, so Bradley had to be driven. It was evening by the time he reached Versailles, and, here, far from the Ardennes, he finally received word of a major German offensive, which had forced a massive bulge into the VIII Corps sector. Bradley picked up the phone and ordered Patton to send an armored division to Middleton's aid. Having resumed the eastbound offensive in his own sector, some 40 miles south of Bastogne, Patton protested that parting with a entire division now would weaken his effort. Bradley's insistence, however, clicked with Patton's own intuition of the situation around Middleton's corps at Bastogne, and he had the division moving within the hour.

The next day, December 17, Patton did not wait for further orders from Bradley, but prepared a massive and rapid reinforcement of the Ardennes. He summoned John Millikin, in command of III Corps, and told him that he would probably be called on to move north to lead a counterattack against the German offensive. He advised Millikin to prepare his corps and to make himself familiar with the ground.

Patton was often accused of being impulsive. In terms of his emotional makeup, the accusation was justified, but, where his profession was concerned, he was a careful planner who believed in advance preparation. Once an operation was under way, Patton focused on action, typically an unremitting combination of advance and attack. However, he always took care to distinguish between haste and speed. For him, haste characterized spontaneous or at least inadequately planned operations. Thorough preparation made haste unnecessary and enabled speed, an operation carried out swiftly as well as efficiently. A big part of conducting operations at high speed was preparing for them in advance. Patton was proactive rather than reactive and wanted, wherever possible, to choose the time and place for battle instead of letting the enemy dictate these terms. Good preparation helped to ensure that unfolding events would not steal the march on the commander's will and initiative. H. Norman Schwarzkopf and the others responsible for the success of the first Gulf War put this Patton principle into action in 1990–1991. The lightning war that was Operation Desert Storm had been preceded by the meticulous preparation of Operation Desert Shield.

When Bradley returned from Versailles to his Luxembourg headquarters on the morning of December 18, he summoned Patton, together with his top staff. The men of Lucky Forward were on their way within 10 minutes of Bradley's call. When they arrived, Bradley took them to a map and showed them the bulge. It was now clear to him that the Germans intended to break through to the Meuse River and, ultimately, to advance against Antwerp, the recently hard-won port through which much of the Allied supplies and troops were now flowing.

This was a major crisis, and it quickly cured every case of Allied victory fever. Bradley asked Patton what he could send and when. Without hesitation, Patton replied that he could send three divisions immediately, one starting off at midnight, the next at first light, and the third within 24 hours, all led by Millikin. Additionally, if Jacob Devers, who was south of Patton's position, could cover XII Corps, Patton could send that entire corps, under Manton Eddy, as well. It was a remarkable promise to make. What it meant was that a very large portion of Third Army, which was heading steadily eastward, was to be turned on a dime, 90 degrees to the north, and marched at full speed into desperate battle. Executing such a complex turn, with about 250,000 men, their vehicles, and equipment, in winter, during ice and snow storms, and at very high speed, wagered the highest possible stakes. Any massive object, whether it is an 18-wheeler semi or a 250,000-man army, has momentum and inertia. It resists sudden stops, starts, and changes in direction. Bradley was skeptical, but he needed what Patton was offering, and he responded by asking Patton to meet him at Verdun on the nineteenth for an 11:00 A.M. conference with Eisenhower.

After preparing himself in conference with his key staff as well as the principal field commanders, Millikin and Eddy, at 7:00 A.M., Patton conferred with his full staff at 8:00 A.M., then set off for Verdun. Eisenhower, whom Patton had earlier accused of lacking "the stuff," rose brilliantly to the occasion. After his intelligence officer opened the meeting by painting the Ardennes situation in the darkest possible terms, Ike rose and cleared the air. "The present situation is to be regarded as one of opportunity to us and not of disaster," he declared. "There will be only cheerful faces at this conference table." This prompted Patton to break out with "Hell, let's have the guts to let the ____ _ ____ go all the way to Paris. Then we'll really cut 'em off and chew 'em up." In his account, Eisenhower chastely substituted one long, one short, and one long blank for Patton's favorite expletive: sons of bitches. The remark broke the tension, and everyone present grinned, but, just so there would not be any misunderstanding, Eisenhower countered that the enemy "would never be allowed to cross the Meuse."[1]

Ike turned to Patton and "said he wanted me to get to Luxembourg and take command of the battle and make a strong counterattack with at least six divisions. The fact that three of these divisions exist only on paper did not enter his head." By this time, the three divisions in the Ardennes had been decimated by the German attack. Eisenhower continued, asking Devers how much of the defensive line he could take over while XII Corps was diverted to the north. "Devers made a long speech on strictly selfish grounds and said nothing," Patton complained to his diary, adding that "Bradley said little." Finally, Ike turned back to Patton: "When can you attack?" On December 22, he promised, with three divisions: the 4th Armored, the 26th, and the 80th.[2]

"Don't be fatuous, George," an irritated Eisenhower responded. "If you try to go that early, you won't have all three divisions ready and you'll go piecemeal. You will start on the twenty-second and I want your initial blow to be a strong one! I'd even settle for the twenty-third if it takes that long to get three full divisions."[3]

But Patton insisted that he could make an effective attack on the twenty-second. Some of the British officers present at the conference laughed. Others nervously shuffled their feet and, realizing Patton was dead serious, straightened in their chairs.

More than any other single point in his career, this was Patton's defining moment. He proposed to turn almost an entire army 90 degrees to the north, force-march it through ice and snow 40 miles or more, then, without rest, commit it to a counterattack against an enemy tasting victory for the first time in many months.

Patton appreciated Eisenhower's fear that an attack by three divisions "was not strong enough," but "I insisted that I could beat the Germans with three divisions, and if I waited [to get more divisions into the effort], I would lose surprise."[4] It was part and parcel of Patton's firmest conviction that war was about opportunity, not perfection.

Despite his misgivings, Eisenhower approved Patton's proposal, and the time of the attack, by III Corps, was fixed at 0400, December 22. "On the twenty-first, I received quite a few telephone calls from various higher echelons, expressing solicitude as to my ability to attack successfully with only three divisions. I maintained my contention that it is better to attack with a small force at once, and attain surprise, than it is to wait and lose it."[5]

Patton strode to the map and fixed his eyes on Bradley. "Brad, the Kraut's stuck his head in a meatgrinder." Thrusting his fist into the map, he ground it into the bulge. "And this time I've got hold of the handle."[6] This was a metaphor for his proposed strategy. He wanted to allow the Germans to drive another 40 or 50 miles into the bulge, then he would aim his attack well to the northeast with the objective of pinching off the entrance to the bulge, which was also the avenue of retreat. He would then attack the trapped Germans mainly from the rear. Like Patton's proposal during Operation Cobra to effect a deep envelopment in order to bag every German north of the Loire, he wanted now to trap and destroy as much of the German army as possible in the Ardennes. Like his earlier proposal, however, this one was rejected as well. Bradley was less concerned about killing large numbers of the enemy than he was about preventing those already in the bulge from overrunning Bastogne, which the 101st Airborne Division and other U.S. units were holding on to so desperately. Bradley understood that the town commanded a major road junction. Whoever held it had access to the points farther west. Therefore, Bradley directed Patton's proposed counterattack squarely on Bastogne.

Even Patton seemed to appreciate that, under the circumstances, this more conservative approach made some sense. Instead of using all his resources against the base of the bulge, Patton ordered Millikin, with three divisions, to relieve the German siege. He would, however, reserve Eddy's divisions, when they arrived, for use farther east, to seize the handle of the meatgrinder.

With the priority of the attacks having been settled, Patton threw himself into the complex task of managing the movement of more and more men into the Ardennes while Millikin, as Patton had promised, made his attack early on the morning of December 22. Patton choreographed the entire operation via telephone, the receiver to his ear all day.

Throughout the fall and winter of 1944, the weather in northern Europe was the worst in 20 years, and some of the most severe conditions prevailed during Millikin's attack. He had a front 20 miles wide through which he advanced and fought in heavy snow and frigid temperatures. If the weather made going on the ground difficult, it rendered support from the air impossible, which seriously threatened the American counteroffensive. At Bastogne, the surrounded 101st Airborne continued grimly to hold out. On the morning of December 22, a party of two German officers and two noncommissioned officers, under a white flag, approached with a surrender ultimatum. The message was brought to the acting division commander, Brigadier General Anthony McAuliffe. Surrounded and pounded as the 101st was, McAuliffe nevertheless initially assumed that the Germans were coming to surrender to *him*. When he was told that, on the contrary, they were demanding that the 101st surrender, McAuliffe laughed and said: "Us surrender? Aw, nuts!" The singular American expletive *"Nuts!"* was conveyed to the Germans as McAulliffe's reply to their surrender demand.

The "Nuts!" story quickly spread throughout Third Army and into enduring legend, but Patton knew that it would take more than a gesture of defiance, no matter how magnificently laconic, to save Bastogne. He was becoming frustrated at having to fight the Germans and the weather too. Without air support, a breakthrough was nearly impossible. Back in November, during another siege of bad weather, a frustrated Patton phoned the Third Army chaplain, Monsignor (Colonel) James H. O'Neill, and asked him if he had "a good prayer for weather." Patton was hardly a conventionally pious man, but he took religion seriously and believed he had a very personal relationship with God, to whom he often prayed. Patton believed God was on his side. A weather prayer would serve simply to remind Him of that fact. Discovering that no standard weather prayer existed, Chaplain O'Neill wrote one himself in the space of an hour:

Almighty and most merciful Father, we humbly beseech Thee, of Thy great goodness, to restrain these immoderate rains with which we have had to contend. Grant us fair weather for battle. Graciously hearken to us as soldiers who call upon Thee that, armed with Thy power, we may advance from victory to victory, and crush the oppression and wickedness of our enemies, and establish Thy justice among men and nations. Amen.

Patton had liked it and saved it, and he now ordered it printed on 250,000 wallet-size cards, which were distributed to the soldiers of the Third Army. On the reverse side of each card was a Christmas greeting, which O'Neill had composed on Patton's behalf:

To each officer and soldier in the Third United States Army, I wish a Merry Christmas. I have full confidence in your courage, devotion to duty, and skill in battle. We march in our might to complete victory. May God's blessing rest upon each of you on this Christmas Day.

G. S. Patton, Jr.
Lieutenant General
Commanding, Third United States Army

As Patton explained to O'Neill, he was

a strong believer in prayer. There are three ways that men get what they want; by planning, by working, and by praying. Any great military operation takes careful planning or thinking. Then you must have well-trained troops to carry it out: that's working. But between the plan and the operation there is always an unknown.

That unknown spells defeat or victory, success or failure. It is the reaction of the actors to the ordeal when it actually comes. Some people call that getting the breaks; I call it God.

God has His part, or margin in everything. That's where prayer comes in.[7]

On December 23, the weather broke sufficiently to allow, at long last, massive Allied air strikes, as Millikin closed in around Bastogne. "A clear cold Christmas," Patton wrote in his diary, "lovely weather for killing Germans, which seems a bit queer, seeing Whose birthday it is." Then, on December 26, Patton received a call from Hugh Gaffey, commanding one of Millikin's divisions. Gaffey reported that he could break through to Bastogne and make contact with the 101st by a rapid advance. It was, of course, risky. "I told him to try it," Patton recorded in his diary. "At 1845 they made contact, and Bastogne was liberated. It was a daring thing and well done. Of course they may be cut off, but I doubt it. . . . The speed of our movements is amazing, even to me, and must be a constant source of surprise to the Germans."[8]

Patton was proud of Gaffey, proud of the Third Army, and proud, too, of Chaplain O'Neill. When the weather broke, Patton exclaimed, "Hot dog! I guess I'll have another 100,000 of those prayers printed." He then summoned O'Neill, told him he was "the most popular man in this headquarters. You sure stand in good with the Lord and soldiers." As O'Neill recalled, Patton then "cracked me on the side of my steel helmet with his riding crop. That was his way of saying, 'Well done.'"[9] Patton also decorated O'Neill with the Bronze Star, making him the only U.S. Army chaplain to receive the honor for writing a prayer. It was a gesture that would not be out of place in today's army, in which religious faith plays an increasingly visible role.

Meanwhile, the fighting continued, as the Germans simultaneously persisted in menacing Bastogne while fiercely resisting attempts at encirclement, but by December 29, Patton was confident enough to write to Beatrice: "The relief of Bastogne is the most brilliant operation we have thus far performed and is in my opinion the outstanding achievement of this war. Now the enemy must dance to our tune, not we to his."[10]

As successful as the counteroffensive had been, Patton wanted more. He wanted to keep attacking to prevent the Germans from withdrawing from the bulge. Once again, he found himself up against what he deemed the excessive conservatism, even the timidity, of both Bradley and Eisenhower, who were allowing too many of the enemy to escape. They feared driving the troops beyond endurance, but Patton believed that, in the clutch, war was all about driving troops beyond endurance, forcing them to find the strength to achieve a rapid victory. Yet once the threat to Bastogne had been vanquished, the other commanders, especially Eisenhower and Bradley, lost the momentum that had been created by the crisis.

Patton's gloom deepened in February, when Eisenhower transferred the principal thrust of the collective Allied offensive from the American army to the British under Montgomery. "You may hear that I am on the defense," he wrote to Beatrice on February 4, 1945, "but it was not the enemy who put me there. . . . I feel pretty low to be ending the war on the defensive." From Eisenhower, Patton sought recognition and praise, but received none. When he met with Ike in Bastogne on February 5, he came away "surprised when Eisenhower failed to make any remark about my Bastogne operation. . . . So far in my dealings with him, he has never mentioned in a complimentary way any action that myself or any other officer has performed. . . . He had on his new five stars—a very pretty insignia." Turning to Beatrice by way of letter, Patton sought a sympathetic ear. He bemoaned the fact that "too many 'safety first' people" were running things. "I don't see much future for me in this war."[11]

CHAPTER 13

The Final Advance

After the Battle of the Bulge, Patton wrote to his son, George, about leadership : "I have it—but I'll be damned if I can define it." This was not bragging or pride. It was a statement of fact about his own nature. "It" was not an achievement or a skill; "it" was simply an irreducible element that could not be accounted for. In any case, publicly, Patton gave all the credit for victory to his officers and troops, telling the press on January 1 that the relief of Bastogne "sounds like what a great man George Patton is, but I did not have anything to do with it. . . . The people who actually did it were the younger officers and soldiers. When you think of those men marching all night in the cold, over roads they had never seen, and nobody getting lost, and everybody getting to the place in time, it is a very marvelous feat; I know of no equal to it in military history . . . I take my hat off to them. . . . To me it is a never ending marvel what our soldiers can do."[1]

By the middle of February, as Third Army closed in on the Rhine, Patton's post-Battle of the Bulge let-down began to lift. Whereas on February 4, he had whined to Beatrice about being forced to end the war on the defensive, on February 10, he responded with defiance when, through Bradley, Eisenhower asked how soon Third Army could go on the defensive and yield more troops to Montogomery's 21st Army Group. Patton replied to Bradley that he would resign before he would relinquish the offensive at this point in the war. Bradley conveyed Patton's ultimatum to Eisenhower, who backed down to the extent of permitting Bradley (and, therefore, Patton) to assume a posture of what he called "aggressive defense." As Patton noted, "I chose to view it as an order to 'keep moving' toward the Rhine with a low profile." Indeed, Patton pressed the attack, albeit very quietly. "Let the gentlemen up north learn what we're doing when they see it on their maps."[2]

On leaving Luxembourg, Third Army moved through the Eifel sector of Germany's West Wall, the formidable defenses of the Siegfried Line. The terrain, stubbornly defended, was heavily forested, rugged, and cut up by the Moselle, Our, and Saur rivers. Of the fighting and progress through the Eifel, Patton wrote to Beatrice on February 14: "Some times I get so mad with the troops for not fighting better and then they do something superb. The forcing of the crossing of the Sauer and Our Rivers . . . was an Homeric feat."[3]

On February 14, Patton and his aide, Charles Codman, left for a few days of relaxation in Paris, where Patton took time to spend an evening at the Folies Bérgère, which (he recorded in his diary) "is perfectly naked, so much so that no one is interested."[4] Patton also went hunting with Ike's chief of staff, Bedell Smith, bagging three ducks, one pheasant, and three hares, and then talked Smith into backing his request for more troops to use in his low-profile offensive. Patton managed to persuade Bradley to return the 10th Armored Division to the Third Army; however, Bradley conspired with Patton to keep Eisenhower and the rest of SHAEF (Supreme Headquarters Allied Expeditionary Force) in the dark. He cautioned Patton to stay off the phone for the next few days until it was too late for

SHAEF to recall the division. If he was unavailable to receive an order, he could neither obey nor disobey it.

Patton advanced on the principal city of the Eifel, Trier (which, he observed with pleasure, had once been captured by the Roman legions). It fell to the 10th Armored and an infantry division on March 1. Shortly after this, Patton resumed answering the telephone and soon picked up an order to bypass Trier. He sent a message in reply: "Have taken Trier with two divisions. Do you want me to give it back?"[5]

Soldiers of the 6th Army Group had been fighting just west of the Rhine since November. At last, on March 7, 1945, elements of the 9th Armored Division under Brigadier General William M. Hoge, captured an intact railway bridge at Remagen and quickly crossed the Rhine, establishing a bridgehead on the east bank. The Third Army finally reached the Rhine on that same day, at Coblenz, but the Germans had left no bridges intact here. Although Patton was disappointed that his was not the first army to cross the Rhine, he was pleased that at least an American army had beaten Montgomery across. Patton's engineers set to work bridging the Rhine and, during the night of March 22, Patton stealthily slipped a division across the river—a day in advance of Montgomery, whose much-trumpeted crossing had been delayed by the overly elaborate preparations he made. "God be praised," Patton recorded in his diary on the twenty-third. He immediately composed Third Army General Orders 70, addressed to the "officers and men of the Third Army and to our comrades of the XIX TAC [Tactical Air Command]," tallying their achievements from January 29 to March 22, including the capture of Trier, Coblenz, Bingen, Worms, Mainz, Kaiserslautern, and Ludwigshafen; the capture of 140,112 enemy soldiers; and the killing or wounding of 99,000 more, "thereby eliminating practically all of the German Seventh and First Armies. History records no greater achievement in so limited a time. . . . The world rings with your praises. . . . Please accept my heartfelt admiration and thanks for what you have done, and remember that your assault crossing over the Rhine . . . assures you of even greater glory to come."[6]

The day after writing this exultant general order, Patton recorded in his diary: "Drove to the river and went across on the pontoon bridge, stopping in the middle to take a piss in the Rhine, and then pick up some dirt on the far side."[7] Picking up the clod of dirt was in emulation of William the Conqueror, who, in 1066, stumbled as he disembarked at Pevesney, then rose up with a fistful of English earth and led his army to the Battle of Hastings. As to Patton's other act, urinating in the Rhine was without doubt a crude gesture, but no less a figure than Winston Churchill would repeat it on his own arrival.

Although Patton and the Third Army had not been the first across the Rhine, he expressed himself quite accurately when he told his soldiers that the world rang with their praises—and it rang with his as well. Once again, Patton was in the limelight and hailed as a great general. And once again, it was at this moment that he chose to gamble on yet another controversial action that risked his reputation.

During the Tunisian campaign, Patton's son-in-law John Waters had been captured. Until early 1945, he was held in a prisoner-of-war (POW) camp in Poland, but (according to intelligence Patton received), as the Soviets approached, he was transferred west to a camp at Hammelburg, Germany. Hammelburg was believed to hold 5,000 POWs, including 1,500 Americans, many desperately ill, all near starvation. Patton decided to launch a rescue mission.

Patton discussed the matter with Manton Eddy. Hammelburg lay well within enemy-held territory, and Patton wanted to detach a 4,000-man armored combat command to do the job. Eddy persuaded him that a much smaller highly mobile detachment, just 306 men and 10 medium tanks, 6 light tanks, 27 half-tracks, 7 Jeeps, and 3 motorized assault guns, would be better suited to a hit-and-run raid. Reluctantly, Patton agreed. Captain Abraham Baum was assigned to command the detachment, and Patton asked (but did not order) his aide Alexander C. Stiller, who knew Waters and would be able to recognize him, to go along. Stiller hopped into Baum's Jeep. His presence would raise serious questions about Patton's motive. Was he risking 306 men (307, including Stiller) to liberate 5,000 Allied POWs, including his son-in-law? Or was he risking them to liberate his son-in-law, who incidentally happened to be in company with 5,000 other prisoners?

The raiding party rushed headlong to Hammelburg, on the way engaging and defeating an enemy tank unit, destroying some locomotives and military equipment on flatcars, liberating 700 Soviet POWs, then fighting through to the camp. The commandant surrendered, sending out a surrender party of four, including Waters. A nervous German guard fired at the party, however, seriously wounding Waters. Baum liberated the camp and loaded as many of the freed prisoners into his vehicles as he could. On the return trip, however, the raiders were ambushed by a superior force. In a fierce firefight, Baum was wounded three times, and the rescue party, vastly outnumbered, surrendered. Most of the prisoners walked back to the camp. The raiders were taken back to Hammelburg, except for Stiller, who was sent to a prison in Nuremberg. A week after the raid, a number of officers who had managed to escape during the firefight found their way back to U.S. lines and confirmed that Waters was a prisoner. Just two days after this, on April 5, the 14th Armored Division reached Hammelburg and liberated the prisoners still there, including Waters. He recovered and continued his military career. Stiller was not liberated until later in April.

In some ways, the hardest-hit casualty of the operation was Patton. The same newspapers that, weeks earlier, had hailed him as Grant, Lee, and Napoleon rolled into one now carried stories of how Patton had sacrificed a heroic force of soldiers for the sake of his son-in-law. Both Eisenhower and Bradley were furious, but, this time, there would be no official repercussions. "I did not rebuke [Patton] for it," Bradley wrote in his postwar memoir, *A Soldier's Story.* "Failure itself was George's own worst reprimand."[8]

In Patton's corner of the war, southern Germany, resistance was rapidly folding, and Third Army units were scooping up prisoners of war. By early April, their bag of more than 400,000 exceeded the number of prisoners captured by any other Allied army. By the end of April, the Third Army had processed more than a million POWs. That same month, Manton Eddy's XII Corps liberated the Merkers industrial salt mine and there found the entire gold bullion reserve of the Third Reich. Eddy reported to Patton that the mine, some 2,100 feet underground, also contained vaults belonging to the Reichsbank. When Eddy hesitated to investigate, Patton in no uncertain terms ordered him to "blow open that fuckin' fault and see what's in it."[9]

What was in it warranted a special tour by Eisenhower, Bradley, and Patton. The three generals were lowered into the mine aboard a superannuated elevator suspended by single cable. As they slowly descended through the darkness, Patton could not resist the bravado of gallows humor: "If that clothesline should part, promotions in the United States Army would be considerably stimulated."

Ike was not amused. "O.K., George, that's enough. No more cracks until we are above ground again."[10]

The generals beheld 4,500 25-pound gold bars (worth at the time about $57.6 million); millions more in currency, including marks, British pounds, and American dollars; and many hundreds of paintings that the Nazis had looted from the museums and great homes of the nations they had conquered. "We examined a few of the alleged art treasures," Patton remarked. "The ones I saw were worth, in my opinion, about $2.50, and were of the type normally seen in bars in America."[11] The generals also saw something far more sinister: many thousands of gold and silver dental fillings, eyeglasses, and other gold and silver items taken from victims of what Hitler and his henchmen called the Final Solution and what the world would soon call the Holocaust.

Patton came face to face with it that very afternoon. Accompanied by Eisenhower and Bradley, he visited the just-liberated Ohrduf concentration camp. It was, Patton said, "the first horror camp any of us had ever seen. It was the most appalling sight imaginable." The generals were shown the gallows, the whipping table ("which was about the height of the average man's crotch. The feet were place in stocks on the ground and the man was pulled over the table . . . while he was beaten across the back and loins"), and pile upon pile of naked bodies, some out in the open, some jammed into a shed, all "in the last stages of emaciation." The generals also saw "a sort of mammoth griddle of 60 cm. railway tracks laid on a brick foundation." As the Americans had approached the camp, the German guards had ordered the inmates to exhume the many dead and pile the corpses on this "griddle." The idea was to cremate the abundant evidence of war crimes and crimes against humanity. "The attempt," Patton remarked, "was a bad failure. . . . one could not help but think of some gigantic cannibalistic barbecue."[12]

Just how powerfully Patton was affected by the sights and smells of the "horror camp" is not apparent from his diary, letters, or other writings. An American diplomat who was present at Buchenwald, which the Third Army also liberated and which Patton visited, noted that the general "went off to a corner thoroughly sick."[13]

Patton's tour of the death camps not only sickened him, it brought on renewed depression, which deepened further when Eisenhower assigned Third Army to turn away from Berlin and instead drive southeast into Czechoslovakia by way of Bavaria. It was believed that hard-line Nazis were gathering there for a last desperate stand. As for the German capital, Eisenhower informed Patton that Berlin would taken by neither the American nor the British army, but by the Red Army. Patton was shocked, disgusted, and dispirited by the news. He believed that the Soviets were an even bigger threat to the United States and its western allies than the Germans had been. To have won the war militarily only to lose politically by giving away so important a prize was, as he saw it, a tragedy of staggering dimensions.

Still reeling from the news about Berlin, Patton tuned to the BBC on the night of April 12 to get the correct time so that he could set his watch. That is how he heard of the death of Franklin D. Roosevelt, who had succumbed to a cerebral hemorrhage at the "Little White House" in Warm Springs, Georgia. Patton immediately conveyed the news to Eisenhower and Bradley, and, as he recorded in his diary, "we had quite a discussion as to what might happen." A man without personal political ambitions, Patton was nevertheless, like most career officers, a conservative Republican (his father had been a Democrat), but he appreciated FDR's charismatic style of leadership. He now complained to his diary about how, through "political preference, people are made Vice Presidents who were never intended, neither by Party nor by the Lord to be Presidents." Patton would live just long enough, however, to come to a more balanced estimation of Harry S. Truman.[14]

Hoping to improve his gloomy mood, Patton, with Codman, flew to Paris to visit Waters in the hospital. Patton spent the night with Everett

Hughes, who, at breakfast the next morning, passed him *Stars and Stripes,* the army's official newspaper. Patton took a cursory look and passed it back. Hughes gave it to him again and, pointing to an article, said, "Read that."

"Well," Patton said, looking up from the paper. "I'll be goddamned." He had received the fourth star of a full general.[15]

┼══╾┼

Third Army's V Corps, under Clarence Huebner, reached Pilsen, Czecho-slovakia, on May 5. When Patton telephoned Bradley for permission to advance to Prague, Bradley, after checking with Eisenhower, said no. Pilsen would be the extent of Third Army's advance. Patton had desperately wanted to liberate the Czech capital as Third Army's final prize. He would not have the chance. At 2:41 in the morning of May 7, 1945, a delegation of German officers signed an unconditional surrender at Rheims.

Patton wanted urgently to be transferred to the Pacific theater, but, clearly, that part of the world was not big enough for both a Douglas MacArthur and a George S. Patton. As early as February, Patton had begged Marshall for a Pacific command, saying that he was willing to serve in any capacity, from division on up. Marshall replied that he would send him to China if the Chinese managed to secure a major port for his entry. That, Patton knew, was highly unlikely. Marshall's reply, therefore, was the polite equivalent of no.

On May 8, Patton bade farewell to the Third Army war correspondents and invited their questions for the last time. One question would soon come back to haunt him. "Are SS troops [taken prisoner] to be handled any differently?" Patton replied: "No. SS means no more in Germany than being a Democrat in America—that is not to be quoted." Yet again, Patton had made a politically inept statement to the press, briefly thought the better of it, but then went on to put his foot further into his mouth. "I mean by that initially the SS people were special sons-of-bitches, but as the war progressed, they ran out of sons-of-bitches and then they put anybody in there. Some of the top SS men will be treated as criminals, but there is no reason for trying someone who was drafted into this outfit." The statement was part and parcel of Patton's immediate postwar attitude toward the defeated enemy. He had seen and felt German savagery. He had been sickened by the death camps. And yet, in the coming days and weeks, he would propose privately to his military colleagues that Britain and America should now engage a defeated Germany as an ally against the Soviet Union. To the war correspondents on May 8, Patton also spoke of those who had given their lives "from North Africa to the Channel. . . . I wonder how the dead will speak today when they know that for the first time in centuries we have opened Central and Western Europe to the forces of Genghis Khan"—by which he meant Joseph Stalin. "I wonder how they feel now that they know there will be no peace in our times and that Americans, some not yet born, will have to fight the Russians tomorrow, or ten, 15 or 20 years from tomorrow."[16]

Toward the middle of May, Patton flew to Paris and then to London for rest. In June, he returned to the United States for an extended leave with his family before beginning his new assignment as the occupation forces' military governor of Bavaria. He landed at Bedford Airport on June 7, outside of Boston, where Beatrice and his children were there to greet him. All along the 25-mile drive from Bedford to the city, cheering throngs lined the streets. Standing upright in the car, he waved to them all, all the way to Boston and the Hatch Shell on the Charles River Esplanade, where 20,000 people waited to hear him speak. The people of Boston, like those throughout America, were thankful for victory and craved the presence of heroes. All controversy dissolved—at least for the moment.

As usual, when he spoke publicly, Patton gave the credit for victory to the soldiers. Looking at some 400 wounded Third Army veterans, who were sitting in a specially reserved section at the front of the shell, he declared: "With your blood and bonds, we crushed the Germans before they got here. This ovation is not for me, George S. Patton—George S. Patton is simply a hook on which to hang the Third Army." Then, to honor the wounded men, he said that most people believe the hero is the man who dies in battle. The truth is, Patton said, the man who dies in battle is often a fool. He pointed to the wounded veterans: "These men are the heroes."[17]

Instead of bringing universal praise, the speech released an avalanche of angry and anguished letters from Gold Star mothers and fathers (the parents of slain soldiers were entitled to display a gold star in their window) to General Marshall, to Secretary of War Stimson, and to others in authority. Patton had managed, yet again, to create outrage in the midst of adulation.

Patton spent less than a month on leave in the States, visiting Boston, speaking in Denver, and appearing in Los Angeles to address a crowd of 100,000 at the city's Coliseum before making an official visit to Washington. Patton then returned to Europe, arriving on July 4. Although he was relieved to be back among soldiers, he was not looking forward to performing an administrative and political task for which he, a fighter, not a bureaucrat, was eminently unsuited.

Indeed, it was peace itself for which Patton was unsuited. To those who had served with him in battle and were now serving with him in peace, he looked old and tired, a man doing his best just to go through the motions. When word came to him on August 10 that Japan had surrendered and World War II was over, he wrote to Beatrice: "Now the horrors of peace, pacafism, and unions will have unlimited sway. I wish I were young enough to fight in the next one . . . killing Mongols [the Russians]." In his diary, he expressed himself even more bleakly: "Another war has ended and with it my usefulness to the world. . . . Now all that is left to do is to sit around and await the arrival of the undertaker and posthumous immortality. Fortunately, I also have to occupy myself with the de-Nazification and government of Bavaria."[18]

De-Nazification was precisely the issue that would be Patton's final undoing. Under Allied military administration, the process proceeded rapidly throughout Germany. Nazi clergy were purged. Nazi street names were expunged. Nazi were memorials dismantled. Former Nazi party members were excluded from business, banking, and industry as well as from the professions. The communications sector—radio, telegraph, and telephone—was swept clean of former Nazis. In Patton's region, Bavaria, however, de-Nazification proceeded at a markedly slower pace. In contrast to other military administrators throughout the country, Patton was unenthusiastic about the process. The issue came up at a press conference held at his headquarters, in Bad Tölz, on September 22. Why were Nazis retaining key governmental positions in Bavaria? a reporter asked.

Patton's aide Hap Gay vigorously shook his head, signaling to his chief to avoid answering the question. Patton pointedly ignored the signal, replying: "In supervising the functioning of the Bavarian government, which is my mission, the first thing that happened was that the outs accused the ins of being Nazis. Now, more than half the German people were Nazis and we would be in a hell of a fix if we removed all Nazi party members from office." That may have sounded reasonable to some, but it was not the answer Eisenhower and the politicians wanted. Patton went on: "The way I see it, this Nazi question is very much like a Democratic and Republican election fight. . . . Now we are using [former Nazi party members] for lack of anyone better until we can get better people."[19] Patton had a population to feed; electricity, heat, and water to supply. He had to begin reconstruction of basic infrastructure. Practically the only ones who knew how to do these jobs had served during the Hitler regime as bureaucrats and administrators, and party membership was a job requirement at the time. The papers, however, looked no further than Patton's comparison between the Nazis and the American political parties, announcing in their headlines the shocking news that Patton found no difference between Nazis and the Democratic and Republican parties.

Predictably, Eisenhower exploded. Patton defended himself by claiming that he had been misquoted. Strictly speaking, he had not been misquoted but quoted out of context. Eisenhower asked him to hold another press conference to set the record straight. In compliance, Patton carefully prepared a written statement, but instead of reading it verbatim, he embellished the speech, ad-libbed in a defiant tone, and ended up simply reiterating his rationale for retaining former Nazis in administrative positions.

Patton had been raised during a time and in a social milieu in which class prejudice, racism, and anti-Semitism were the rule rather than the exception. His exposure to the death camps, the horrific evidence of the Holocaust, had not softened these inbred and long-cultivated views. True, he was sickened by Nazi inhumanity, yet he also tended to blame the Jews for allowing themselves to be victimized. Now, under fire from the press and politicians, he became ugly and downright delusional in his prejudice. He saw no fault in himself, but declared in a letter to Beatrice on September 25 that the "Devil and Moses" had joined forces against him. In another letter to her, he wrote that the "noise against me is only the means by which the Jews and Communists are attempting with good success to implement a further dismemberment of Germany." He noted, in his diary, "a very apparent Semitic influence in the press. They are trying to do two things: First, implement Communism, and second, see that all business men of German ancestry and non-Jewish antecedents are thrown out of their jobs." He went on to draw a sharp line between the Jewish-dominated press and what he saw as his own heritage of values: "They have utterly lost the Anglo-Saxon conception of justice and feel that a man can be kicked out because somebody else says he is a Nazi."[20]

On September 28, 1945, Eisenhower summoned Patton to his headquarters in the IG Farben Building in Frankfurt. After a heated exchange among Patton, Eisenhower, and Bedell Smith, Eisenhower quietly, even gently, made what he carefully termed a suggestion. The so-called Fifteenth Army—really nothing more than a small headquarters and staff—had been formed to compile the history of the war in Europe. It was an important job, Eisenhower insisted, and the Fifteenth required a good commanding general. He asked Patton to take charge. Patton's first impulse was to resign his commission on the spot, but he held his tongue. Perhaps it was his love of history and the opportunity to exercise come control over how the history of the war would be written—whatever his reasons, he decided to relinquish the storied Third Army and accept command of this new "paper army."

Lucian Truscott, old comrade and trusted subordinate, who had performed for Patton at first reluctantly but then brilliantly in the capture of Messina, Sicily, relieved him of Third Army command on October 7 at the army's headquarters in Bad Tölz. During the somber change-of-command ceremony, Patton spoke to his officers: "All good things must come to an end," he said. "The best thing that has ever happened to me thus far is the honor and privilege of having commanded the Third Army."[21]

Assuming his new command, Patton wasted no time in putting the personnel of Fifteenth Army, housed in a hotel at Bad Nauheim, to work on gathering the documents necessary for writing the war's history. But he quickly lost interest in his assignment. As his staff started their research, Patton left, traveling to Paris, Rennes, Chartres, Brussels, Metz, Reims,

Luxembourg, and Verdun. Everywhere he was welcomed as a hero and given civic certificates and military decorations. He even traveled to Stockholm, scene of his Olympic glory in 1912, where he met with the surviving members of the Swedish Olympic team of that now-distant year.

Patton decided to go home for Christmas 1946 and to never return to Europe or the Fifteenth Army. Perhaps he would remain in the military, in some stateside post, perhaps he would retire. It was something he needed to discuss with Beatrice. He was scheduled to fly aboard Ike's plane to Southampton, England, and to sail from there to New York on December 10. On the eighth, Hap Gay, looking to lift Patton's spirits, suggested the two of them drive out to an area west of Speyer for some pheasant hunting. Patton was pleased, and, early on Sunday morning, December 9, Private First Class Horace L. Woodring prepared the general's 1938 Model 75 Cadillac staff car. They left Bad Nauheim at nine. Just before quarter to noon, Woodring stopped at a railroad crossing outside of Mannheim to let a train pass. He then crossed the tracks. From the opposite direction, a two-and-a-half-ton truck driven by Technical Sergeant Robert L. Thompson suddenly turned left to enter a quartermaster depot. At precisely 11:45, Patton remarked on the numbers of derelict vehicles that littered the road. "How awful war is," he said. "Think of the waste." Apparently attending to the general's words, Woodring glanced away from the road, then looked up to see Thompson's turning vehicle looming in front of him. He slammed on the brakes and turned the steering wheel, hard, to the left. Gay, who saw what was coming, said, "Sit tight." He braced for the collision. Patton, contemplating the waste of war, was oblivious to what was happening.[22]

Under the circumstances, Woodring had reacted well, so that the collision, though it had not been avoided, was minor. Neither driver was hurt and Gay suffered only slight bruises. Patton, however, was bleeding profusely from a bad gash to the head. He had hit the glass partition separating the backseat passengers from the driver, and he probably also hit a diamond-shaped interior light on the car's head liner.

Patton's first question was if Gay and Woodring were hurt. After they both replied no, he calmly said, "I believe I am paralyzed. I am having trouble breathing. Work my fingers for me. Take and rub my arms and shoulders and rub them hard." Patton could feel nothing. "Damn it, rub them." Gay, recognizing that Patton was badly injured, told him not to move while they called for help.

"This is a helluva way to die," Patton said.[23]

The general was transported to a hospital in Heidelberg. He never lost consciousness, and to the physicians and orderlies who buzzed about him, he joked, "Relax, gentlemen, I'm in no condition to be a terror now."[24]

The diagnosis was a fracture and dislocation of the third and fourth cervical vertebrae: a broken neck with spinal cord damage. Patton was placed in traction, in the hope that the injury would heal or at least that some movement and sensation would return as inflammation subsided. An eminent neurosurgeon was flown in from Oxford University, and Eisenhower placed an airplane at the disposal of Beatrice Patton. With Dr. R. Glen Spurling, a noted American neurosurgeon, himself recently discharged from the army with the rank of colonel, she flew to Patton's bedside.

To Beatrice, Patton presented a cheerful front. However, when he was alone with Dr. Spurling, he asked for the unvarnished truth.

"Now, Colonel, we've known each other during the fighting and I want you to talk to me as man to man. What chance have I to recover?"

Spurling answered that his prognosis depended on what happened during the next several days.

"What chance have I to ride a horse again?"

"None."

"In other words, the best I could hope for would be semi-invalidism."

"Yes."

"Thank you, Colonel, for being honest."[25]

For the following 13 days Patton lived, totally paralyzed, as a model patient, who never complained, never expressed anger, never said a rude word to anyone. On the afternoon of December 21, his wife read to him until about four, when he drifted into sleep. His breathing became irregular, and she summoned Dr. Spurling. By quarter past five, his breathing had improved, and he now seemed peacefully asleep. Beatrice and Dr. Spurling went to dinner. At six, Dr. William Duane Jr. appeared in the hospital mess and summoned them both to Patton's room. The walk took no more than a few minutes, but by the time they reached his bedside,

General George Smith Patton Jr., United States Army, was dead. On the day the war had ended in Europe, Patton had remarked to an aide: "The best end for an old campaigner is a bullet at the last minute of the last battle."[26] Injured in a fender bender dreary months after that last battle, Patton succumbed to pulmonary edema and congestive heart failure. He was 60 years old.

CHAPTER 14

The Patton Problem
and the Patton Legacy

DURING THE SICILY CAMPAIGN, Patton confided to his diary that he had a "feeling of being a chip in a river of destiny." It was a feeling and a metaphor he would often use, with variations (sometimes he was a leaf blown by the winds of destiny), throughout the war. Patton's sense of personal destiny was a constant throughout his life. A chip, a leaf, floating, blowing—this is not the vocabulary of a leader known for an aggressive, hands-on style of command, a hunger for glory, and an absolute determination to win. It is the language of passive surrender.[1]

Perhaps the paradox of this metaphor provides a clue to his genius as a warrior. "Old Blood and Guts" was outwardly a fierce athlete and a profane killer, but inwardly a religious mystic who saw fate as a stream flowing through time and who conceived of himself as having lived, fought, and died in the past even as he fought now in the present and doubtless would fight again in the future. At times, this vision of himself was conventionally religious; he saw himself as an instrument of God's will. Often, however, the vision was more idiosyncratically mystical. His role was not providential, but rather driven by a more impersonal destiny in which God seemed to play no part. In either case, whether he was an instrument of God or a chip in the river of destiny, there was nothing passive about the fulfillment of providence or of destiny. It required his utmost exertion, courage, boldness, and exercise of personal will.

The coexistence of passivity and aggressive activity, of surrender and victory, of mystical spirituality and bloodthirsty profanity in a military commander was difficult for Patton's contemporaries to accept and, for the leaders of an army serving a rational democracy, nearly impossible to tolerate. Although American history is in very large part a saga of war and warlike violence, Americans have never been entirely comfortable with their warriors, and their historical reluctance to maintain large standing armies reflects a national revulsion against fostering anything resembling a warrior class, the very class to which Patton believed he belonged.

Steeped as we are in a culture strongly influenced by romantic notions of inspiration, most of us readily accept the idea that a great composer, artist, scientist, or inventor—Beethoven, say, or Michelangelo, or Edison—may be inspired by sources and forces beyond the rational, everyday self. Many of us have difficulty accepting that a warrior might be similarly inspired. Yet that was precisely the case with Patton, and that, for his contemporaries, was the Patton problem. Had Patton consistently identified the source of his inspiration as God, this might have been less of a problem—although even Chaplain O'Neill was uncomfortable when Patton ordered him to write a weather prayer, enlisting God's aid in killing Germans. In today's army, the more conventional aspects of Patton's spirituality would likely find ready acceptance. Many soldiers find strength in the belief that they are fighting on the side of God, and, in recent years, as the conservative politicians who shape American foreign policy, including America's wars, claim to be guided by their faith, the role of religion in the military is more visible than ever before.

But Patton was no simple soldier of God. He was more akin to the disturbingly complex military characters of Shakespeare, to such figures as the Bard's Julius Caesar, Othello, and Titus Andronicus—inspired captains all—on whom civilization itself depends in time of war but whom civilization cannot abide in time of peace. As it was with Shakespeare's captains, so it was with Patton. Civilization at peace could not tolerate him, and he could not live at peace in a peaceful civilization. Soldiers such as Eisenhower and Bradley endured no such conflict. They claimed no inspiration, divine or driven by destiny, but rather aspired to be neither more nor less than professional men-at-arms in service to their country. For Patton, these men frequently represented a frustrating intrusion of the values of peaceful civilization into his sphere—all-out war. Patton's all-or-nothing boldness in battle was often countermanded by Bradley or Eisenhower.

It is no accident that Bradley and, even more, Eisenhower enjoyed exceptional success in the postwar world. Whereas Patton died before he could write his memoirs (his *War as I Knew It* consists of notes edited and shaped by other hands), Eisenhower and Bradley lived to write widely read memoirs conveying their own versions and visions of the war. During the war they also skillfully managed the popular press to their advantage: Bradley was consistently portrayed as the earthy "G.I. general," Eisenhower as the smiling executive manager of Allied strategy. Patton, for whom image was central (he had been practicing his "war face" since his cadet days), was rarely able to maintain control of his image, at least not once the press got hold of it. Incapable of suppressing his impulsive nature even in the presence of reporters, he was time and again at the mercy of newspapers, lifted by them to the heights on one day, only to be cast into the depths on the next. Patton would have appreciated the modern army's struggle with the media over control of its image. Problems of direction and command as well as stories of atrocities were frequently in the news during the Vietnam War and contributed to the collective American revulsion against that war, and Operation Iraqi Freedom, which began in 2003, has likewise been plagued by worldwide news stories of prisoner abuse, torture, and even homicide. Yet Patton might have observed that even though the news media of World

War II was far more tightly controlled than it is today, the papers always managed to publish something damaging about George S. Patton while other potentially embarrassing stories were effectively censored.

All of this suddenly changed on the day Patton died. The controversy was swept aside, if not forgotten, in a rush to depict Patton as a very great general, perhaps the greatest of World War II. The American people, by and large, sincerely mourned him, even those who had called for his resignation after the slapping incidents, the Knutsford speech, and the de-Nazification comments. During the bewildering and anxious aftermath of World War II, when (as Patton, Churchill, and others had warned) the erstwhile Soviet ally loomed as a new and terrible threat, the popular image of Patton as a heroically simple and direct man of action became most seductively appealing.

For army officials, the death of Patton presented most immediately a problem of protocol. During the war, no American officer or enlisted man had been sent home for burial. How would the public react, especially all those Gold Star mothers and fathers, if an exception were made in the case of Patton? When the issue was raised with Beatrice Patton, she responded instantly: "Of course he must be buried here! Why didn't I think of it? Furthermore, I know George would want to lie beside the men of his army who have fallen."[2] Beatrice chose the U.S. military cemetery at Hamm, Luxembourg, not far from Bastogne, site of the desperate battle of which her husband was proudest. Thus Patton was not only removed from life and all the controversies life engenders, even his mortal remains, the last vestige of his physical presence, were buried in a place remote from the people of his country. Dead heroes make the best heroes, because, for them, time has stopped, and there is no more of the messy business of life to interfere with the collective cultural projection that is myth.

Upon his death, Patton was enshrined in the American mythic imagination. As mentioned in the introduction, discussions of Patton still elicit controversy. Yet the name of Patton has never lost its magic. It would not be difficult to argue that Eisenhower, Bradley, and MacArthur were more central to the Allied victory than Patton, but it could not be argued that they were superior warriors, and none of them has entered the realm of mythic imagination.

And that is another aspect of the Patton problem. Figures of myth largely represent the meaning we endow them with. To the extent that he has entered into American mythology, this is true of Patton, and the mythic Patton all too readily overshadows the historical Patton, a soldier and a leader of soldiers, obscuring the important question that needs to be asked: What is Patton's legacy to the army of today?

Command Presence

With many of history's most important commanders, answering this question is a matter of ticking off strategic, tactical, and doctrinal contributions. In the case of Patton, however, his most important contribution was less quantifiable but even more important than any he made in these traditional areas. Patton bequeathed to the army the ideal of the warrior leader. He wanted a modern army, equipped with the best and latest weapons, served by the most modern logistics, aided by the most advanced technology of reconnaissance and communication, but he also sought to inspire his army with his own ancient and even atavistic soul. The modern military calls this command presence. It is the ability of a commander to create a cohesive and highly motivated force in large part through the power of his or her personality. An effective army identifies with its leader, and it is the responsibility of the leader to project a presence most likely to create a victorious force. Today's military planners call any element that dramatically increases the effectiveness of a military organization a force multiplier. Patton demonstrated that the persona of the commander could be among the greatest force multipliers of all. This does not mean that today's commanders simply imitate Patton. It does mean that each leader must find his own warrior soul and project that onto the force he or she commands. This is a lesson not readily learned at the War College, but it is a lesson embodied in the example of Patton.

Tactics

If all great generals project an effective command presence, most are also significant strategists. This was not the case with George S. Patton, a fact his seniors recognized. They gave him a subordinate role in planning

Operation Torch, the Allied invasion of North Africa, and Operation Husky, the invasion of Sicily, and they gave him no part in planning Operation Overlord, the invasion of Normandy. This did not greatly displease Patton, who was usually content to execute the strategy set by others, provided that he was given a free hand in the execution. He believed that brilliant strategy could never compensate for inadequate tactics. A plan was only as good as its execution. Conversely, he sincerely believed that good tactics, skillfully and violently executed, could even compensate for poor strategy.

Under the best of circumstances, when he was able to choose the time and place of an attack, Patton was a peerless tactician. In the case of his breakout and advance during Operation Cobra, which expanded Bradley's rather modest strategy into a juggernaut of unprecedented speed and extent, Patton's tactics became strategy, transforming a vast portion of the European theater by suddenly reclaiming all of France north of the Loire. Beginning with the Louisiana and Texas maneuvers on the eve of America's entry into World War II and culminating in Operation Cobra, Patton provided the model for mobile warfare on the grandest of scales and at speeds that made an ally rather than an adversary of time. The ambitious scope and drive of Patton's Cobra breakout were reprised by a later generation of commanders in the first Gulf War, which was characterized by the rapid movement of massive ground forces spearheaded by tanks.

Patton's tactics were always distinguished by boldness and daring. He planned carefully. He gathered intelligence meticulously and believed that the fresher the intelligence, the better. But he never adhered slavishly to any plan; once an attack was launched, he kept himself open to opportunity and was always prepared to improvise, if doing so would enlarge the victory. Plans enabled him; he never let them limit him.

Another hallmark of Patton's tactics was speed and coordination of forces. His objective was to create the greatest effect in the least time, so that his forces were exposed to enemy fire as briefly as possible. He understood that advances in mobile warfare—modern tanks and other vehicles—and in air support as well as rapid communications enabled speed of execution. Since Patton's time, much of the technology of warfare has been devoted to increasing the tempo of operations. This means that Patton's attitude toward time in combat has become more important than ever. Whereas the first Gulf War was a dramatic example of the application of speed and coordination of forces, the second war in the Gulf, Operation Iraqi Freedom, has demonstrated the limitation of this tactical principle. Employing a Pattonesque ground advance, the invasion of Iraq was accomplished in a remarkably brief period during 2003. This phase of the war, however, was followed by an insurgency to which no one, as of 2005, can see a definitive end. Patton's tactics were developed on and for vast battlefield spaces occupied by large conventional armies. They are not effective in asymmetrical warfare scenarios, in which time, which a determined insurgency can draw out almost infinitely, becomes for the much larger invading force an enemy rather than an ally.

Redefinition of Military Professionalism

Patton also bequeathed to the American military tradition a new definition of professionalism. Although he, more than most of his contemporaries, believed that the profession of arms partook of ancient and honorable traditions, he also insisted that the modern military commander place himself squarely in the real world by becoming thoroughly familiar with all the weapons systems at his disposal, including the newest and still-emerging ones. Patton was not only a master of tank doctrine and tactics, he thoroughly understood the mechanics of his tanks, their armor plating, endurance, fuel demands, speed, and capabilities over various terrain. The nuts and bolts of war were not to be left to noncommissioned technicians. Patton insisted that these details also be made the province of each and every commander.

Attaining the level of Patton's technical proficiency has become increasingly difficult as the technology of warfare has become more complex. The consequences of failure to understand the capabilities and limitations of battlefield equipment was made embarrassingly evident during the invasion of Grenada in 1983. Commanders failed to adequately understand the communications infrastructure of the forces they led. The result was that much of the mission's radio equipment was incompatible across services: The army's radios could not talk with those of the marines, and the air force could not communicate adequately with the forces on the ground. At one point, officers in the field were compelled to communicate with higher headquarters via private or even pay telephones. In the first Gulf War, an inadequate understanding of weapons capability marred operations, when commanders relied on the Patriot missile system to defend against Iraqi Scud missile attacks. The Patriot had not been designed as an antimissile weapon and proved woefully inadequate in this role, a fact that was not understood until after the war had ended.

Updating the Cavalry Idea

In pioneering advanced war-fighting doctrine for modern armor, Patton never forgot the traditional lessons he had learned as a cavalryman. He transferred time-honored cavalry ideals of speed, highly flexible mobility, a hard-hitting raider's mentality, and a keen sense of the "ground" (the topography) of the battlefield to armor tactics and doctrine. In this sense, he brought cavalry into the twentieth century. As Patton redefined the tactics and doctrine of horse soldiery in terms of the light and medium tank, the mobile weapons par excellence of World War II, so Vietnam-era army tacticians redefined cavalry yet again in terms of the mobile weapon most closely identified with the Vietnam War, the helicopter. The "air cavalry" was developed as an assault force that functioned much like the traditional cavalry, penetrating enemy territory to conduct hit-and-run raids and reconnaissance in force. Patton loved horses and loved the idea of fighting from the saddle, but, in World War I, he immediately recognized the superiority of the light tank over the horse. Instead of clinging nostalgically to an outmoded weapons system, he salvaged what was best from that system and applied it to a new modality. Through Patton, the idea of the cavalry survived and was available to a later generation of warriors in Vietnam, who were fighting a very different kind of war with yet another means of armed mobility.

Combined Arms Approach

Although he loved the cavalry and was a passionate advocate of armor, Patton never limited himself to a single arm. He was an early advocate and practitioner of what is today called the "combined arms" approach to warfare. He integrated armor, infantry, artillery, and air in each of his major World War II operations. All played a role, and none was subordinated to any other. Thanks to commanders like Patton in Europe and MacArthur in the Pacific, World War II became a vast laboratory in which combined arms doctrine was developed. The doctrine emerged as so central to modern warfare that, in 1947, the War Department was replaced by the Department of Defense, a cabinet-level office charged with coordinating combined arms on the largest scale, bringing together the army, air force, navy, and marines. Within each of these services, combined arms has also steadily become more important, and all major military operations since World War II have been conceived and executed in terms of combined arms.

Patton used the combined arms approach to carry out his favorite tactic, which he frequently described as holding the enemy by the nose while kicking him in the pants. This involved locating and exploiting enemy weakness, attacking that weakness with great speed and maximum violence, pursuing the enemy to his destruction, then continuing the advance, also with great speed. Typically, Patton used infantry to hold the enemy by the nose, while the tanks swung round, usually covering great distances, to deliver the kick in the pants. This use of masses of tanks to make long, sweeping end runs around the enemy to hit his flank was spectacularly effective in World War II. Patton's tactic was employed by H. Norman Schwarzkopf in the so-called Hail Mary end run into the vulnerable flank of the main Iraqi ground force, thereby bringing the Gulf War of 1991 to a speedy and devastating conclusion. In that brief conflict, it was marines who held the enemy's nose with an amphibious assault while the main coalition army force, spearheaded by tanks, delivered the kick in the pants.

The Principle of Speed

Patton brought to a high state of perfection an exceptionally limber version of the blitzkrieg tactics the German army had used so devastatingly against Poland, France, and the Soviets. His ideal was to create warfare that combined speed and destructiveness so that a battle could be won with a minimum loss to one's own personnel and equipment. Conservative war fighting, Patton preached, gave the illusion of safety but ultimately cost more lives. The only way to achieve victory and at the same time minimize casualties was to defeat the enemy as quickly as possible, exposing one's forces to fire as briefly as possible.

The first Gulf War applied the Patton principle impressively. A large coalition force was built up over time, then used in a swift, relentless, and highly coordinated manner to minimize duration under fire. The result was massive destruction of the Iraqi army with very minimal coalition casualties. The use of a strong, coordinated force in a bold and violent offensive is most effective against a conventional enemy, as in the first Gulf War.

Reduction of Collateral Damage

Limiting the duration of time under fire not only saves the lives of the attacker's troops, it has the added benefit of limiting what is today called collateral damage, the destruction visited on civilian populations, the innocent bystanders in all wars. "Old Blood and Guts" was deeply disturbed by the sight of wounded soldiers and also by the magnitude of civilian devastation he witnessed. His detractors might be loath to recognize it, but Patton brought a significant measure of humanity to warfare.

The modern trend toward the deployment of "smart weapons" has not only made war more destructive against enemy military forces, but has enabled war fighters to minimize collateral damage. This was demonstrated in the air assault against Baghdad during the initial phase of Operation Iraqi Freedom. However, faulty intelligence can easily lead to the misapplication of "smart" technology, as when U.S. forces, relying on outdated intelligence, mistakenly directed a smart bomb attack against the Chinese embassy in Belgrade in 1999. During the first hours and days of Operation Iraqi Freedom, smart weapons were employed against sites mistakenly believed to harbor Iraqi dictator Saddam Hussein. Intelligence, not the weapons, was at fault when these attacks resulted in high collateral damage and the loss of innocent lives. Patton abhorred the waste of war and, in principle, would have approved of smart weapons technology as a tool capable of reducing that waste; however, he would have condemned the kind of political and military thinking that relies exclusively on air strikes employing such high-tech weaponry. There is no substitute, he would doubt-less point out, for the eyes, ears, brains, and valor of troops on the ground.

Training

Given Patton's glorious and controversial record in combat, it is all too easy to forget that, at the outbreak of war, General Marshall and other members of high command saw Patton's greatest value as a trainer of soldiers rather than as a combat leader. In creating and commanding the Desert Training Center at Indio, California, Patton trained America's first generation of desert fighters. The tactical triumph of the first Gulf War and of the initial desert combat phase of Operation Iraqi Freedom were built on foundations Patton laid at Indio training an army to defeat Rommel in the desert of North Africa.

Beyond training troops for a particular environment, Patton elevated training in general to a new status, putting it at the heart of the army. Patton far preferred serving in the heat and danger of combat than he did training troops, but perhaps no commander in the American service since Friedrich von Steuben in the American Revolution accorded training as central a role as Patton did. Today the American military accepts as a given that high-quality training is the most valuable commodity the force possesses. Beyond the basic training every soldier receives, the modern United States Army maintains, through its Training and Doctrine Command (TRADOC), 33 major schools and centers at 16 army installations. As of 2005, the schools were staffed by 9,141 instructors and offered 1,753 courses, enrolling more than 300,000 soldiers. Patton's central contributions to training the first generation of tank soldiers and commanders and the first generation of desert warriors are pioneering examples of the kind of special-applications training that has become commonplace in today's American military.

Leadership

Patton stands high among all other commanders as an example of leader-ship. He was a master of motivation, and he could motivate the men he commanded to perform beyond what they themselves conceived as their utmost. He had the ability to create the image of victory as well as the capacity to impart to his men the will, the emotions, and the mind-set to realize that image. Military leaders as well as leaders in business and civil government study Patton's speeches and other pronouncements on leadership to learn something of his motivational technique. To the extent that Patton put his technique into words, it can be studied. But, absent Patton himself, his style of leadership is at best semi-tangible, just as the work of a great actor, without that actor's physical presence, can be only partially appreciated. Call it charisma or call it what Patton himself called it—"*it*"—this is the intangible part of leadership, which can be admired, marveled at, and even, to an extent, conveyed, but it cannot be taught.

Key to Patton's effectiveness as a leader was his uncanny ability to "think like an army," to use historian Eric Larrabee's phrase. He instinctively knew what an army could achieve in a given situation and, just as important, what it could not achieve. As John Ingles, a Third Army lieutenant, put it, Patton had an unequaled "sense of what was possible on the battlefield." Ingles said that "we knew what General Patton expected us to do, and we believed that if we did it we would win." If Patton could not understand why other superb soldiers, such as Eisenhower or Bradley, did not always allow him to do with the Third Army everything he knew it could do, it was because he could not conceive what it was like to lack the intuition that was part of his very being. [3]

Professional historians, soldiers, and military buffs have long speculated on what would have happened had Patton been given a freer hand. What would have resulted had Patton been allowed to make a deeper penetration beyond the Falaise-Argentan pocket during the culminating phase of Operation Cobra? It is likely that far more of the German army would have been killed or captured much earlier in the European campaign. And what of the Ardennes counteroffensive? What if Patton had been permitted to direct more of his attack against the base of the German salient, the "bulge"? To have done so would surely have risked the fall of Bastogne and, ultimately, even Antwerp, but, had such an attack succeeded, the Battle of the Bulge would have been far less costly and even more effective than it was. For that matter, we can only imagine what was lost to the Allied war effort by keeping Patton inactive for some 11 months after the slapping incidents. Over the years since the end of World War II, many experts, amateurs, generals, and armchair generals have suggested that the war in Europe would have ended in 1944 if Patton had been given more of the authority—and the gasoline—he asked for.

As it was, Patton accomplished enough to make himself instrumental in winning the war in Europe. Had Eisenhower and Bradley really been the mediocre commanders Patton at times privately thought they were, he would not have been given any of the opportunities he invariably converted into victories. As Eisenhower observed, "He was one of those men born to be a soldier."[4]

Notes

Introduction

1. Rundstedt quoted in Martin Blumenson, *Patton: The Man Behind the Legend, 1885–1945* (New York: Quill/William Morrow, 1985), 296.
2. Stalin quoted in Blumenson, *Patton,* 296.
3. Lucian K. Truscott, *Command Missions* (New York: E. P. Dutton, 1954), 509; Carlo D'Este, *Patton: A Genius for War* (New York: HarperCollins, 1995), 440 and 800.
4. Dwight Macdonald quoted in John Phillips, "The Ordeal of George Patton," *New York Review of Books,* December 31, 1964; Andy Rooney quoted in D'Este, *Patton,* 813.
5. Alan Axelrod, *Patton on Leadership: Strategic Lessons for Corporate Warfare* (Paramus, N.J.: Prentice Hall Press, 1999), 8–9.
6. Dwight David Eisenhower, *Crusade in Europe,* reprint ed. (Baltimore: The Johns Hopkins University Press, 1997), 180–81.
7. Alfred D. Chandler, Jr., ed., *The Papers of Dwight David Eisenhower: The War Years* (Baltimore: The Johns Hopkins University Press, 1970), III: 1594–95.

Chapter 1

1. George S. Patton, Jr., *War as I Knew It,* reprint ed. (Boston: Houghton Mifflin, 1995), 92 and 111; Carlo D'Este, *Patton: A Genius for War* (New York: HarperCollins, 1995), 320 and 324.
2. Patton, letter to Frederick Ayer, January 3, 1909, in Martin Blumenson, ed., *The Patton Papers 1885–1940,* reprint ed. (Bridgewater, N.J.: Replica Books, 1999), 157–58.

3. Martin Blumenson, *Patton: The Man Behind the Legend, 1885–1945* (New York: Quill/William Morrow, 1985), 16.
4. Patton, field notebook, quoted in Alan Axelrod, *Patton on Leadership: Strategic Lessons for Corporate Warfare* (Paramus, N.J.: Prentice Hall Press, 1999), 74.
5. Blumenson, *Patton,* 31.
6. Patton, letter to Beatrice Ayer, January 10, 1903, in Blumenson, ed., *The Patton Papers 1885–1940,* 45.
7. Patton, "My Father as I Knew Him" (unpublished manuscript), in Blumenson, ed., *The Patton Papers 1885–1940,* 58.

Chapter 2

1. Patton, "My Father as I Knew Him" (unpublished manuscript), in Martin Blumenson, ed., *The Patton Papers 1885–1940,* reprint ed. (Bridgewater, N.J.: Replica Books, 1999), 61.
2. Father, letter to Patton, September 27, 1903, in Blumenson, ed., *The Patton Papers 1885–1940,* 61.
3. Patton, "My Father as I Knew Him" (unpublished manuscript), in Blumenson, ed., *The Patton Papers 1885–1940,* 62; Patton, letter to Father, December 13, 1903, in Blumenson, ed., *The Patton Papers 1885–1940,* 62.
4. Father, letter to Patton, in Blumenson, ed., *The Patton Papers 1885–1940,* 83–84.
5. Strother, letter, January 31, 1904, in Blumenson, ed., *The Patton Papers 1885–1940,* 84–85 and 77.
6. Patton, letter to Mother, June 21, 1904, in Blumenson, ed., *The Patton Papers 1885–1940,* 89.
7. Patton, letter to Father, July 3, 1904, in Blumenson, ed., *The Patton Papers 1885–1940,* 90.
8. Patton, letters to Father, July 31, 1904; "end of November" 1904; January 27, 1905; Patton, letter to Father, April 9, 1905; Patton, telegram to Father, June 12, 1905; Father, telegram to Patton, June 13, 1905, in Blumenson, ed., *The Patton Papers 1885–1940,* 93, 106, 110, 113, and 116.
9. Patton, undated notebook entry, quoted in Martin Blumenson, *Patton: The Man Behind the Legend, 1885–1945* (New York: Quill/Morrow, 1985), 53.
10. Patton, letter to Beatrice, quoted in Blumenson, *Patton,* 54.
11. George S. Patton Jr., *War as I Knew It,* reprint ed. (Boston: Houghton Mifflin, 1995), 187.
12. Patton, letter to Beatrice, February 22, 1908, in Blumenson, ed., *The Patton Papers 1885–1940,* 141.
13. Patton, letter to Beatrice, February 16, 1909, in Blumenson, ed., *The Patton Papers 1885–1940,* 166.
14. Captain Francis C. Marshall quoted in Blumenson, *Patton,* 63.
15. Blumenson, *Patton,* 63
16. Blumenson, *Patton,* 64

17. Patton, letter to Beatrice, February 28, 1910, and Patton, letter to Mother, March 6, 1910, in Blumenson, ed., *The Patton Papers 1885–1940*, 197 and 199.
18. "My Father as I Knew Him" (unpublished manuscript), quoted in Carlo D'Este, *Patton: A Genius for War* (New York: HarperCollins, 1995), 134.
19. "My Father as I Knew Him" (unpublished manuscript), quoted in D'Este, *Patton*, 134.

Chapter 3

1. Patton, letter to Beatrice, quoted in Martin Blumenson, *Patton: The Man Behind the Legend, 1885–1945* (New York: Quill/William Morrow, 1985), 75.
2. Patton, letter to Father, April 19, 1914, in Martin Blumenson, ed., *The Patton Papers 1885–1940*, reprint ed. (Bridgewater, N.J.: Replica Books, 1999), 273.
3. Patton, letter to Beatrice, quoted in Blumenson, *Patton*, 76.
4. Blumenson, *Patton*, 78.
5. Blumenson, *Patton*, 78.
6. Patton, letter to Father, April 19, 1914, in Blumenson, ed., *The Patton Papers 1885–1940*, 307.
7. Ladislas Farago, *The Last Days of Patton* (New York: McGraw-Hill, 1981), 285.
8. Quoted in Carlo D'Este, *Patton: A Genius for War* (New York: HarperCollins, 1995), 161.
9. Patton, letter to Father, quoted in D'Este, *Patton*, 163.
10. Patton, letter to Father, quoted in D'Este, *Patton*, 163.
11. Patton, "Personal Glimpses of General Pershing" (unpublished manuscript), quoted in D'Este, *Patton*, 168.
12. Patton, letter to Father, April 17, 1916, quoted in D'Este, *Patton*, 173; Patton, diary entry, quoted in Blumenson, *Patton*, 83.
13. Patton's account of the episode is given in D'Este, *Patton*, 172–177.
14. Patton, diary, May 18, 1916, in Blumenson, ed., *The Patton Papers 1885–1940*, 339.
15. Patton quoted in Frank E. Vandiver, *Black Jack: The Life and Times of John J. Pershing* (College Station: Texas A&M University Press, 1997), II: 658.
16. Patton, letter to Beatrice, October 7, 1916, quoted in D'Este, *Patton*, 181.
17. Pershing, letter to Patton, October 16, 1916, in Blumenson, ed., *The Patton Papers 1885–1940*, 354.

Chapter 4

1. Patton, letter to Beatrice, October 2, 1917, in Martin Blumenson, ed., *The Patton Papers 1885–1940*, reprint ed. (Bridgewater, N.J.: Replica Books, 1999), 426.

2. Patton, undated diary entry, and Patton, letter to Pershing, October 3, 1917, in Blumenson, ed., *The Patton Papers 1885–1940*, 426 and 427.
3. Patton, diary, November 3, 1917, in Blumenson, ed., *The Patton Papers 1885–1940*, 429.
4. Patton, letter to Father, November 6, 1917, in Blumenson, ed., *The Patton Papers 1885–1940*, 432–33.
5. Patton, letter to Beatrice, November 26, 1917, in Blumenson, ed., *The Patton Papers 1885–1940*, 445–46.
6. Patton, diary, December 15, 1917, in Blumenson, ed., *The Patton Papers 1885–1940*, 459.
7. Patton, instructions to troops, September 11, 1918, in Blumenson, ed., *The Patton Papers 1885–1940*, 581–82.
8. Martin Blumenson, *Patton: The Man Behind the Legend, 1885–1945* (New York: Quill/William Morrow, 1985), 109.
9. Blumenson, *Patton*, 110.
10. Patton's account is given in Blumenson, ed., *The Patton Papers 1885–1940*, 613–14.
11. Patton, letter to Beatrice, quoted in Blumenson, *Patton*, 114.

Chapter 5

1. Martin Blumenson, *Patton: The Man Behind the Legend, 1885–1945* (New York: Quill/William Morrow, 1985), 121.
2. Blumenson, *Patton*, 121.
3. Patton, "The Obligation of Being an Officer," quoted in Blumenson, *Patton*, 122.
4. Carlo D'Este, *Patton: A Genius for War* (New York: HarperCollins, 1995), 339.
5. Blumenson, *Patton*, 128.
6. Patton, "Federal Troops in Domestic Disturbances," unpublished paper (ca. 1932) quoted in Martin Blumenson, ed., *The Patton Papers 1885–1940*, reprint ed. (Bridgewater, N.J.: Replica Books, 1999), 898.
7. The incident is narrated in Blumenson, *Patton*, 136.

Chapter 6

1. Martin Blumenson, *Patton: The Man Behind the Legend, 1885–1945* (New York: Quill/William Morrow, 1985), 140.
2. George C. Marshall, letter to Patton, September 23, 1939, in Martin Blumenson, ed., *The Patton Papers 1885–1940*, reprint ed. (Bridgewater, N.J.: Replica Books, 1999), 994.
3. Blumenson, *Patton*, 151.
4. Blumenson, *Patton*, 156.

5. George S. Patton Jr., *War as I Knew It*, reprint ed. (Boston: Houghton Mifflin, 1995), 335.

6. Patton, "Notes on Tactics and Techniques of Desert Warfare (Provisional)," July 30, 1942, in Martin Blumenson, ed., *The Patton Papers 1940–1945*, reprint ed. (New York: Da Capo, 1996), 74.

7. Patton, farewell address to troops, Desert Training Center, in Blumenson, ed., *The Patton Papers 1940–1945*, 73.

Chapter 7

1. Patton, diary, August 9, 1942, in Martin Blumenson, ed., *The Patton Papers 1940–1945*, reprint ed. (New York: Da Capo, 1996), 82.

2. Robert Coram, *Boyd: The Fighter Pilot Who Changed the Art of War* (Boston: Little, Brown, 2002), 424; George S. Patton Jr., *War as I Knew It*, reprint ed. (Boston: Houghton Mifflin, 1995), 348.

3. Patton, diary, August 11, 1942, and other comments, in Blumenson, ed., *The Patton Papers 1940–1945*, 82–83.

4. Patton, letter to Beatrice, August 11, 1942, in Blumenson, ed., *The Patton Papers 1940–1945*, 83.

5. Patton, diary, September 24, 1942, in Blumenson, ed., *The Patton Papers 1940–1945*, 86.

6. Patton, letters to Mrs. Francis C. Marshall, André W. Brewster, James G. Harbord, and Frederick Ayer, quoted in Blumenson, ed., *The Patton Papers 1940–1945*, 91–92.

7. Patton, *War as I Knew It*, 7–8.

8. Martin Blumenson, *Patton: The Man Behind the Legend, 1885–1945* (New York: Quill/William Morrow, 1985), 172.

9. Blumenson, *Patton*, 174.

10. Patton, diary, November 30, 1942, and letter to Beatrice, December 2, 1942, in Blumenson, ed., *The Patton Papers 1940–1945*, 130–131.

11. Blumenson, *Patton*, 176 and 180.

12. Eisenhower, Secret Memorandum to Patton, in Alfred D, Chandler, Jr., ed., *The Papers of Dwight David Eisenhower: The War Years* (Baltimore: Johns Hopkins University Press, 1970, II: 1010–11.

13. The incident is narrated in Blumenson, *Patton*, 185.

14. Eisenhower, letter, April 14, 1943, in Blumenson, ed., *The Patton Papers 1940–1945*, 220; Marshall quoted in Blumenson, *Patton*, 189; Patton, diary, April 15, 1943, in Blumenson, ed., *The Patton Papers 1940–1945*, 221.

Chapter 8

1. Patton, letter to Beatrice, April 29, 1943, in Martin Blumenson, ed., *The Patton Papers 1940–1945*, reprint ed. (New York: Da Capo, 1996), 237.

2. Patton, diary, May 3, 1943, quoted in Carlo D'Este, *Patton: A Genius for War* (New York: HarperCollins, 1995), 494–95.

3. Patton, letter of instruction to subordinate officers, June 5, 1943, in Blumenson, ed., *The Patton Papers 1940–1945*, 262–63.

4. Patton, message to men while at sea, July 1943, in Blumenson, ed., *The Patton Papers 1940–1945*, 274–75.

5. Martin Blumenson, *Patton: The Man Behind the Legend, 1885–1945* (New York: Quill/William Morrow, 1985), 198.

6. Patton, diary, July 10, 1943, in Blumenson, ed., *The Patton Papers 1940–1945*, 280.

7. Patton quoted in Harry Semmes, *Portrait of Patton* (New York: Paperback Library, 1970), 160–61.

8. Gay's deception is documented in D'Este, *Patton,* 519.

9. Patton, letter to Beatrice, March 1944, in Blumenson, ed., *The Patton Papers 1940–1945,* 296.

10. Patton, letter to Troy Middleton, July 28, 1943, in Blumenson, ed., *The Patton Papers 1940–1945,* 306.

11. Patton, diary, August 10 and 11, 1943, in Blumenson, ed., *The Patton Papers 1940–1945,* 319–20.

12. Patton, letter to Beatrice, August 11, 1943, in Blumenson, ed., *The Patton Papers 1940–1945,* 320.

13. British officer quoted in Blumenson, ed., *The Patton Papers 1940–1945,* 323.

14. Patton, comment to Arvin H. Brown (Patton's cousin), and Patton, Seventh Army General Orders 18, August 22, 1943, in Blumenson, ed., *The Patton Papers 1940–1945,* 328 and 334.

15. Patton, Seventh Army General Orders 18, August 22, 1943, in Blumenson, ed., *The Patton Papers 1940–1945,* 334.

Chapter 9

1. Roosevelt, Alexander, Marshall, and Montgomery quoted in Martin Blumenson, ed., *The Patton Papers 1940–1945,* reprint ed. (New York: Da Capo, 1996), 326–27.

2. Patton, diary, August 2, 1943, August 10, 1943, and August 6, 1943, in Blumenson, ed., *The Patton Papers 1940–1945,* 311, 318, and 315.

3. Patton, letter to Beatrice, August 18, 1943, in Blumenson, ed., *The Patton Papers 1940–1945,* 325.

4. Lt. Col. Perrin H. Long, Medical Corps, letter to The Surgeon, NATOUSA, August 16, 1943, in Blumenson, ed., *The Patton Papers 1940–1945,* 330–31; Patton, diary, August 3, 1943, quoted in Carlo D'Este, *Patton: A Genius for War* (New York: HarperCollins, 1995), 533.

5. Charles H. Kuhl quoted in Blumenson, ed., *The Patton Papers 1940–1945,* 336–37.

6. Patton, memorandum, August 5, 1943, quoted in D'Este, *Patton,* 533.

7. Lt. Col. Perrin H. Long, Medical Corps, letter to The Surgeon, NATOUSA, August 16, 1943, in Blumenson, ed., *The Patton Papers 1940–1945*, 331–32.

8. Patton's remarks after the incident are quoted in D'Este, *Patton*, 534.

9. Patton, diary, August 20, 1943, and Eisenhower, letter to Patton, August 17, 1943, in Blumenson, ed., *The Patton Papers 1940–1945*, 332 and 329.

10. Patton, diary, August 20, in Blumenson, ed., *The Patton Papers 1940–1945*, 332; Patton's comment on his motive and Patton's remarks to assembled troops quoted in Martin Blumenson, *Patton: The Man Behind the Legend, 1885–1945* (New York: Quill/William Morrow, 1985), 213.

Chapter 10

1. Patton, letters to Beatrice, February 9, 1944, and March 6, 1944, in Martin Blumenson, ed., *The Patton Papers 1940–1945*, reprint ed. (New York: Da Capo, 1996), 413 and 421.

2. Patton, letter to Beatrice, February 3, 1944, in Blumenson, ed., *The Patton Papers 1940–1945*, 411.

3. Patton, letter of instruction to officers, March 6, 1944, in Blumenson, ed., *The Patton Papers 1940–1945*, 423.

4. Patton, letter of instruction to officers, March 6, 1944, and letter of instruction to officers, April 3, 1944, in Blumenson, ed., *The Patton Papers 1940–1945*, 424 and 432–34.

5. Patton, letter of instruction to officers, March 6, 1944, in Blumenson, ed., *The Patton Papers 1940–1945*, 424.

6. Patton, letter of instruction to officers, March 6, 1944, in Blumenson, ed., *The Patton Papers 1940–1945*, 424.

7. Third Army soldier quoted in Martin Blumenson, *Patton: The Man Behind the Legend, 1885–1945* (New York: Quill/William Morrow, 1985), 220.

8. Patton's address quoted in Blumenson, *Patton*, 220–21.

9. Patton, remarks to the Knutsford Welcome Club, April 25, 1944, in Blumenson, ed., *The Patton Papers 1940–1945*, 440–41.

10. Marshall, cable to Eisenhower, quoted in Blumenson, ed., *The Patton Papers 1940–1945*, 446.

11. Carlo D'Este, *Eisenhower: A Soldier's Life* (New York: Henry Holt, 2002), 508.

12. D'Este, *Eisenhower*, 509.

13. Patton, speech, quoted in Blumenson, *Patton*, 228.

14. See Carlo D'Este, *Patton: A Genius for War* (New York: HarperCollins, 1995), 744. The truth about Patton and Jean Gordon will probably never be known for certain. What is certain is that early in January 1946, weeks after her husband died, Beatrice Patton confronted Jean Gordon in a meeting she arranged at a Boston hotel. Beatrice fixed her eyes on Jean, leveled a finger at her, and recited a curse she had picked up in Hawaii: "May the Great Worm gnaw your vitals and may your bones rot joint by little joint" (D'Este, *Patton*, 806).

No one knows what else the two women said to one another, but on January 8, 1946, a few days after the meeting, Jean Gordon, not yet 31, put her head in the oven at a friend's New York City apartment and turned on the gas.

15. D'Este, *Patton*, 613–14.
16. Patton's plea to Bradley, quoted in D'Este, *Patton*, 616; Patton, letter to Beatrice, July 22, 1944, quoted in Blumenson, *Patton*, 486; Patton's criticism of Bradley, Hodges, and Eisenhower cited in Blumenson, *Patton*, 228.

Chapter 11

1. Patton, diary, August 15, 1944, in Martin Blumenson, ed., *The Patton Papers 1940–1945*, reprint ed. (New York: Da Capo, 1996), 511.
2. Patton, letter to Beatrice, August 16, 1944, in Blumenson, ed., *The Patton Papers 1940–1945*, 512.
3. Patton, diary, August 30, 1944, in Blumenson, ed., *The Patton Papers 1940–1945*, 531.
4. Patton, diary, September 1, 1944, in Blumenson, ed., *The Patton Papers 1940–1945*, 533.
5. Transcript of Patton press conference, September 7, 1944, in Blumenson, ed., *The Patton Papers 1940–1945*, 540.
6. Patton, diary, November 24, 1944, in Blumenson, ed., *The Patton Papers 1940–1945*, 582.

Chapter 12

1. Dwight David Eisenhower, *Crusade in Europe*, reprint ed. (Baltimore: The Johns Hopkins University Press, 1997), 350.
2. Patton's account of the meeting is excerpted in Martin Blumenson, ed., *The Patton Papers 1940–1945*, reprint ed. (New York: Da Capo, 1996), 599.
3. Carlo D'Este, *Patton: A Genius for War* (New York: HarperCollins, 1995), 680.
4. Patton quoted in Blumenson, ed., *The Patton Papers 1940–1945*, 600.
5. George S. Patton Jr., *War as I Knew It*, reprint ed. (Boston: Houghton Mifflin, 1995), 197.
6. Quoted in D'Este, *Patton*, 681.
7. The prayer and Christmas message are quoted in D'Este, *Patton*, 685–86, as is Chaplain O'Neill's account, "The Story Behind Patton's Prayer."
8. Patton, diary, December 25 and 26, in Blumenson, ed., *The Patton Papers 1940–1945*, 606–607.
9. O'Neill, "The Story Behind Patton's Prayer," quoted in D'Este, *Patton*, 688.
10. Patton, letter to Beatrice, December 29, 1944, in Blumenson, ed., *The Patton Papers 1940–1945*, 608.
11. Patton, diary, February 5, 1945, and letter to Beatrice, February 4, 1945, in Blumenson, ed., *The Patton Papers 1940–1945*, 635 and 634.

Chapter 13

1. Patton, letter to son George, January 16, 1945, and Patton, press conference, January 1, 1945, in Martin Blumenson, ed., *The Patton Papers 1940–1945,* reprint ed. (New York: Da Capo, 1996), 625 and 612.
2. Patton, diary, February 26, 1945, quoted in Carlo D'Este, *Patton: A Genius for War* (New York: HarperCollins, 1995), 706.
3. Patton, letter to Beatrice, February 14, 1945, in Blumenson, ed., *The Patton Papers 1940–1945,* 638,
4. Patton, diary, February 1945, in Blumenson, ed., *The Patton Papers 1940–1945,* 634.
5. Harry Semmes, *Portrait of Patton* (New York: Paperback Library, 1970), 240.
6. Patton, Third Army General Orders 70, March 23, 1945, in Blumenson, ed., *The Patton Papers 1940–1945,* 660–61.
7. Patton, diary, March 24, 1945, in Blumenson, ed., *The Patton Papers 1940–1945,* 661.
8. Omar N. Bradley, *A Soldier's Story* (New York: Henry Holt, 1951), 542–43.
9. Ladislas Farago, *The Last Days of Patton* (New York: McGraw-Hill, 1981), 45.
10. Farago, *Last Days of Patton,* 46.
11. George S. Patton Jr., *War as I Knew It,* reprint ed. (Boston: Houghton Mifflin, 1995), 292.
12. Patton, *War as I Knew It,* 293.
13. Robert Murphy, *Diplomat among Warriors* (Garden City, N.Y.: Doubleday, 1964), 255.
14. Patton, diary, April 12, 1945, in Blumenson, ed., *The Patton Papers 1940–1945,* 685.
15. Martin Blumenson, *Patton: The Man Behind the Legend, 1885–1945* (New York: Quill/William Morrow, 1985), 265.
16. Patton, press conference, May 8, 1945, in Blumenson, ed., *The Patton Papers 1940–1945,* 700; Larry G. Newman, "Gen. Patton's Premonition," *American Legion Magazine* (July 1962), quoted in D'Este, *Patton,* 734.
17. Patton, speech in Boston, June 7, 1945, quoted in Blumenson, ed., *The Patton Papers 1940–1945,* 721.
18. Patton, letter to Beatrice, August 10, 1945, and diary, August 10, 1945, in Blumenson, ed., *The Patton Papers 1940–1945,* 735 and 736.
19. The press conference was recorded by Robert S. Allen in "The Day Patton Quit," *Army* (June 1971) and quoted in D'Este, *Patton,* 766.
20. Patton, letter to Beatrice, September 25, 1945, and diary, September 22, 1945, in Blumenson, ed., *The Patton Papers 1940–1945,* 772–73 and 766.
21. Patton, speech to officers and men of Third Army, October 7, 1945, in Blumenson, ed., *The Patton Papers 1940–1945,* 792.
22. Account of Hobart R. Gay, quoted in D'Este, *Patton,* 785.
23. Account of Hobart R. Gay, quoted in D'Este, *Patton,* 785.
24. Patton quoted in Blumenson, *Patton,* 292.

25. Farago, *Last Days of Patton,* 276–77.
26. Robert S. Allen, *Lucky Forward* (New York: Vanguard Press, 1964), 401–402.

Chapter 14

1. Patton, diary, June 8, 1943, in Martin Blumenson, ed., *The Patton Papers 1940–1945,* reprint ed. (New York: Da Capo, 1996), 263–64.
2. R. Glen Spurling's recollections ("The Patton Episode"), in Carlo D'Este, *Patton: A Genius for War* (New York: HarperCollins, 1995), 798.
3. Eric Larabee, *Commander in Chief* (New York: Harper & Row, 1987), 487; John Ingles is quoted in D'Este, *Patton,* 819.
4. Eisenhower quoted in Brenton G. Wallace, *Patton and His Third Army* (Nashville: The Battery Press, 1981), 206.

Index

Lake Vineyard (Patton childhood home), 9, 11
Langres (France), Patton establishes U.S. tank school at, 49–53
Larrabee, Eric, appraisal of Patton of, 182
Labienus, 12
Lawrence, Justus "Jock," 130
leadership, Patton's military legacy and, 181–182
League of Nations, 62
Lear, Benjamin, 81
Leclerc, Jacques, 141
Lee, J. C. H, 25
Lee, Robert E., 12
Lend Lease, 79–80
Licata mule-shooting incident, 107
logistical problems, Allied, 141–142
Loire River, Patton's operations near, 137
Long, Perrin H., 115
Lorient, Patton's unsuccessful assault on, 136–137
Lucky and Lucky Forward (Third Army headquarters code names), 125, 147
Lucky 6 (Patton's personal code name), 125
Lusitania, sinking of, 35, 46
Luxembourg City (Bradley's headquarters), 146, 147

MacArthur, Douglas, 6, 25, 55, 68, 69, 70, 162, 174, 178
Macdonald, Dwight, condemnation of Patton by, 2
Madero, Francisco, 34, 38
Maknassy Pass, Battle of, 97
Marshall, Francis C., 26, 36
Marshall, George C., 5, 49, 52–53, 74, 75, 82, 84, 87, 89, 99, 121, 164
  congratulates Patton on Sicily campaign, 114
  response to Knutsford Incident, 129
Marshall, Mrs. Francis C., Patton's letter to, 90

Master of the Sword, Patton named, 32
McAuliffe, Anthony, 150
  replies "Nuts!" to German surrender demand, 150
McCoy, Frank, 48
McNair, Lesley J., 80, 84
mechanized warfare, Patton as advocate and pioneer of, 2, 67–67, 78, 80
Meeks, George, 91, 124
Mercer, Anne Gordon (great-great grandmother), 10
Mercer, Hugh (great-great-great grandfather), 10
Merkers industrial salt mine, liberation of, 159–160
Messina
  captured by Patton, 3, 110, 123
  Patton races Montgomery to, 105–110
Metropolitan Club (Washington, D.C.), 31
Metz, captured by Patton, 142
Meuse River, Third Army runs out of gasoline at, 141
Meuse-Argonne Offensive, Patton's role in, 57–58
Middleton, Troy, 107, 133, 136, 137, 144, 145, 146
military legacy, Patton's, 175–182
military professionalism, Patton's legacy and, 177–178
Millikin, John, 146, 147, 150
"Mistreatment of Patients in Receiving Tents of the 15th and 93rd Evacuation Hospitals" (Long report), 115–118
mobile warfare,
  Patton as exponent of, 2
  Patton's military legacy and, 176–177
Montgomery, Bernard Law, 3, 95–96, 97, 101, 102, 104, 105, 107, 138–139, 140, 143, 156

Patton, George Smith II (father), 9, 10,
    11, 17–18, 19, 46
  death of, 67
  defeated in Senate election, 43
Patton, George Smith IV (son), 66
Patton, George Smith, Jr.
  appointed aide to Secretary of War
    Stimson, 29
  ambition of, 21–22, 34–35, 38,
    49–50, 91
  anti-British attitude of, 89, 103, 153,
  anti-Semitism of 20, 165–166
  appraisals of, 1–3, 5, 25, 43–44, 67,
    120, 172
  attack and advance philosophy of,
    29, 53–54, 80, 90, 98, 103,
    130–131, 139
  audacity, belief in, 82, 109, 176
  as Bavaria's military governor,
    163–166
  birth of, 9
  burned in accident, 43
  named cadet adjutant at West Point,
    23–24
  childhood of, 9–13
  command presence of, 126,
    132–133, 175, 182
  contradictory personality of, 4,
    171–174
  courage, preoccupation with, 15, 23,
    55, 57–58, 66, 103, 126, 168
  cowardice, fear of, 15, 116–118
  credit for achievements, Patton
    liberally assigns, 81, 106,
    155–156, 163
  death of, 2, 168–169
  decorations awarded to, 61, 115
  depression of, 4–5, 143, 153
  destiny, belief in, 21, 49, 55, 58, 77,
    88–89, 91, 92, 102–103, 114,
    171
  discipline, philosophy concerning,
    22–23, 43, 48, 52, 76, 77, 84,
    96, 103, 125

  discussion and dissent, encourages
    among subordinates, 84
  drinking by, 70–71
  dyslexia of, 4, 11, 13, 18, 34, 68
  education of, 11–25
  energy of, 77
  fatal automobile accident of,
    167–168
  as fox hunt rider, 70
  frustration of, 35, 48, 62, 140, 143,
    149, 153
  glory, craving for, 19, 25–26, 35, 81,
    104, 106, 116
  "Green Hornet" tanker's uniform of,
    79
  heritage of, 4, 10–13
  as hero, 42, 58–59, 121, 158
  heroes of, 11, 12, 42–43
  history, interest in, 11–12, 94
  humor of, 160, 168
  as hunter, 156
  impulsiveness of, 77, 173
  intelligence, belief in importance of,
    126
  ivory-handled revolver of, 41, 91, 132
  jaundice, contracts, 49
  Knutsford Incident, 127–130
  Leadership, philosophy and practice
    of, 54, 57–58, 66, 77, 96, 99,
    103, 104–105, 125–126, 146,
    156
  legacy of, 6–7, 175–182
  legend of, 27, 76–77, 96, 106–107,
    121–122
  loyalty, importance of, 43, 52
  marriage of, 28, 70–71
  as Master of the Sword, 4, 32
  maxims of, 13, 81, 82, 85, 89, 91,
    92, 103, 109, 125–126, 143, 169
  mechanized warfare and, 2–3, 4, 42,
    48–49, 50
  military courtesy, importance of, 19,
    48
  military tradition, and, 65